THE BRITISH IMPERIAL EXPERIENCE

THE BRITISH IMPERIAL EXPERIENCE

ROBERT A. HUTTENBACK

California Institute of Technology

Harper & Row, Publishers

NEW YORK AND LONDON

Library of Congress Catalog Card Number: 66-15671

For my mother and father

Contents

List of Maps

Introduction

THE ENGLAND OF THE TUDORS was a brash, virile, and self-confident nation. It gave vent to its aggressive patriotism and youthful exuberance by sending merchants and sailors across the seas to chastise the Spaniard and to capture from him his gold and the markets of the world. The Elizabethan Age and subsequent decades witnessed the establishment of many joint-stock companies. Organized for various purposes but encouraged by a mercantilist doctrine of state, they planted the British flag on the eastern seaboard of North America and on the sugar islands of the West Indies.

This was the so-called "First British Empire" which died toward the close of the eighteenth century. It was an empire of settlement—of colonies peopled by British immigrants. The "Second British Empire," whose birth overlapped the death of the first, was founded on ambitions for increased Far Eastern trade. Ideally, it was to have been a chain of trading posts protected by strategically placed naval bases. Commercial profit was to be its purpose, but profit undiminished by the expense and responsibility of colonization which had proved so frustrating in North America.

The actual development of the Second Empire turned out to be of a quite different nature. Collisions with the French and Dutch could not be prevented. The West Indian sugar islands remained significant, and connection with North America was unavoidable, although Canada had originally been conquered from France to protect the now-lost lands further south. Australia and New Zealand were rediscovered and occupied, and the population explosion of the nineteenth century peopled these new possessions with British immigrants. In India the stable structure of the Mogul empire, under whose aegis the East India Company had once securely conducted its business, had collapsed, leaving a vacuum into which the British were forced to move.

Once committed, however unwillingly, the British government

thought it necessary to protect these new possessions. Thus the British nation embarked on a whole new sea of troubles when the Cape of Good Hope was finally wrested from the Dutch in 1814 to facilitate the journey to India. As it turned out, British occupation of Africa was not to be limited to the Cape. In time a number of different factors prompted further expansion. Greed, humanitarianism, missionary zeal, fear of foreign intervention, and that curious phenomenon "prestige imperialism," which toward the end of the nineteenth century filled Englishmen with an inordinate yearning to paint the map red, all played their part.

Much of the early expansionist activity was accomplished without the direct intervention of the British government. But with increased colonial responsibilities and with the growth of liberalism and humanitarianism in Britain itself, the British government found itself forced to admit that an empire had been acquired and to develop for it a philosophy in keeping with the prevailing climate of opinion. This was no easy matter. The new Empire, as it grew, was far from homogeneous. On the one hand were the colonies of white settlement, such as Canada, Australia, and New Zealand, increasingly demanding control of their own destinies; on the other, the colonies that became known as the "Dependent Empire," predominantly nonwhite, centered at first in Asia but including by the end of the nineteenth century large tracts of Africa. Two divergent paths of development were followed, and possibly the greatest problems the British faced in the later days of the Empire were how to extend to the Dependent Empire the privileges granted to the colonies of settlement, and how to guarantee equal rights and opportunities to all British subjects regardless of race, creed, or country of origin. In time, this dilemma and the strengthening of colonial nationalism prompted significant changes in the structure of the Empire, until it essentially disappeared to be replaced by the much more loosely knit Commonwealth.

The purpose of this book is not to give a full chronological history of the Empire and the Commonwealth. It is rather to analyze those incidents, persons, and movements that altered the character of the Empire and influenced its governing philosophy. Chapters are consequently devoted to the changing face of both the Dependent Empire and the Empire of white settlement, to the scramble for Africa, and to the evolution of the imperial organization from Empire to Commonwealth. Historians have never agreed as to the nature of imperialism, and several chapters therefore discuss the motivations for imperial expansion, the nature of British imperialism, and the role of the imperial proconsul. Finally, an attempt is made to dissect the intellectual content of imperialism. Was there a viable imperial philosophy dedicated to the betterment of man? Or was imperialism merely a manifestation of national ego? Was there, indeed, any substance to the "imperial idea"?

I am most grateful to Mr. Bernard Kotkin; to Mr. Robert Conhaim of the Extension Division of the University of California at Los Angeles; to Professor Richard Wilde of the History Department, California State College, Long Beach; and to Professor John Galbraith of the History Department of the University of California at Los Angeles, all of whom read and offered most useful advice on the whole manuscript. Professor L. M. Thompson of the last-named department kindly read and criticized the chapter on Indians in South Africa. I am also indebted to Miss Penelope Mason, Mrs. Ned Hale, Mrs. Virginia Kotkin, and Mrs. Lucille Lozoya, who undertook the tedious task of typing the manuscript.

In addition, the author wishes to thank the following: Macmillan & Co., Ltd., London, for permission to quote from George Otto Trevelyan, *Cawnpore* (1865); The Public Trustee and the Society of Authors, London, for permission to quote from G. B. Shaw, "The Man of Destiny," in *Plays, Pleasant and Unpleasant*, vol. 2, Constable & Co., Ltd. (1957); St. Martin's Press, Inc., New York, and Chatto & Windus, Ltd., London, for permission to quote Sir Harry Johnston's "A Cannibal's Ode to His Aunt," from Roland Oliver, *Sir Harry Johnston and the Scramble for Africa* (1957); Mrs. George Bambridge, The Macmillan Company of Canada, Metheun & Co., Ltd., London, A. P. Watt & Son, London, and Doubleday & Co., Inc., New York, for permission to quote a stanza from Rudyard Kipling, "The White Man's Burden," in *Rudyard Kipling's Verse*, Definitive Edition (1940).

ROBERT A. HUTTENBACK

Pasadena, California

THE BRITISH IMPERIAL EXPERIENCE

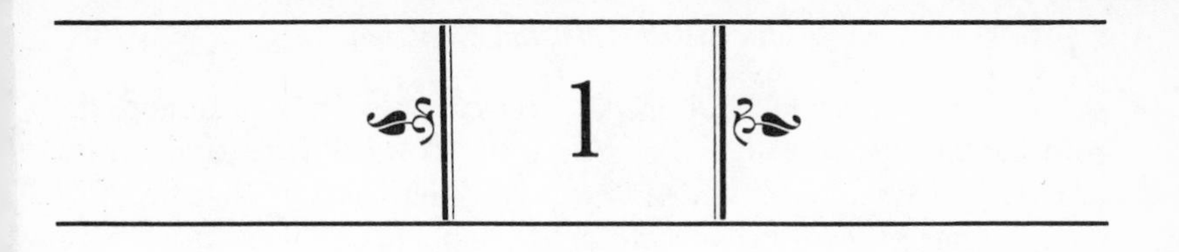

1

Robert Clive, Warren Hastings, and the Changing British Attitude Toward India

ON THE LAST DAY of December 1600, Queen Elizabeth I granted a charter to "the Governor and Company of merchants of London trading into the East Indies," or what became commonly known as the East India Company. The new trading organization was born into difficulties. England was at war with Spain, and the Company's ordained area of activities was already frequented by the Dutch, Portuguese, and Spanish. The Company started with only 217 subscribers and a total capital of £68,373; yet it was to prosper and within a few short years had established several trading stations in India. By the end of the next century, the voyage of a single vessel would bring in more net profit than the total assets of the Company had been at its inception: in 1784 the Company ship *Berrington* carried to India a cargo of lead, copper, steel, woolen clothes, and naval stores, which were traded for cotton piece goods, cotton yarn, indigo, redwood, silk, and saltpeter; since the outgoing cargo cost the Company £27,300 and the incoming cargo was sold for £119,304, the Company realized a net profit of over £90,000.[1]

If the Company in London garnered large dividends from the India trade, what of its servants in India? Certainly the pay was meager.

[1] According to most estimates, the purchasing power of the pound sterling in the period 1783–1793 was about 20 times its present-day equivalent.

Before 1773, a "writer," or clerk, received only £5 a year and the governor of Bengal only £200. Yet men returned from India with vast fortunes acquired in only a few years. The fact was that the East India Company expected its officers to supplement their income by private trading and tolerated all manner of disreputable schemes not directly associated with official duty. It was a type of life that attracted the ambitious, the impecunious, the unscrupulous, and the low-born rather than the idealist or the moneyed aristocrat; and it was frequently pleasant as well as rewarding. The daily routine for the newcomer, or "griffin," began shortly after dawn with a two- or three-hour ride. After breakfast came two hours of language study and an hour's visit to the office. Dinner, which consisted of "plain" food accompanied by four or five glasses of the best Madeira, was at two or three in the afternoon, followed by a rest. An hour before sunset the griffin bathed and took an airing. As the day drew to an end, two more hours were devoted to language study before a light repast and more Madeira encouraged the coming of sleep. For the veteran in the Company's service, life was even less demanding, and much of the time was given over to social intercourse.

In the early days, the Company had been a purely commercial venture, depending for protection on the orderly might of the Mogul empire which dominated all but the southern tip of India. In the three presidencies of Bombay, Madras, and Bengal, the Company conducted its affairs largely unfettered by the British government, the subject of regular inquiry only at the time of the periodic charter renewal. All appointments emanated from the Company's Court of Directors in London, but there was no supreme authority in India with jurisdiction over the Company's activities in all three presidencies.

By 1707, when the Emperor Aurangzeb died and the Mogul regime was deteriorating, the Company found its position imperiled not only by the growing internal anarchy, but also by the French *Compagnie des Indes,* which, backed by the might of the French government, was attempting to increase its influence in South India. It was in this atmosphere of turmoil, at the end of May 1744, that the East Indiaman *Winchester* dropped anchor in the roads of Madras. On board was a young clerk named Robert Clive. Of fiery temperament and reckless courage, this ambitious youth from an impoverished family had come to make his fortune in India. But it was hardly an inspiring scene that met the eyes of the new arrival—a landscape scorched by an unrelenting sun, in the foreground the unimposing façade of Fort St.

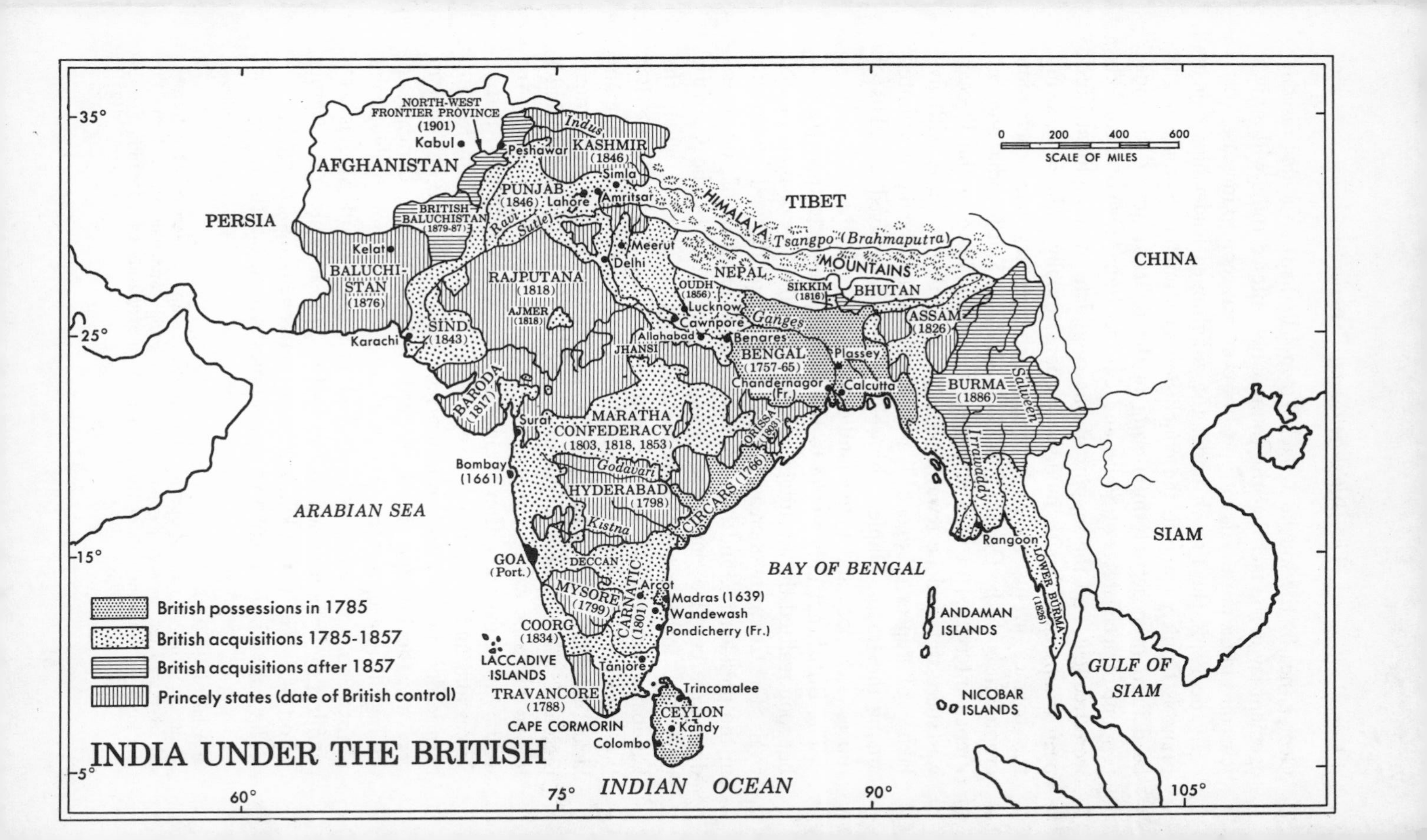
INDIA UNDER THE BRITISH
British possessions in 1785
British acquisitions 1785-1857
British acquisitions after 1857
Princely states (date of British control)
0
200
400
600
SCALE OF MILES
35°
25°
15°
5°
60°
75°
90°
105°
PERSIA
AFGHANISTAN
NORTH-WEST FRONTIER PROVINCE (1901)
Kabul
Peshawar
KASHMIR (1846)
Indus
Simla
PUNJAB (1846)
Lahore
Amritsar
BRITISH BALUCHISTAN (1879-87)
Ravi
Sutlej
Kelat
BALUCHI-STAN (1876)
Karachi
SIND (1843)
RAJPUTANA (1818)
AJMER (1818)
Meerut
Delhi
TIBET
HIMALAYA
Tsangpo (Brahmaputra)
MOUNTAINS
NEPAL
SIKKIM (1816)
BHUTAN
CHINA
OUDH (1856)
Lucknow
Cawnpore
Ganges
Allahabad
Benares
JHANSI
BENGAL (1757-65)
Plassey
Chandernagor (Fr.)
Calcutta
ASSAM (1826)
BURMA (1886)
Salween
Irrawaddy
Rangoon
LOWER BURMA (1826)
BARODA (1817)
Surat
MARATHA CONFEDERACY (1803, 1818, 1853)
ORISSA (1803)
Bombay (1661)
Godavari
HYDERABAD (1798)
CIRCARS (1766)
ARABIAN SEA
Kistna
GOA (Port.)
DECCAN
MYSORE (1799)
CARNATIC (1801)
Arcot
Madras (1639)
Wandewash
Pondicherry (Fr.)
COORG (1834)
LACCADIVE ISLANDS
Tanjore
TRAVANCORE (1788)
Trincomalee
CEYLON
Kandy
CAPE CORMORIN
Colombo
BAY OF BENGAL
ANDAMAN ISLANDS
NICOBAR ISLANDS
SIAM
GULF OF SIAM
INDIAN OCEAN

George, nearby the squalid "Black Town." Perhaps an added discouragement lay in the fact that the young Clive entered India with only a few coins in his purse. His fortune, however, was soon to increase.

In the 1740s, the French under the enlightened leadership of Jean Francois Dupleix came to the conclusion that immense profits might be derived from actively interfering in the political life of the independent princely states of South and Central India. Dynastic conflicts were frequent, and the support of one candidate by disciplined European troops, armed with modern weapons, usually sufficed to swing the balance in his favor. In 1749 such disputes over succession erupted in both the Deccan and the Carnatic in South India, and the French intervened in both struggles. Their candidate in the Deccan was successful, and he rewarded the *Compagnie des Indes* with five lakhs[2] of rupees (£50,000), a similar amount being distributed among the troops. Dupleix, himself, it is said, received 20 lakhs of rupees (£200,000) and a large land grant.

The British not only awoke to the French danger to their position but soon realized the advantages of the political policy of their French rivals. The Company increased its own meager military establishments in the presidencies, and by mid-century large numbers of Indian soldiers were enrolled under the Company's banner.[3] In the Carnatic these new forces actively opposed the French influence when the Company supported a candidate of its own on the field of battle. But the war went against it, for, unused to military action, the Company lacked talented officers. To Robert Clive the Company's predicament presented a heaven-sent opportunity. He had abandoned the clerk's life, to which he was so temperamentally unsuited, for a career in the military in 1745—soon after the outbreak of the War of the Austrian Succession, and the campaigns in the Carnatic proved him to be a born leader and an intuitive military genius. His defense of Arcot in 1751 was the key episode of the war in the Carnatic, dramatically turning the tide against the French. In 1753 he sailed for England, and in 1755, only 11 years after he had first set foot in Madras as a penniless clerk, he returned to India—this time as lieutenant governor of Fort St. David, with a king's commission as lieutenant colonel.

The war with the French was by no means over, but the key to final

[2] A lakh is 100,000.

[3] In 1748 the regular European corps of the Company's service were formed, and six years later the first regular British army troops landed in India. From this time forth, British regiments of the line served on a rotating basis in India.

victory lay far from the scene of actual combat—to the north in Bengal. Here both the British and French held trading stations by permission of the nawab of Bengal—the British at Calcutta and the French at Chandernagor. The British were aware that Bengal was the richest province in India, and they were becoming progressively more restive at not controlling a greater percentage of the rich Bengal trade. Nor was the nawab, Siraj-ud-daula, pleased with the situation. In 1756 he attacked Calcutta with 50,000 men, forcing the British to surrender and perpetrating a deplorable deed by which some 123 British prisoners died in the course of a hot Indian summer night after being incarcerated with 23 others in a stifling cell about 18 by 15 feet square—an event immortalized in history as the "Black Hole of Calcutta." The Company immediately responded by sending a punitive force from Madras, under the leadership of Clive, which recaptured Calcutta with little difficulty and wrested large concessions from the nawab. Next, Chandernagor was wrested from the French. Finally, Clive decided that it might be most profitable to give clandestine support to a rival claimant to the throne in Bengal, a certain Mir Jafar, then in the service of the nawab.

There followed a period of the most devious and disreputable scheming which bore shameful testimony to the nature of official morality in the Company's India of the eighteenth century. To conduct the negotiations with Mir Jafar successfully, Clive required an intermediary, and the noted intriguer Aminchand (Omichand), who assumed this role, appreciated fully the delicacy of the situation. If Siraj-ud-daula were to discover that the East India Company was plotting to overthrow him, the results could prove highly embarrassing to the British. Consequently, Aminchand, realizing the power of his position, demanded a large consideration from the Company as a reward for his services and discretion. To guard himself against any possible treachery, he insisted that a clause be inserted in the treaty with Mir Jafar specifically committing the Company to reward him, Aminchand, from the Bengal treasury once Siraj-ud-daula was overthrown. But Aminchand was no match for Clive, who prepared two versions of the treaty—the genuine one which made no mention of Aminchand and a forged version containing the agreed-upon clause. The latter was shown to the deluded Aminchand.

Clive, having completed his web of treachery, now moved against the nawab. At Plassey, he sealed the success of his venture in battle, and as a result the Company appointed him governor and commander-in-chief in Bengal. Mir Jafar, the new nawab, confirmed all privileges previously granted by Siraj-ud-daula, entered into an offensive-defensive alliance with the British, promised to exclude the French from Bengal, and undertook to compensate both the Company and the European inhabitants of Calcutta for the earlier loss of the city. As for the unfortunate Aminchand, he was so shocked at his betrayal that he is said to have lost his sanity; an Indian gentleman of that day might expect double-dealing from his fellow countrymen, but he would never expect an Englishman to break his word, even when it was given as a result of virtual blackmail. Bengal proved to be the key to all of India. Enriched and encouraged, the Company, by 1761, was able to drive its French rival almost entirely from the subcontinent.

If the ethics of these actions, including the deposing of Siraj-ud-daula and the tricking of Aminchand, was dubious, the private transactions of Clive himself were even more suspect. Admittedly, the eighteenth century was an age when public officials were frequently rewarded with large purses by Parliament or the Crown, and when prize money was considered a perfectly legitimate reward for successful warfare. In like spirit, the East India Company allowed its servants virtual *carte blanche* to enrich themselves as best they could. But never had a high official, merely by virtue of his position, made a fortune comparable to Clive's. Through private agreements with Mir Jafar in conjunction with their official treaty, Clive received outright the sum of £234,000. Later, as a result of a thinly veiled hint, he was granted the quit-rent of £30,000 paid by the Company to the nawab for the lands south of Calcutta—this at a time when the treasury of Bengal was so low that the official debt to the Company had to be discharged in installments and the nawab's own troops were mutinous because there was no money with which to pay them.

Meanwhile the British government's attitude towards the Company's rule in India and the conduct of its officials was undergoing a profound reappraisal. It was primarily a matter of political morality; but the profligate habits and poor taste of the *nouveaux riches* who returned to Britain (the so-called "nabobs") added force to the rising wave of objection. At the news of Clive's transactions, these feelings of concern for the first time came into focus. Nevertheless, upon his return from India in 1760, Clive received a hero's welcome. He was elected to the House of Commons in 1761 as the member from Shrewsbury; in the following year he was created Baron Clive of Plassey, but, as his elevation was to the Irish peerage, he was able to retain his seat in the Commons. By 1764 conditions in Bengal had become so deplorable that by popular demand Clive was returned to Calcutta to "cleanse the Augean stables," as he put it.

In January 1767 Clive, shattered in health and depressed in spirit, left India for the last time. During his second governorship he had carried through a number of necessary reforms, but much still remained to be done, and Parliament, incensed at the behavior of retired servants of the East India Company, many of whom had purchased seats in Parliament, and annoyed at the conditions in India which permitted the accumulation of such vast wealth, was becoming increasingly restive. In January 1770 Lord Chatham addressed the House of Lords on the subject. "For some years past," he declared,

> there has been an influx of wealth into this country, which has been attended with many fatal consequences, because it has not been the regular natural produce of labour and industry. The riches of Asia have been poured in upon us, and have brought with them not only Asiatic luxury but, I fear, Asiatic principles of government. Without connexions, without any natural interest in the soil, the importers of foreign gold have forced their way into Parliament by such a torrent of corruption as no private hereditary fortune could resist.

Two years later, a Select Committee of 31 members and a Secret Committee of 13 inquired into Indian affairs. Among other things, the committees investigated the affairs in Bengal between 1757 and 1760. Needless to say, Clive himself, although still a member of the House of Commons, occupied much of the committees' time. He thought himself shabbily treated—"like a sheep stealer," he said—but he defended himself forcefully. When his integrity was impugned for the presents he had received from Mir Jafar, Clive wondered:

> Am I not deserving of praise for the moderation which marked my proceedings? Consider the situation in which the victory of Plassey had placed me. A great prince dependent on my pleasure; an opulent city lay at my mercy; its richest bankers bid against each other for my smiles; I walked through vaults which were thrown open to me alone, piled on either hand with gold and jewels!

But in spite of the boldness of his defense, the committees' reports tended to condemn Clive's actions. And in early May 1773 the attacks on him reached their climax when Colonel John Burgoyne (later, of Saratoga fame) moved three resolutions in the Commons condemning the acquisition by private persons of vast emoluments that, as a result of war, should really have accrued to the state. These resolutions were carried, as was inevitable. But ten days later Burgoyne abandoned the field of the abstract to open an attack on Clive himself:

> . . . through the influence of the powers with which he was intrusted as . . . commander-in-chief of the British forces [he] did obtain and possess himself of the sum of £234,000; and that in so doing the said Robert Clive abused the power with which he was intrusted to the evil example of the servants of the public and to the dishonour and detriment of the state.

Clive again defended himself with vigor and passion. "Before I sit down," he concluded, "I have one request to the House, and it is that when they come to decide upon my honour they will not forget their own."

Feeling in Commons was strongly sympathetic to Clive personally, and as a result Burgoyne's motion was amended so that all reflections on Clive's character were removed; but the fact that he had received £234,000 in his capacity as commander-in-chief in Bengal was put in the record—a condemnation in itself, albeit a relatively mild one. To conclude the proceedings, the House unanimously passed the resolution: "That Robert Lord Clive did, at the same time, render great and meritorious services to this country."

Although Clive himself escaped virtually unscathed from the Parliamentary investigations, the resolutions that were passed were indicative of the changing attitude in Britain towards Indian affairs. Not surprisingly, legislation was proposed incorporating new concepts. Two acts were passed in 1773. The first one granted the East India Company a state loan to relieve its financial difficulties but limited the Company's dividends and obliged it to submit its accounts to the Treasury for scrutiny. The second, the Regulating Act, provided a new constitution for the Company, specifying a different procedure for the election of the Company's directors. The administration of Bengal was vested in a governor general and a council of four members. In the deliberations of the government of Bengal, majority opinion was to prevail, the governor general having only the advantage of a casting vote. The governor general's powers over the presidencies of Madras and Bombay were also severely circumscribed, being limited to matters concerned with the waging of war and the concluding of peace. The act provided for the creation of a supreme court in Bengal and specifically named the first governor general and councilors, although all future appointments were to be made by the Company.

Of great significance was the establishment of a scale of salaries sufficiently high to allow the Company's servants to gain a fair return for their efforts without having to engage extensively in unofficial activities. Where the governor of Bengal had received a remuneration of £200 a year, he was in the future to get £25,000. Despite its desirable features, the Regulating Act of 1773 was still a vague and inadequate piece of legislation. It failed to define clearly the relationship between the various organs of government in India, and, for that matter, between the Company and the Crown. It was, however, the first attempt to place some Crown control over the Company's rule of India and was to lead to more beneficial and coherent enactments.

The "governor-general of Fort William in Bengal" (there was as yet no governor general of India) named in the act of 1773 was Warren Hastings. Like Clive, he came from a Tory family in straitened circumstances, and the careers of the two men contain many parallels. But in personality and temperament, they differed greatly. Clive had been a rough and headstrong boy who had developed into a passionate, ruthless, dictatorial, and uncultivated man. Warren Hastings was, in contrast, reserved, careful, and prudent, a scholar who developed a lasting affection for the learning of India. He had arrived in India in 1750 under conditions similar to Clive's—as a £5-a-year clerk—and, like Clive, he rose quickly. In 1757, at the age of twenty-five, he was appointed to the important post of Company representative at the court of the nawab of Bengal in Murshidabad. Following Clive's return to England in 1760, Hastings served on the council in Calcutta. In 1765 he too sailed for England, returning again to India in 1769 as deputy to the governor of Madras, with a seat on the council. Finally, at the close of the year 1771, he was appointed to the governorship of Bengal, a post which he still held when the Regulating Act came into effect in 1774.

Altogether, Hastings served 11 years as governor general, and they were not easy years. Beset by enemies in India and England, he conducted himself with courage and dignity and, above all, with great circumspection and skill. Due to the unfortunate provisions of the Regulating Act, he was frequently at odds with the other members of the council. His relations with the presidencies of Madras and Bombay were equally difficult. Armed with an only limited supervision of their activities, he was frequently unaware of their policies—a situation that the jealous local governors did their best to encourage. Madras at one time suspended from duty its agent at the court of Hyderabad for having "betrayed the secrets of his trust to the Governor General and Council of Bengal."

Beyond the borders of Bengal, Hastings was faced with the hostility of the Marathas and the states of Hyderabad and Mysore, with the sporadic presence of French naval squadrons ready to support hostilities directed against the Company's position. Yet through patience, determination, and consummate diplomatic acumen, Hastings managed to prevail against the forces, both internal and external, which threatened him. But he made enemies, on the council and in England, who were to take advantage of four questionable episodes during his tenure as governor general to hound and harry him in later years.

In the 1730s a tribe of Afghan freebooters, the Rohillas, had seized a fertile stretch at the foot of the Himalayas and to the north of the state of Oudh. They were considered of no great consequence by either the Company or the rulers of Oudh. In 1772, however, the Marathas invaded Rohilkhand (as the Rohillas called their state), remaining only briefly; the following year they invaded again and were only induced to withdraw by a combined Oudh-Company force and by their recall to central India because of internal dissensions within the Maratha ranks.

Although the Rohillas were in alliance with Oudh against the Marathas, they behaved in an ambiguous manner when the Marathas actually appeared. The nawab wazir of Oudh used this as a pretext to eliminate his somewhat unreliable neighbors. He gained Hastings' support by paying the Company 50 lakhs of rupees (£500,000) for the restoration to Oudh of Korah and Allahabad from the dwindling possessions of the Mogul emperor to whom they had been assigned by Clive. The nawab wazir also promised to pay the Company 40 lakhs of rupees (£400,000) for its support in a war against the Rohillas and 210,000 rupees (£21,000) for the "rental" of one brigade of Company troops.

Hastings was not too concerned about the morality of his actions. He saw nothing wrong in hiring out Company troops to fight in a war with which the Company was not intimately concerned. Neither he nor his council doubted that the Rohillas, by their equivocal conduct during the Maratha invasions, had justified the actions being taken against them. As Hastings himself later said:

I own that the convenience of possessing the Rohilla country was not sufficient reason for invading it. I never said it was; but if they had afforded a just provocation for invading their country, and we saw advantages in invading it, though neither cause was alone sufficient to produce that effect, yet both united would certainly justify it, and the most rigid speculators would approve so fair a conclusion. The war was successful, a troublesome neighbour was removed, an ally strengthened and a neat profit was made in the bargain. This was justification enough.

Three new members of the council appointed under the Regulating Act arrived in India during the concluding stages of the Rohilla war. They were determined to undermine, thwart, and even supplant the governor general. Of these new arrivals, the ambitious and vindictive Sir Philip Francis was not only the most able but the most determined, and he was to persecute Hastings venomously throughout his career. Francis's two allies were General Sir John Clavering and Colonel George Monson, and from 1774 to 1776 Hastings was generally outvoted and overruled in the council.

The first action of the new councilors was to condemn the Rohilla war, and their general hostility encouraged Hastings' enemies in Calcutta to come to the surface. Several charges of peculation and dishonesty were filed against him. Finally, in March 1775, Nandakumar (known at the time as Nuncomar), an old Brahmin adversary of Hastings', laid before the council a letter accusing the governor general of having received numerous bribes, but particularly one of three and a half lakhs of rupees (£35,000) from the widow of Mir Jafar. This accusation was seized upon with avidity by Francis, Monson, and Clavering, who further stated that "there is no species of peculation from which the Governor-General has thought it reasonable to abstain." Hastings, in a rare state of fury, replied:

I will not sit at this Board in the character of a criminal, nor do I acknowledge the members of the Board to be my judges. I am induced on this occasion to make the declaration that I look upon General Clavering, Colonel Monson and Mr. Francis as my accusers.

When the council summoned Nandakumar to give evidence, Hastings declared the council closed and left the room.

The Chief of this administration, your superior, gentlemen, appointed by the legislature itself, shall I sit at this Board to be arraigned in the presence of a wretch whom you all know to be one of the basest of mankind? . . . Shall I sit to hear men collected from the dregs of the people give evidence at his dictating against my character and conduct? I will not. You may, if you please, form yourselves into a Committee for the investigation of such matters, in any manner which you may think proper, but I will repeat that I will not meet Nundcoomar at the Board nor suffer Nundcoomar to be examined at the Board; nor have you a right to do it, nor can it answer any other purpose than that of vilifying and insulting me to insist upon it.

But insist upon it they did. Hastings withdrew, along with Richard Barwell, his only ally on the council, and the other members proceeded to examine Nandakumar.

Although Nandakumar's accusation was indeed false, it managed to rally all the enemies of the governor general behind the council. Nor could Hastings expect any help from the Company or the British government, neither of which bore him any great love. But matters were soon to take a dramatic new turn. Hastings, with Sir Elijah Impey, the chief justice of Bengal, on his side, counterattacked by having Nandakumar arraigned and convicted for conspiracy on rather flimsy evidence. Next Nandakumar was charged with forgery. Of his guilt there was little doubt, although he was merely indulging in a practice not uncommon in the India of his day. The case was heard before Impey and a European jury. Nandakumar was found guilty of forgery—his greater crime, of course, was to have attacked the governor general.

If the conviction of Nandakumar for forgery was not surprising, the sentence of death was. Certainly this was the punishment prescribed by British law, but it had never been implemented in Bengal, where forgery was a common practice in business and at worst a venial offense. Even if Nandakumar were being punished for affronts to the governor general, the sentence of death was excessive, and no one thought it would actually be carried out. But the council, whose tool Nandakumar was, did not come to his aid, and the whole unlikely drama proceeded inexorably towards a grim and unexpected end. Thomas Babington Macaulay, the famous nineteenth-century historian, essayist, and administrator, eloquently described the morning of the execution in the *Edinburgh Review* (October 1841):

Grief and horror were on every face; yet to the last the multitude could hardly believe that the English really purposed to take the life of the great Brahmin. At length the mournful procession came through the crowd. Nuncomar sat up in his palanquin, and looked round him with unaltered serenity. He had just parted from those who were most nearly connected with him. Their cries and contortions had appalled the European ministers of justice, but had not produced the smallest effect on the iron stoicism of the prisoner. The only anxiety which he expressed was that men of his own priestly caste might be in attendance to take charge of his corpse. He again desired to be remembered to his friends in the Council, mounted the scaffold with firmness, and gave the signal to the executioner. The moment that the drop fell, a howl of sorrow and despair rose from the innumerable spectators. Hundreds turned away their faces from the polluting sight, fled with loud wailings towards the Hoogley, and plunged into the holy waters, as if to purify themselves from the guilt of having looked on such a crime.

Yet Hastings did not fall in the popular estimation: perhaps having successfully avenged himself on an enemy who had grievously injured him, he gained greater public respect.

The execution of Nandakumar was for Hastings the harbinger of victory over the council, and from 1777 on he was once more in the ascendancy. He was able to renovate the administration of Bengal but found himself embroiled in a series of wars with the Marathas and with Hyder Ali of Mysore who was supported by the French. These wars were naturally expensive, but the Company in London, far from sending the necessary funds, demanded money from India for the payment of dividends to its stockholders. The House of Commons, for its part, passed a vote of censure on the governor general's conduct.

Hastings, with his coffers dwindling, was forced to turn elsewhere. The raja of Benares had at one time owed fealty to the state of Oudh, but by a treaty of 1775 he had gained his lands from the Company and tendered it his allegiance. As part of this arrangement, the raja, Chait Singh, paid the Company an annual tribute of 22½ lakhs of rupees (£225,000). In 1778, under the financial pressures of war, Hastings felt justified in demanding a special contribution of five lakhs of rupees (£50,000) from the raja. Chait Singh asked that the exaction be limited to one year and was punished for this effrontery by being ordered to pay immediately, rather than in installments. When Chait Singh begged for a postponement of seven months, he was given five days and informed that if he did not pay within that time he would be treated as if he had refused to pay altogether. In the following year a similar sum was demanded of the raja. He was aghast and claimed that his agreement with the Company exempted him from all payments beyond the original annual tribute. In this he was correct, for in 1775 it had been specified that as long as Chait Singh paid the tribute, "no demands shall be made upon him by the Honble. Company, of any kind, on any pretence whatsoever, nor shall any person be allowed to interfere with his authority or to disturb the peace of the country." Nevertheless, in 1779 British troops marched on Benares and Chait Singh paid the five lakhs of rupees, plus 20,000 more rupees for the expenses of the troops. Again, in 1780, a demand for an extra five lakhs of rupees was made. This time, the raja sent a special agent to Calcutta to offer Hastings a present of 20,000 rupees, which the governor general accepted on behalf of the Company; but he also exacted the five lakhs of rupees, and, it is rumored, levied an additional fine for attempted bribery as well.

The sorely tried Chait Singh was still not to be relieved of anxiety: he was next ordered to furnish the Company with 2,000 cavalry. When he protested vehemently against this, the number was reduced to 1,000, and he finally produced 500 infantry, armed with matchlocks. Hastings had meanwhile determined to impose upon the Company's wretched tributary the staggering fine of 50 lakhs of rupees (£500,000). "I was resolved," he wrote, "to draw from his guilt the means of relief to the Company's distresses. In a word, I had determined to make him pay largely for his pardon, or to exact a severe vengeance for his past delinquency." Chait Singh, whose written defense was found inadequate as well as impudent by Hastings (though this seems hardly to have been the case), was arrested and compelled to submit to the governor general's demands. But the raja's soldiers in Benares rose in protest and massacred a contingent of British troops, forcing the unfortunate Chait Singh to flee. He was deposed by Hastings and his territories were forfeited to his nephew, who had in the future to pay an annual tribute of 40 lakhs of rupees (£400,000) to the Company instead of the 22½ lakhs formerly demanded. It is true that in this whole business Hastings acted in the best traditions of oriental monarchy, but, as Sir Alfred Lyall, the noted English historian of India and biographer of Hastings, later pointed out, "whenever the English in India descend to the ordinary level of political morality among Asiatic potentates they lose all the advantages of contrast."

Hastings' desperate quest for funds was not limited to the squeezing of the unhappy Chait Singh. The nawab wazir of Oudh, Asaf-ud-daula, was in considerable arrears with the tribute he owed the Company. His mother and grandmother, the so-called begums of Oudh, held large estates and had inherited a considerable fortune from the late nawab. Asaf-ud-daula claimed that this wealth was justly his, and in 1775 the widow of Shuja-ud-daula, the previous nawab, agreed to pay her son 30 lakhs of rupees (£300,000) in addition to the 26 lakhs (£260,000) already given him, on condition that both he and the Company agreed to make no further demands on her. Although Hastings himself opposed the signing of such an agreement, he was overruled by the council, and the pledge was duly given.

In 1781 Asaf-ud-daula asked that the agreement be abrogated so that he could pay his debt to the Company, and Hastings, who was as usual in severe financial straits, consented, using the so-called rebellious conduct of the begums as provocation. But the nawab was afraid of the "uncommonly violent temper of his female relations" and began to lose his enthusiasm for the venture. Consequently, he had to be forced into action by Hastings, whose appetite had now become thoroughly whetted. British detachments were sent to support the nawab's movements, and, by means of several modes of persuasion, the eunuch servants of the begums were forced to yield the treasure. All in all, about 105 lakhs of rupees (£1,050,000) were thus obtained, most of which was turned over to the Company. It was at best an ignoble undertaking, and Hastings was ordered by the directors to make at least partial restitution to the begums.

The torrent of criticism which had been unleashed in British official circles by the conduct of Clive was strengthened by these actions of his successor. In 1784, impressed with the inadequacies of the Regulating Act of 1773, William Pitt the Younger introduced his India Bill, which was to set the basis for future British rule in India. The East India Company officially remained the ruling agency but was effectively placed under government regulation through the establishment of the Board of Control, whose president became the chief author, in England, of Indian policy. In India itself, the presidencies were finally made subordinate to Bengal in all questions of war, revenue, and diplomacy, and the supreme power was placed in the hands of a governor general and a council of three.

Hastings himself returned to England in June 1785, only to fall into the waiting arms of his enemies. The attack in Parliament was led by Edmund Burke and Charles James Fox, both old antagonists of the Company. The Commons acquitted Hastings of having acted improperly in the case of the Rohilla and Maratha wars, and it appeared that Hastings was going to weather the storm. When, in mid-June 1786, Fox presented the charges of extortion regarding Chait Singh, Hastings' supporters were in complacent high spirits. Pitt rose and began by generously praising Hastings, who he felt was quite justified in fining Chait Singh. But just as the House had settled back to watch the inevitable defeat of the charge, Pitt concluded by saying that although Hastings had a right to assess Chait Singh, the amount collected was "utterly disproportionate and shamefully exorbitant," as was the imposing of the final 50 lakhs of rupees (£500,000) fine. So saying, Pitt announced his intention of voting for Fox's motion. The effect was electric, a complete change in the situation was effected, and the vote on the motion, whose loss had been considered a foregone conclusion, resulted instead in its passage by 119 votes to 79. The House was now committed to the impeachment of Warren Hastings, and a resolution condemning him for his despoliation of the begums of Oudh was passed by an even larger majority. Many other charges of peculation were agreed upon, and in May 1787, almost a year after the decisive vote, Hastings was arrested and brought before the bar of the House of Lords.

The trial itself began in Westminster Hall in February 1788, and again the words of Macaulay, in his essay on Hastings in the *Edinburgh Review,* bring the memorable scene to life:

The place was worthy of such a trial. It was the great hall of William Rufus, the hall which had resounded with acclamations at the inaugurations of thirty kings, the hall which had witnessed the just sentence of Bacon and the just absolution of Somers, the hall where the eloquence of Strafford had for a moment awed and melted a victorious party inflamed with just resentment, the hall where Charles had confronted the High Court of Justice with the placid courage which has half redeemed his fame. Neither military nor civil pomp was wanting. The avenues were lined with grenadiers. The streets were kept clear by cavalry. The peers, robed in gold and ermine, were marshalled by the heralds under Garter King-at-arms. The judges in their vestments of state attended to give advice on points of law. Near a hundred and seventy lords, three-fourths of the Upper House as the Upper House then was, walked in solemn order from their usual place of assembling to the tribunal. The junior Baron present led the way, George Eliott, Lord Heathfield, recently ennobled for his memorable defence of Gibraltar against the fleets and armies of France and Spain. The long procession was closed by the Duke of Norfolk, Earl Marshal of the realm, by the great dignitaries, and by the brothers and sons of the King. Last of all came the Prince of Wales, conspicuous by his fine person and noble bearing. The grey old walls were hung with scarlet. The long galleries were crowded by an audience such as has rarely excited the fears or the emulations of an orator. There were gathered together, from all parts of a great, free, enlightened, and prosperous empire, grace and female loveliness, wit and learning, the representatives of every science and of every art. There were seated round the Queen the fairhaired young daughters of the House of Brunswick. There the Ambassadors of great Kings and Commonwealths gazed with admiration on a spectacle which no other country in the world could present. There Siddons, in the prime of her majestic beauty, looked with emotion on a scene surpassing all the imitations of the stage. There the historian of the Roman Empire thought of the days when Cicero pleaded the cause of Sicily against Verres, and when, before a senate which still retained some show of freedom, Tacitus thundered against the oppressor of Africa. There were seen side by side the greatest painter and the greatest scholar of his age. . . . There appeared the voluptuous charms of her to whom the heir of the throne had in secret plighted his faith. . . . There were the members of that brilliant society which quoted, criticized, and exchanged repartees, under the rich peacock-hangings of Mrs. Montague. And there the ladies whose lips, more persuasive than those of Fox himself, had carried the Westminster election against palace and treasury, shone around Georgiana Duchess of Devonshire.

The Serjeants made proclamation. Hastings advanced to the bar, and bent his knee. The culprit was indeed not unworthy of that great presence. . . . He looked like a great man, and not like a bad man. A person small and emaciated, yet deriving dignity from a carriage which, while it indicated deference to the court, indicated also habitual self-possession and self-respect, a high and intellectual forehead, a brow pensive, but not gloomy, a mouth of inflexible decision, a face pale and worn, but serene. . . .

But neither the culprit nor his advocates attracted so much notice as the accusers. In the midst of the blaze of red drapery, a space had been fitted up with green benches and tables for the Commons. The managers [of the impeachment], with Burke at their head, appeared in full dress. The collectors of gossip did not fail to remark that even Fox, generally so regardless of his appearance, had paid to the illustrious tribunal the compliment of wearing a bag and sword.

The other managers of impeachment besides Burke and Fox were Richard Brinsley Sheridan, William Windham, and Charles (later Earl) Grey, who was the youngest at the age of twenty-three.

It was an age of elaborate and verbose oratory. The reading of the charges alone took two complete days. On the third, Burke rose and occupied the next four sittings with his opening speech which served as a general introduction to the charges. It was apparently as eloquent as it was long. With deep emotion he concluded:

Therefore, hath it with all confidence been ordered, by the Commons of Great Britain, that I impeach Warren Hastings of high crimes and misdemeanours. I impeach him in the name of the Commons' House of

Parliament, whose trust he has betrayed. I impeach him in the name of the English nation, whose ancient honour he has sullied. I impeach him in the name of the people of India, whose rights he has trodden under foot, and whose country he has turned into a desert. Lastly, in the name of human nature itself, in the name of both sexes, in the name of every age, in the name of every rank, I impeach the common enemy and oppressor of all!

But the high sense of drama that pervaded the openings of proceedings was not to continue. Dissension within the ranks of the managers of the impeachment themselves, acrimonious debates on the admissibility of evidence, and the Lords' preoccupation with more pressing business extended the affair interminably. The verdict was finally given in April 1795, in the eighth year of the impeachment, and only 29 peers had heard enough of the trial to feel themselves qualified to vote. Hastings was acquitted on all charges.

Warren Hastings was to live for 23 more years in retirement at his old family seat at Daylesford, Worcestershire. But he returned to Westminister one final time in 1813, when the renewal of the charter of the East India Company was being debated. By this time old animosities were forgotten and Hastings was remembered for what he basically was—a talented, loyal, and tenacious imperial public servant. As he withdrew, he wrote in his diary that "all the members, by one simultaneous impulse rose with their heads uncovered, and stood in silence till I passed the door of the chamber."

Robert Clive and Warren Hastings were the two ablest servants of the East India Company during the eighteenth century. They established the basis of British power in India. Yet they were both tried for behaving according to the accepted standards of their day. This would seem a paradox were it not that the real importance of these proceedings lay not with the individuals concerned, but rather in the changes in public attitude of which they were symptomatic. They indicated the dissatisfaction of Parliament with the conduct of affairs in India. Clive's career in India presaged the Regulating Act of 1773, and the governor generalship of Hastings presaged the India Act of 1784. These acts ensured that a commercial company would no longer be allowed virtually unfettered political control over vast and rich lands. Nor would its adventurous servants continue to make fortunes in activities which took them well beyond the bounds of their official duties. With the appointment of Lord Cornwallis as governor general in 1786, a different type of Englishman was to serve in India. Frequently a member of the upper class, he was bound by a new morality to live on his official earnings and whatever private means he might have. As a product of the age of William Wilberforce and the evangelical antislavery movement, he was more concerned with religion, morals, and the welfare of those he governed than his forebears had been. But whether this new type of official was really an improvement over his unprincipled, rapacious predecessor we shall have to see in later chapters.

The Durham Report and the Establishment of Responsible Government in Canada

THE AMERICAN REVOLUTION not only deprived the British Empire of most of its possessions in North America; it also placed in doubt heretofore accepted principles of imperial administration, and its aftermaths forced changes in imperial policy towards the colonies of white settlement even more profound than those effected in India after the administrations of Clive and Hastings. It became generally accepted that colonies should not in future be taxed from Britain. But whether the American Revolution was the result of too much permissiveness on the part of the home government or not enough was a matter of considerable controversy. The consensus, however, seemed to be that while Britain's imperial future might lie in the East, already established colonies in other areas should be retained and should be under the strict control of Westminster. As William Knox, a former undersecretary in the Colonial Department stated: "It was better to have no colonies at all than not to have them subservient to the maritime strength and commercial interests of Great Britain." Such being the reasoning, Britain's overseas possessions were in future to be kept under a tight rein.

Whereas the new concept of the taxing power of the state was a wise one, the principle of more rigid imperial control over the remain-

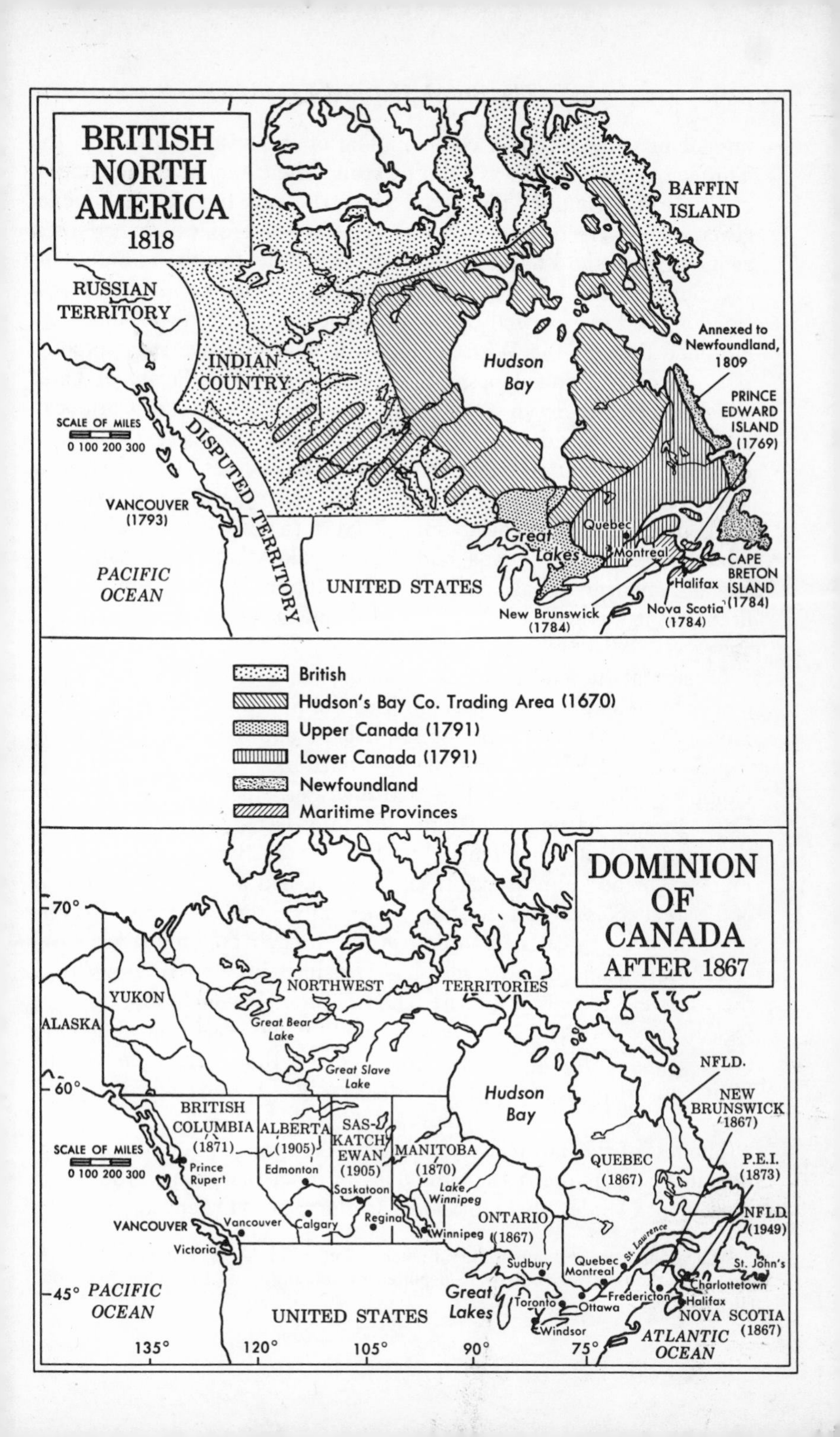
BRITISH NORTH AMERICA 1818
RUSSIAN TERRITORY
INDIAN COUNTRY
DISPUTED TERRITORY
BAFFIN ISLAND
Hudson Bay
Annexed to Newfoundland, 1809
PRINCE EDWARD ISLAND (1769)
CAPE BRETON ISLAND (1784)
Quebec
Montreal
Great Lakes
Halifax
Nova Scotia (1784)
New Brunswick (1784)
SCALE OF MILES
0 100 200 300
VANCOUVER (1793)
PACIFIC OCEAN
UNITED STATES
British
Hudson's Bay Co. Trading Area (1670)
Upper Canada (1791)
Lower Canada (1791)
Newfoundland
Maritime Provinces
DOMINION OF CANADA AFTER 1867
70°
60°
45°
YUKON
ALASKA
NORTHWEST TERRITORIES
Great Bear Lake
Great Slave Lake
Hudson Bay
NFLD.
NEW BRUNSWICK (1867)
BRITISH COLUMBIA (1871)
ALBERTA (1905)
SAS-KATCH-EWAN (1905)
MANITOBA (1870)
QUEBEC (1867)
P.E.I. (1873)
NFLD. (1949)
ONTARIO (1867)
Prince Rupert
Edmonton
Saskatoon
Lake Winnipeg
Calgary
Regina
Winnipeg
Vancouver
Victoria
VANCOUVER
St. Lawrence
Sudbury
Quebec
Montreal
St. John's
Charlottetown
Fredericton
Ottawa
Toronto
Windsor
Halifax
NOVA SCOTIA (1867)
Great Lakes
PACIFIC OCEAN
UNITED STATES
ATLANTIC OCEAN
135°
120°
105°
90°
75°

ing colonies was merely a compounding of the mistakes made in the Thirteen Colonies and was almost to cause the complete disintegration of the British Empire. The arena where the new theories of imperial government were to be tested was Canada, most of which had been acquired from the French in the wars of the eighteenth century. This vast northern territory was, however, not considered of much value in London. Still mesmerized by the principles of mercantilism, most Englishmen thought the West Indies, with their lucrative sugar production, the ideal colonial possessions. Thus, when the Treaty of Paris, which ended the Seven Years' War in 1763, returned the Caribbean sugar island of Guadeloupe to France but upheld British possession of Canada, consternation reigned in the financial houses of the city. One interested observer remarked: "The Peace of Paris is like the Peace of God, it passeth all understanding." Nevertheless, the British maintained possession of Canada, and the new colony became the object of several American attacks during the Revolution. But its defenses held firm, and it was still solidly in British hands at the end of the war in 1783.

Canada at the end of the Revolution consisted of the province of Quebec, stretching from the mouth of the St. Lawrence to the Great Lakes; Nova Scotia; Cape Breton Island and Isle St. John (later Prince Edward Island); and the vast territories of the Hudson's Bay Company in the north. The maritime settlements—Nova Scotia,[1] Cape Breton Island, and Prince Edward Island—contained a few thousand British inhabitants, but the rest of their population was French. Quebec, almost exclusively French, had a population in 1783 of between 80,000 and 100,000. The end of the American Revolution, however, threatened to destroy the French predominance. Over 50,000 American colonists who had remained loyal to Britain during the war were forced to find new homes after its conclusion, and the logical place for them to go was Canada. In the years following 1783, some 35,000 "United Empire Loyalists," as they were soon known, settled in Nova Scotia and the adjacent islands and 20,000 in Quebec.

The loss of the Thirteen Colonies and the changed population equation in Canada forced the promulgation of a new constitutional arrangement. Under the provisions of the Canada Act of 1791, the

[1] There had been about 10,000 French colonists in Nova Scotia (Acadia) in 1755. Six thousand of them were deported by the British in that year, but 3,000 later returned.

western half of Nova Scotia, where most of the loyalists had settled, was detached from the rest of the province and established as a separate province of New Brunswick. The solution in Quebec was more difficult. Although most of the new colonists had settled in the western part of Quebec—between Montreal and the Great Lakes—a significant number had also decided to stay in the predominantly French east and south. Thus, although the act divided the old province of Quebec into a predominantly French Lower Canada (present-day Quebec) and a predominantly British Upper Canada (present-day Ontario), the former harbored a strong British minority. A bitter rivalry developed between the agricultural French and the mercantile British, based on national, social, religious, and, above all, economic differences. The British merchant class, for instance, advocated a land tax as the best method for raising revenue, while the French farmers preferred a duty on imports. The act of 1791 stipulated that Upper and Lower Canada were each to have its own governor appointed by the Crown and its own assembly, laws, language, and established church. The governor of Lower Canada was also to be the governor general of British North America—a post of little real substance.

Under the new constitution, members of the Legislative Assembly, the lower house, were to be elected by all freeholders with lands worth 40 shillings a year, and the members of the Legislative Council, the upper house, were to be appointed by the governors. The Canada Act was a conscious effort to put into effect the prime lesson Englishmen thought they had learned from the American Revolution. It was a system intended to prevent Canadians from having the latitude of action that had been the cause of all the problems further south: conservative government was to operate with little scope for the popular expression of ideas.

If this was the objective of the new system, it worked admirably. In the legislatures of both Upper and Lower Canada, reactionary cliques predominated—the Family Compact, made up of United Empire Loyalists, in Upper Canada, and the similarly constituted Château Clique in Lower Canada. The center of their control was the Legislative Council, where the elective principle was not in operation and which consequently tended to remain unchanged through the years. Any possible independence of the legislature from the executive was obviated by the presence of the same men in both the governor's Executive Council and the Legislative Council. The governor, under the act, had a suspensory veto over all legislation. This in effect meant that long delays would often occur in the legislative process, for after the governor had suspended a piece of legislation, it had to be referred to London for a final decision.

Although the lower house of each province could initiate tax policy, the governor again had a veto, making it possible to bring the wheels of administration to a complete halt. Adding to the difficulties, no good system of land distribution was established by the act. Instead, it provided for the assignment of vast tracts of the land to the Anglican Church and to the Crown. Large grants were in turn made to favored individuals within the ruling cliques. The whole situation was one calculated to create the maximum of frustration. Legitimate settlers had to buy land from privileged persons at excessively high prices. The legislature could debate but could not really act. Meanwhile, to compound already existing problems, the population of Canada increased from 150,000 in 1773 to 600,000 in 1830, and many of these new settlers came from the United States where they were accustomed to a different set of political circumstances.

Things went from bad to worse. In Lower Canada the situation was exacerbated by the fact that control of the upper house was in the hands of English appointees, while the French continued to control the lower house. Reformers constantly demanded unhampered legislative control of the revenue, an elective upper house, curbs on the power of the executive, and an improved system of land allocation. Some minor concessions were made by the British government, but most of the Canadian appeals fell on deaf ears. In Upper Canada, the Family Compact maintained control of the Executive Council from governor to governor and continued irresponsibly to allocate the revenue and distribute the public lands.

While the British government persisted in adhering theoretically to the principle of rigid control of colonial areas from London, in practice imperial administration was far different. Canadian affairs were studiously ignored, and the governors appointed by Whitehall were all too often nonentities of little talent. Whereas British neglect of the Thirteen Colonies had allowed representative institutions with considerable power to evolve, in Canada a similar development was prevented by the constitution of 1791.

In November 1837 popular discontent became too great, and open revolt broke out in Lower Canada. It was a protest against British "coercion and despotism," manifested by the continued efforts of the governor and Legislative Council, representing the British minority, to subjugate the predominantly French Legislative Assembly and *la nation Canadienne.* Upper Canada was also the scene of an uprising in the following month, but it had none of the serious implications of the unrest near Montreal. The Upper Canadian rebellion was an attempt to force the government of the province towards a more democratic constitution, and the governor—to a large degree—encouraged its outbreak in order to provide himself with an excuse for crushing radical agitation.

The two rebellions were of little consequence militarily and were put down without much difficulty, but the effect in London was dramatic. A permissive policy had resulted in revolt in the Thirteen Colonies; the more rigid control of colonial administration from London had brought about revolt in Canada. What was to be done?

In England, the future of the Empire had been a subject of increasing debate. Colonies, it seemed, should either be firmly controlled by the mother country or they should be cut free. There appeared to be no middle road. Responsible government in an imperial context seemed a logical impossibility, since it would place the governor under colonial control and not under the control of the secretary of state in London, or, ultimately, of the British Parliament. Would this not lead inevitably to the dissolution of the British Empire?

Most statesmen thought that it would, and some welcomed the prospect either on philosophical or purely materialistic grounds. Colonies were expensive. A great deal of money was expended on their administration and defense, with very little accruing to the British government in the way of a tangible return. Lord John Russell, the prominent Whig parliamentarian, said in the year of the rebellions that the granting of responsible government in Canada would mean "separate independent powers existing in Great Britain and every separate Colony. It would be better to say at once 'Let the two countries separate' than for us to pretend to govern the Colony afterwards." Although he did not foresee an immediate collapse of the British Empire, Russell conjectured that in the future "our Colonies might with propriety be severed from us and formed into a separate and distinct State." To those who claimed that colonies were necessary for defense, the anti-imperialists answered that colonial bases were only necessary for the defense of other bases, not of England itself. Besides, as Lord Palmerston had once said, if one owned a house in London and a house in York, must one own all the inns on the way?

It would seem that there were only two possible answers to the imperial question: either British overseas possessions had to be strictly controlled from London or they would have to be cut loose, by overt action if necessary. But reducing the issue to these two alternatives would be oversimplifying the case. Very few, even of the most ardent anti-imperialists, favored the complete independence of the colonies from the mother country if it could be avoided, and none wished to cut the profitable Indian connection. They merely wanted to limit Britain's responsibilities—to "loosen the bands."

Real differences nonetheless did exist on the matter of imperial policy, and a group known in history as the Liberal Imperialists developed to bridge the gap between the advocates and opponents of empire. They too were for the loosening of imperial bands and for the transfer of the costs of administration to colonial governments. But they also wished to strengthen, by all means possible, the ties between the colonies and the mother country. They hoped to accomplish both of these purposes by increasing the emotional ties between Britain and its overseas possessions while at the same time giving the colonies greater control over their own destinies. Thus, the colonies, which might indeed share a common heritage with Britain but who were now developing along different lines, would not be alienated by excessive British interference in their affairs, and Britain would in turn not have to bear the costs of colonial defense and administration.

The concept that was to lend substance to their ideas was that of "responsible government" in the colonies. Loosely defined, responsible government meant legislative supremacy. The governor would lose his ultimate authority over the actions of the legislature and could expect no succor from the imperial government in London. The only way he could continue to preside over a functioning government would be always to choose as his prime minister the leader of the majority party in the legislature. The early formulators of this theory did, however, reserve certain areas for the exclusive control of the British government—most notably, foreign affairs.

The Canadian revolts were to give the Liberal Imperialists a chance to advocate their philosophy more strongly and coherently. Even before the uprisings, Lord Melbourne, the British prime minister, had asked Lord Durham, a leading domestic reformer and opponent of the government's colonial policy, to go to Canada to try and ameliorate the situation. As Melbourne wrote to Durham:

The final separation of those Colonies might possibly not be of material detriment to the interests of the mother-country, but it is clear that it would be a serious blow to the honour of Great Britain, and certainly would be fatal to the character and existence of the Administration under which it took place.

One might wonder why Melbourne should contemplate sending on such a mission a man whom he personally disliked and who had been a persistent critic of his régime. But Melbourne no doubt recognized Durham's very real abilities. No doubt he also hoped that Durham's appointment would temper the attitude of the radical members of Parliament who were harrying him continually and no doubt he was well aware that the situation in Canada was so fraught with difficulties that it had already been the political burial place of many politicians and that it might remove the troublesome Durham from the scene permanently—and certainly for the foreseeable future.

John George Lambton, first Earl of Durham, came from an ancient family, the Lambtons of Lambton Castle, whose wealth in later times was solidly based on the ownership of collieries. A thorough aristocrat, he enjoyed the advantages of wealth and status and was once known to remark that a man ought to be able to "jog along on £40,000 a year." He was the son-in-law of Earl Grey, who had been the Whig prime minister from 1830 to 1834. In spite of his affluence, Durham not only interested himself in public affairs, but also entered Parliament as a radical. An early supporter of the Reform Bill, he broke with the Whigs because of their unwillingness to pass further reforms. Durham was brilliant, mercurial, and difficult. He loved his fellow man in the abstract but despised him in the particular. François Guizot, the French ambassador in London in 1840, "perceived in his haughty melancholy a strong imprint of egotism and vanity," while *The Times* described him as "vainglorious and perverse." There was no doubting his great ability, however, and although he was excluded from the highest offices through the fear, jealousy, and genuine dislike of his colleagues, he nonetheless filled several positions of significance.

That Durham was able to hold public office at all was a tribute to his courage and dedication, for his health was so delicate that he suffered frequent collapses and lived from physical crisis to physical crisis. When Melbourne summoned him for the Canadian mission, he was ambassador to St. Petersburg, and as his health had already suffered from two years' exposure to the Russian climate, he refused the appointment. But this was before the Canadian revolts; when news of them reached London in December 1837, Melbourne renewed his plea—this time with added urgency. For two weeks Durham hesitated.

Finally, with great reluctance and at considerable personal sacrifice, he accepted the commission. "I can assure you," Melbourne wrote to him, "that I consider you as making a great sacrifice for the chance of doing an essential service to the country. As far as I am concerned, and I think I answer for all my colleagues, you will receive the firmest and most unflinching support." Durham, for his part, demanded that he not "be stinted with powers or in money and am to have unstinted appointment of all civil officers whom I may think necessary for the efficient execution of my duties."

As a consequence of Durham's acceptance, the constitution of Lower Canada was suspended by Parliament until November 1840, and a special council created, with the advice and consent of which the governor was empowered to promulgate any acts or ordinances within the powers of the suspended legislature. Durham himself was appointed captain-general, high commissioner, and governor-in-chief of all the provinces, including Newfoundland. He took his new titles seriously and for four months prepared for a truly regal journey and arrival in Canada. This long delay took much of the dramatic edge off his mission, but at least Durham also utilized the time in informing himself thoroughly on Canadian affairs. The new governor general's establishment was truly magnificent, and it must be said to his credit that if it was excessively opulent, he at least bore the whole cost himself, not even accepting any salary. An army of grooms and servants, eight aides-de-camp, cases of silver, horses, and ornate furniture were prepared to add luster to the new captain-general's mission, and all this for an undertaking that Durham himself anticipated would not take more than a year.

The staff Durham chose to accompany him was unusual not only from the standpoint of the many and varied talents possessed by its members, but because of their frequently less than orthodox backgrounds. The chief secretary was Charles Buller, a popular and able member of the radical representation in Parliament. He tended to hide his considerable talents and astute judgment behind a mask of unceasing jocularity and *joie de vivre*. At the time of his appointment, he was only thirty-one.

Durham also selected as his aide Edward Gibbon Wakefield, one of the most fertile minds to devote itself to the economic problems of empire and particularly to the all-important question of land tenure. But Wakefield was possessed of a rather curious moral code. Twice, through the most devious means, he had abducted young heiresses whom he subsequently married. On the second occasion, he had induced a young girl at a boarding school, to whom he was a total stranger, to elope with him as the only means of saving her wealthy father from financial ruin—a story which was a complete fabrication. Wakefield was subsequently arrested and sentenced to three years in Newgate Prison, and his marriage was dissolved by act of Parliament. Nevertheless, Durham recognized Wakefield's very significant contributions to the theory of colonial settlement—chiefly through his doctrine of "systematic colonization"—and determined to appoint him commissioner of Crown lands and emigration in Canada. But this was to be done after the party's arrival in Canada to forestall any possible governmental interference.

Another controversial appointment was that of Thomas Turton as legal advisor to the mission. Durham determined on the creation of such a post so that he would be independent of the solicitor general and attorney general of Lower Canada in deliberating upon the revision of the Canadian legal structure. Turton was undoubtedly professionally qualified for the post, but he, like Wakefield, had an unsavory past—he had been the defendant in a notorious divorce suit which his wife had successfully brought, naming her sister as correspondent. Melbourne tried to dissuade Durham from appointing Turton because of the political explosion that would ensue, but Durham was adamant. It was finally decided that Turton could accompany the mission, but with no official appointment from the British government. These then were the most significant members of Lord Durham's mission to Canada. It was ability and talent that were almost the sole criteria for their selection, and it is interesting to note that not only Durham but also Wakefield and Turton served without any remuneration whatever.

The ship carrying Durham and his entourage finally anchored off Quebec in late May 1838, and the next day the new governor general entered the city in triumph. The spectacle was one of splendor unrivaled in the history of Canada. The size of the retinue astounded the inhabitants. The baggage alone took two days to land. Durham himself was clad in a magnificent uniform emblazoned with silver embroidery, around his neck the collar of the Bath. He was mounted on a spirited white horse and through the cheering crowd made his imperious way to the Castle of St. Louis. After taking the oath of office, his first act was to refuse to reappoint the old members of the Executive Council. Next he issued a proclamation inviting the cooperation of all Canadians in the fulfillment of his mission:

> I invite from you the most free, unreserved communications. I beg you to consider me as a friend and arbitrator—ready at all times to listen to your wishes, complaints, and grievances, and fully determined to act with the strictest impartiality. If you, on your side, will abjure all party and sectarian animosities, and unite with me in the blessed work of peace and harmony, I feel sure that I can lay the foundation of such a system of government as will protect the rights and interests of all classes, allay all dissensions, and permanently establish under Divine Providence, the wealth, greatness, and prosperity, of which such inexhaustible elements are to be found in these fertile countries.

Durham gave unstintingly of his energy. He healed a growing breach with the United States which had developed because of attempts by American interlopers to aid the Canadian rebels and counter measures taken by Canadian irregulars. He traveled, read, and investigated endlessly at great cost to his already weakened health. It was difficult totally to dispel the hostility engendered in both Canadas by the revolts as long as 161 rebels in Lower Canada still remained in prison on charges of treason. What to do with them was a perplexing problem because even the most guilty would certainly be acquitted by Canadian juries. Durham solved the difficulty by choosing eight of the most culpable offenders, gaining their confessions in return for sparing their lives, and then banishing them to Bermuda. All other prisoners were pardoned. Thus, justice was in principle done without outraging sensitive Canadian feelings.

But this seemingly masterful act was to be Durham's undoing. He was not beloved by either Tories or Whigs in England and had already come under attack because of his staff appointments. The edict of banishment to Bermuda exceeded Durham's powers, as did the sentencing *in absentia* of certain rebels who had escaped to the United States. At first it seemed that Durham would escape unscathed, and the next few weeks were full of accomplishment. He provided Montreal with a police force, established a system for the registration of land titles, recommended a British government loan for the construction of a canal from Lake Erie to the sea, and appointed a subcommission to deal with the problems of the disposal of Crown lands and immigration. Two other subcommissions were created to study education and municipal and local government. But news soon reached Canada that Durham's parliamentary enemies were determined to pursue the question of the legality of the Bermuda decision. Durham was undisturbed since he had the warm approbation of the prime minister for his recent action to add to the original promise of full support.

The leader of the attack on Durham was his former colleague and friend, Lord Brougham, who introduced into the House of Lords a bill to limit and define more rigidly Durham's powers and to rescind all action taken under the "illegal" Bermuda ordinance. The Crown law officers ruled that Durham's basic decision was perfectly legitimate as he had been conceded full legislative powers, but they concluded that the banishment of the prisoners to Bermuda was certainly illegal. Now Melbourne could either support Durham wholeheartedly, as he had promised, by introducing a bill into Parliament to rectify Durham's minor infraction, or he could give in to the opposition and sacrifice him. Melbourne, thinking the former course would mean defeat and the fall of his ministry, capitulated. The government consequently supported the Indemnity Bill, which, although it did not contain in its final version any limitation on Durham's original powers, nonetheless reversed his Bermuda decision. *The Times* succinctly summed up the affair:

> The time-serving Whigs, in deference to whom the noble Earl had at great personal sacrifice placed himself in the van of their Canadian conflict, have at the first shot deserted, dishonoured and dismissed him.

Durham, shocked and chagrined, had no choice but to resign. The Indemnity Bill had undermined any further effectiveness he could have hoped to have in Canada. He sailed from Quebec in November 1838, less than six months after his arrival. His chief secretary, Buller, movingly described the scene:

> The sky was black with clouds bearing the first snow-storm of the winter, and hardly a breath of air was moving. The streets were crowded; the spectators filled every window and every housetop; and though every hat was raised as we passed, a deep silence marked the general grief for Lord Durham's departure.

Before actually departing, Durham had issued a proclamation in which he announced the disallowance of his ordinance and gave his reasons for resigning. This was an unprecedented action for a colonial governor and only intensified the debate at home. Thus, when Durham landed at Plymouth, it was confidently expected that he would enter the lists against his foes as he had done so many times before in his career. Powerful allies were rallying to his cause, but Durham stayed aloof. Convinced that the sands of his life were running low, he was determined to finish his report and to engage in no controversy that might impede its acceptance. The seriousness of the situation was manifested by the renewal of rebellious outbursts in both Canadas shortly after Durham's departure. Durham concluded his report on January 31, 1839; on February 11, it was submitted to Parliament. Durham himself lingered in semiretirement until his death in July 1840 at the age of forty-eight.

Durham's *Report on the Affairs of British North America* is one of the great imperial state papers, but its reception was hardly enthusiastic. Durham was even accused of not having written much of it. Brougham snidely told Macaulay that "the matter came from a swindler [Wakefield], the style from a coxcomb [Buller], while the Dictator furnished only six letters, D. U. R. H. A. M." Although Durham naturally incorporated many of the ideas of his aides, the *Report* was inimitably his own.

Much of the *Report* was devoted to a description and analysis of the problems in the various provinces of Canada. But it was Durham's recommendations and conclusions which were of greatest significance. The first and most important of these was that responsible government (although the term itself is hardly ever used in the *Report*) should be established in Canada:

Every purpose of popular control might be combined with every advantage of vesting the immediate choice of advisers in the Crown, were the Colonial Governor to be instructed to secure the co-operation of the Assembly in his policy by entrusting its administration to such men as could command a majority; and if he were given to understand that he need count on no aid from home in any difference with the Assembly, that should not directly involve the relations between the mother country and the Colony. This change might be effected by a single dispatch containing such instructions; or if any legal enactment were requisite, it would only be one that would render it necessary that the official acts of the Governor should be countersigned by some public functionary. This would induce responsibility for every act of the Government, and, as a natural consequence, it would necessitate the substitution of a system of administration by means of competent heads of departments for the present rude machinery of an executive council.

The granting of responsible government, Durham argued, would be advantageous not only to the colony, but to the mother country as well, for

if the colonists make bad laws and select improper persons to conduct their affairs, they will generally be the only, always the greatest sufferers; and, like the people of other countries, they must bear the ills which they bring on themselves, until they choose to apply the remedy. But it surely cannot be the duty or to the interest of Great Britain to keep a most expensive military possession of these Colonies, in order that a Governor or a Secretary of State may be able to confer colonial appointments on one rather than another set of persons in the Colonies. For this is really the only question at issue.

The only matters that Durham would reserve for the exclusive jurisdiction of the home government were: "The Constitution of the form of government—the regulation of foreign relations, and of trade with the mother country, the other British Colonies, and foreign nations—and the disposal of the public lands." Three of these areas fell logically under imperial control. The fourth, the retention of British control over the sale of public land, was to ensure a price low enough to encourage immigration but high enough to force new settlers to become part of the labor force for a time before being in a position to buy land. This was Wakefield's doctrine of "systematic colonization" which will be discussed in greater detail in the next chapter.

If the greatest significance of Durham's *Report* in an imperial sense lay in its remarks on responsible government, its suggestions for Canadian union were of only slightly less importance for Canada itself. Durham recommended the immediate legislative union of Upper and Lower Canada, with a provision allowing the Maritime Provinces to join the union at some future date. It was a federal union that Durham at first had in mind, in which the particularist feelings of French Canadians would not be completely thwarted. He had arrived in Canada more sympathetic to the French than to the British, but he soon reversed his position and advised that it would be highly dangerous both for Canada and the Empire to leave the French in charge of Lower Canada. "I believe," he wrote, "that tranquillity can only be restored by subjecting the Province to the vigorous rule of an English majority," and only through a centralized, nonfederal union could this desirable end be achieved. The British population of Upper and Lower Canada outnumbered the French, and the anticipated later adherence of the Maritime Provinces and growing British immigration would increase this majority.

It is perhaps one of the few blemishes on the Durham *Report* that its author suggested nonfederal union because of a desire to submerge *la nation Canadienne* under a flood of Anglo-Saxons. It was a particularly curious attitude for a man, much of whose career had been dedicated to the cause of depressed nationalities such as the Belgians and the Poles. But, despite the uncharitable nature of his motivation, Durham's recommendation for close Canadian union was a good one and his vision of a Canadian nation lofty, especially in view of the time at which he wrote. Canada could only be saved for the Empire and from American absorption, he wrote,

> by raising up for the North American colonist some nationality of his own; by elevating these small and unimportant communities into a society having some objects of a national importance; and by thus giving their inhabitants a country which they will be unwilling to see absorbed even into one more powerful.

There were, of course, many other recommendations in the Durham *Report,* but of by far the greatest significance was its strong advocacy of the establishment of responsible government in a unified Canada.

The final paragraphs of the *Report* conveyed its author's sense of urgency:

> The good effects . . . produced by the responsibility which I took upon myself will be destroyed; all . . . feelings will recur with redoubled violence; and the danger will become immeasurably greater, if . . . hopes are once more frustrated, and the Imperial Legislature fails to apply an immediate remedy to all those evils of which Your Majesty's subjects in America so loudly complain and of which I have supplied such ample evidence.

Parliament did, indeed, accept Durham's recommendation for the union of Upper and Lower Canada by an act of 1840, although the Maritime Provinces remained aloof from it. But Parliament was not yet ready to allow responsible government. By removing the ultimate authority of the Crown in certain areas, responsible government not only denied a basic assumption of the British constitution, but also gave to Canadians rights not yet possessed by Englishmen at home: in the mid-nineteenth century it was still possible for the British monarch to choose a prime minister without complete dependence on relative party strength in the House of Commons.

The result was that for seven years the governors of Canada attempted, through various devices, to gain the cooperation of the legislature. Lord Sydenham, Durham's successor, tried to keep the Assembly so busy that it would not have time to think about responsible government but still could not prevent the presentation of several resolutions urging its establishment. Sydenham's death in 1841 prevented the clash with the Assembly that he had tried so hard to avoid.

His successor, Sir Charles Bagot, soon realized the futility of attempting to coerce the legislature and of working only through the British members while ignoring the French. Bagot in a sense allowed responsible government before the acceptance of the principle by the British government. He asked the leaders of the British and French parties in the Assembly to form a joint cabinet. Despite grave annoyance and dissatisfaction, the British government accepted the *fait accompli* but felt committed only for the period of Bagot's tenure.

Sir Charles Metcalfe, who followed Bagot in 1843, was an autocrat who soon forced the resignation of the cabinet by his actions. In a subsequent national election, the governor did secure a narrow victory by appealing to the loyalty of the British settlers to the Empire and the Crown, but the resulting governmental anemia finally persuaded the home authorities to allow responsible government. No doubt some officials thought the granting of responsible government would cause Canada to drift from the Empire, while others were convinced that it was the only way of preserving the imperial connection. Be that as it may, Lord Elgin was sent to Canada in 1847 with instructions to conduct his actions according to the advice of ministers commanding a majority in the Legislative Assembly.

The single most important of Durham's recommendations was thus at last implemented. It would be a mistake, however, to conclude that British politicians had suddenly achieved a state of grace and had perceived the good sense of Durham's suggestion. The triumph was more one of apathy. By the late 1840s interest in Empire was at a low ebb. Mercantilism was long dead and the proponents of a diametrically opposed philosophy—free trade—were in the ascendancy. To most of them, empire was anathema, and the school of "Little England" emerged which, in opposing the expense of the imperial connection, favored colonial responsibility and autonomy and thus in action, if not in spirit, supported the Liberal Imperialists. In 1841, the prominent anti-imperial theorist George Cornewall Lewis had concluded:

> If a dominant country understood the true nature of the advantages arising from the relation of supremacy and dependence to the related communities, it would voluntarily recognise the legal independence of such of its own dependencies as were fit for independence; it would, by its political arrangements, study to prepare for independence those which were still unable to stand alone.

Some years later Sir James Stephen, permanent undersecretary in the Colonial Office, revealed the triumph of the new attitude over the official mind, when he said:

> It is evidently possible, I think it is probable, that the day will come when our Canadian and our native dependencies will calmly and deliberately insist on being dependencies no longer, but on being as independent in form and in name as they already are in truth and in reality. And when that demand shall be made, is there a man among us who would discharge, I do not say a single cannon, but so much as a single lucifer match, to resist it? May the union be perpetual; but if it shall ever cease to be spontaneous and cordial it will also cease to be valuable.

The opponents of Durham's theories as contained in the *Report* were, however, often proved to have been well justified in their reservations. The amalgamation of Upper and Lower Canada was ill-conceived, and Canadian government did not develop quite in the way Durham had anticipated. With the exception of foreign affairs, the areas that Durham had reserved for exclusive imperial control came quickly under colonial jurisdiction. The Union Act of 1840 conferred on the Canadian legislature both the power to alter its "form of constitution" and to distribute the public lands, and the passage of a protective tariff in 1859 flew in the teeth not only of Durham's recommendation, but of the cherished principles of British free trade as well. The British government had previously disallowed similar enactments by the legislatures of New South Wales in Australia and of New Brunswick, but despite protests by British manufacturers adversely affected by the Canadian law, it did not disallow this measure. Evidently, the voice of Alexander Galt, the Canadian finance minister, had been heard in London:

> . . . the government of Canada acting for its legislature and people, cannot, through those feelings of deference which they owe to the imperial authorities, in any manner waive or diminish the right of the people of Canada to decide for themselves both as to the mode and extent to which taxation shall be imposed. . . . [In] the imposition of taxation it is so plainly necessary that the administration and the people should be in accord, that the former cannot admit responsibility or acquire approval beyond the local legislature.

The passage of the Canadian tariff of 1859 was another step on the road to full colonial autonomy. It was indicative of the changes in even the most sacrosanct principles of the imperial constitution that the growth of colonial nationalism was going to force.

The responsibility for defense, other than in the local sense, remained largely with the imperial government, but this, of course, involved an expense Canada was most happy to avoid. When asked by the British government in the years before World War I to contribute more to its own and the general imperial defense, Canada was most reluctant to do so.

The final union envisioned by Durham came to pass in 1867, when a federation encompassing all Canada was formed.[2] Thus, some 28 years after he had originally submitted his report, Durham's perspicacity and foresight were vindicated with the birth of the Dominion of Canada. But the importance of the Durham *Report* was not limited to Canada. Its seminal principle of responsible government spread rapidly to all the colonies of white settlement (but not to the Dependent Empire) and became the cornerstone for the developing British imperial structure—the delicate compromise that allowed the colonies to become both nations and members of an Empire and later of a Commonwealth.

3

Colonization in the Antipodes: The Settlement of Australia and New Zealand

CANADA, the senior colony of white settlement, was the first dependency within the British Empire to gain responsible government, and it led the way in agitating for further constitutional changes. What Canada achieved, Australia and New Zealand were usually not long in emulating, and their paths toward responsible government are worthy of note as examples of uniform development in an Empire whose constituent parts owed their birth to vastly differing circumstances.

It was at the end of January 1788 that Captain Arthur Phillip of the Royal Navy moored his vessel in Sydney Cove on the southeast coast of Australia and, to the sound of musketry and the quaffing of toasts, established a new British colony. The early settlers whom Phillip transported to the shores of New South Wales were not religious dissenters or farmers deprived of land by the enclosure movement in Britain, but felons and other offenders from the overloaded prisons at home. With the loss of the American colonies and the failure of convict settlements in West Africa, Australia—upon which Captain James Cook, the famous explorer, had reported favorably—seemed a logical place for these deportees.

Phillip, who became governor of the colony, was somewhat of a visionary, and he saw his arrival in Australia as "the foundation of an

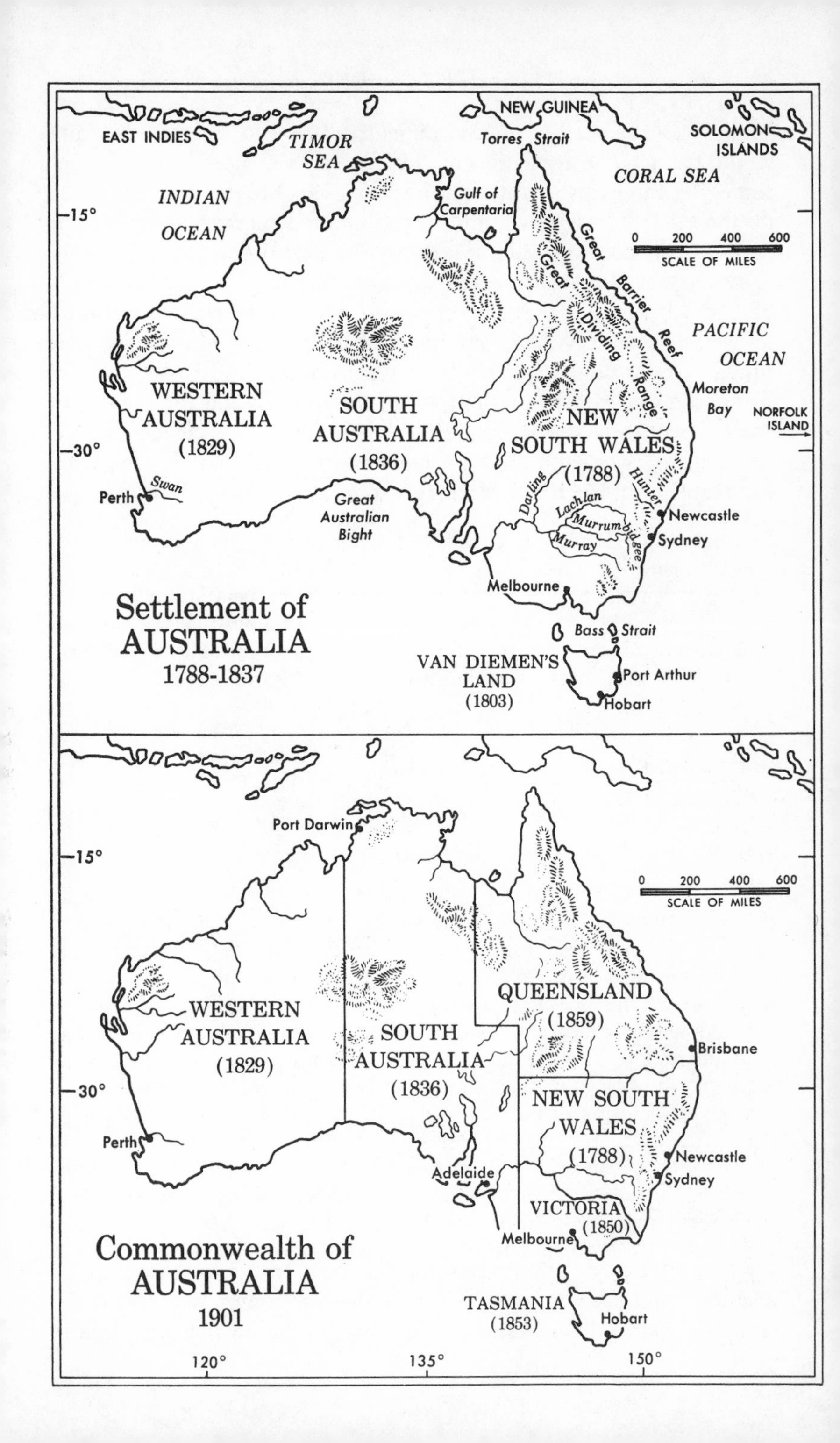
Settlement of AUSTRALIA 1788-1837
EAST INDIES
TIMOR SEA
NEW GUINEA
Torres Strait
SOLOMON ISLANDS
CORAL SEA
INDIAN OCEAN
Gulf of Carpentaria
Great Barrier Reef
Great Dividing Range
PACIFIC OCEAN
Moreton Bay
NORFOLK ISLAND
WESTERN AUSTRALIA (1829)
SOUTH AUSTRALIA (1836)
NEW SOUTH WALES (1788)
Swan
Perth
Great Australian Bight
Darling
Lachlan
Murrumbidgee
Murray
Hunter
Newcastle
Sydney
Melbourne
Bass Strait
VAN DIEMEN'S LAND (1803)
Port Arthur
Hobart
0 200 400 600
SCALE OF MILES
15°
30°
Commonwealth of AUSTRALIA 1901
Port Darwin
WESTERN AUSTRALIA (1829)
SOUTH AUSTRALIA (1836)
QUEENSLAND (1859)
NEW SOUTH WALES (1788)
VICTORIA (1850)
TASMANIA (1853)
Brisbane
Newcastle
Sydney
Adelaide
Melbourne
Perth
Hobart
120°
135°
150°

empire." But it must have been difficult for him to maintain his faith in the future. The formation of this first convict fleet had been welcomed by the British authorities as a long-sought-after opportunity to rid the prisons of the aged, infirm, and mentally deranged—hardly the material for successful colonization. As Francis Bacon had said in the early days of British overseas expansion, "It is a shameful and unblessed thing to take the scum of people, and wicked condemned men, to be the people with whom you plant." Phillip's sentiments were similar, yet his pleas for free settlers went unheeded. To make matters worse, the voyage to Australia took many months, and the embryonic colony frequently found itself short of supplies. The officers of Phillip's garrison were also far from enthusiastic. As Major Robert Ross, commandant of the Royal Marines, wrote:

I do not scruple to pronounce that in the whole world there is not a worse country than what we have yet seen of this. All that is contiguous to us is so very barren and forbidding that it may with truth be said here nature is reversed, and if not so, she is nearly worn out, for almost all the seeds we have put into the ground are rotted, and I have no doubt but will, like the wood of this vile country when burned or rotten, turn to sand.

It was the convict system that gave early Australia its character, and a peculiarly haphazard system it was. Some convicts progressed rapidly from servitude to freedom. Skilled laborers were in the best position. "Convicts who are mechanics," reported a select committee appointed in 1837 to investigate convict transportation to Australia,

are as well, if not better treated, than those, who are domestic servants; for as every kind of skilled labour is very scarce in New South Wales, a convict, who has been a blacksmith, carpenter, mason, cooper, wheelwright, or gardener, is a most valuable servant, worth three or four ordinary convicts; he is eagerly sought after, and great interest is made to obtain him. As a mechanic can scarcely be compelled by punishment to exert his skill, it is for the interest of the master to conciliate his convict mechanic in order to induce him to work well; in too many cases this is effected by granting to the skilled convict various indulgences; by paying him wages; by allotting to him task work, and by permitting him, after the performance of his task, to work on his own account; and lastly by conniving at, or overlooking disorderly conduct; for the most skilled mechanics are generally the worst behaved, and most drunken.

All in all, about 160,000 convicts were transported to Australia, the majority from 1815 to 1852. Most of these prisoners were, until the establishment of the probation system and the end of transportation to

New South Wales in 1840, assigned by the governor to the service of free settlers who had begun to arrive in 1793. On the whole, the convicts assigned to private service did not fare too badly, although there were instances of wanton cruelty. Their terms of servitude were limited, they could not be bought or sold, they could only be flogged upon orders of a magistrate other than their supervisor, and their children were born free.

Not all convicts, however, were so fortunate as to be assigned to private service. Some were kept under direct government control, and of these the vast majority were housed in wretched barracks and placed in road or chain gangs. Worst of all, a convict could be assigned to the remote penal settlement of Norfolk Island or, later, to Port Arthur in Tasmania, although these were usually reserved for convicts who committed a further crime after arriving in Australia. Conditions in the barracks and settlements were so wretched that often the very will to live was extinguished. A Catholic priest who visited Norfolk Island after a mutiny there in 1834 gave his impressions of the place:

I said a few words to induce them to resignation, and I then stated the names of those who were to die; and it is a remarkable fact, that as I mentioned the names of those men who were to die, they one after the other, as their names were pronounced, droppped on their knees and thanked God that they were to be delivered from that horrible place, whilst the others remained standing mute; it was the most horrible scene I ever witnessed.

Much as Governor Phillip wanted free settlers, none landed during his term of office. In 1793 a trickle of free immigrants began to arrive, but their number remained small until about 1815, and they were usually not the most desirable type of settlers. Of the more than 150 free families in the colony in 1804, the colonial surgeon said that he knew

very few indeed between whom and the convict he could draw the smallest discrimination. . . . Some have been people of very suspicious character, and have narrowly escaped being sent out against their inclinations; others, low mechanics who have failed in business, with long families, who had they remained in England, would have become burdensome to their parishes; others, men of dissolute and drunken habits.

These early settlers and those discharged members of the garrison who chose to remain in the colony as farmers were almost always complete failures.

Phillip left New South Wales in 1792, and between his departure and the arrival of his successor, Captain John Hunter, also of the Royal Navy, in 1795, the colony was ruled by the officers of the New South Wales Corps, the colony's garrison. They were an unscrupulous and greedy lot who used their positions to acquire vast estates and amass large fortunes. The most profitable of the Corps' activities was their monopoly of the rum trade which visited all the horrors of London's Gin Lane on the colony. Governors were unable to control the activities of the "Rum Corps," and Hunter, frustrated beyond endurance, declared "an angel from heaven possessing the omniscient attribute of the Divine Being would not have been able as a single individual to prevent [the rum traffic]." The situation was not ameliorated until Colonel Lachlan Macquarie arrived in the colony in 1809 as governor and replaced the New South Wales Corps with his own Highland regiment.

New South Wales was in its early years beset with economic difficulties caused by a lack of water and the inability of the settlers to develop a viable system of agriculture. Wheat did not grow well near the coast. Flax was raised, but the demand was small. Except for cedar, Australian timber could not compete with forest products grown nearer the European markets. Coal was found in usable quantities on the Hunter River, north of Sydney, but again, except for the British stations in India, it appealed to only a very limited market. Sealing and whaling were, indeed, successful industries, but not of the type to provide a solid base for a new and expanding colony.

Wool turned out to be the answer, and in the early development of the Australian wool industry, John Macarthur, at one time an officer of the New South Wales Corps, stands preeminent. From 1801 he tried to interest British manufacturers in Australian wool, but in 1819 Macarthur was still almost the only pastoralist to raise pure Merino sheep, most of the others having tried to combine wool with mutton production. All in all, there were only 100,000 sheep in New South Wales at the time. But the tide was soon to turn. In 1819 J. T. Bigge was sent as commissioner to Australia to inquire into the situation in New South Wales and Van Diemen's Land (Tasmania). Bigge came under the influence of Macarthur, and in his report to the Colonial Office he recommended the increased assignment of convicts to large sheep farms and the elimination of duties on colonial wool. This last was effected in 1825, and subsequent years saw the rise of British investment in New South Wales, an influx of desirable settlers, and a dramatic increase in wool production. In 1821, the first year of Australian wool export to Great Britain, only 175,000 pounds were sent. In 1830 the figure was 2 million pounds; in 1839, 10 million pounds; and in 1845, 24 million pounds. By 1850 the Australian colonies were supplying more high-quality wool to British looms than Germany and Spain combined.

With the sudden explosion of the Australian economy, social and political conditions could not remain static. Until 1823 New South Wales was ruled by a governor unchecked by a council, and Van Diemen's Land, technically a part of New South Wales, was administered by a lieutenant governor generally responsible to the governor of New South Wales. The governor's powers were very vague and more associated with the duties of a warden than with those of a chief executive of a colony of free men. As the convicts became proportionately fewer, the dissatisfaction with the constitutional position of the colony increased. Lord Bathurst, the colonial secretary, accurately described the prevailing Australian sentiment in 1817:

> The settlers feel repugnance to submit to the enforcement of regulations which necessarily partaking much of the nature of rules applicable to a penitentiary, interfere materially with the exercise of those rights which they enjoyed in this country, and to which as British subjects they conceive themselves entitled in every part of His Majesty's dominions.

Some relief was given as the result of Bigge's report when an act of Parliament in 1823 established a nominated council of from five to seven members to advise the governor. The governor was confirmed in his power, with the council's advice, to make laws, but before their official promulgation he had to obtain a certificate from the chief justice of the colony that any law passed was not repugnant to the laws of Great Britain insofar as conditions in New South Wales would permit. The legislation of 1823 also declared former convicts to be in every sense free men, for their status had been called into question by a legal decision in 1820.

In 1828 the council was enlarged to 15 members and given greater power to influence the legislation of the colony. The council was, however, largely an instrument to lend legality to the governor's actions and not really a step on the ladder leading to responsible government. The governor himself was also not in too happy a position. He was responsible to the Colonial Office for the general administration of the colony, to the Home Office for the convicts, and to the War

Office for the military establishment. He was thus often forced to implement policies that he personally opposed.

Opposition to the autocratic rule of the governor might have been more pronounced had it not been for a peculiar social and political rift that divided the population of New South Wales. On one side were the free settlers and their descendants, the so-called "Exclusives," led by Macarthur. Ranged against them were the "Emancipists," the ex-convicts and their progeny. What the Exclusives were for, the Emancipists were usually against, and the converse was equally true. The rivalry between these two groups became increasingly unrealistic as both Exclusives and Emancipists approached the same economic level and as an association with a convict ancestry became more remote for the Emancipists. Yet the animosity continued until the decade 1830–1840, when John Macarthur and William Wentworth, respectively the leaders of the Exclusives and the Emancipists, found themselves sitting on the same platform during a political campaign.

The reason for the reconcilation lies partly in the history of the other colonies of Australia and the way their experience in due course affected New South Wales. The Swan River and South Australian colonies were both experimental ventures. The former was inspired by the glowing description of the Swan River, the present site of Perth in Western Australia, rendered by its discoverer, Captain James Stirling. Thomas Peel and three other London financiers based their decision to found a speculative colony there on his alluring phrases and in 1829 applied to the British government for a monopoly on 4 million acres in the Swan River area. In return, the syndicate that Peel and his colleagues intended to establish would spend £300,000—one shilling sixpence an acre—to bring out 10,000 settlers and sufficient livestock to establish the colony on a sound footing. The British government was, however, prepared to grant only 1 million acres and not on the basis of the monopoly which the syndicate needed to remain viable: any private settler who was so inclined could, if he wished, buy land at the rate of one shilling sixpence an acre. Peel's three companions withdrew from the scheme, but Peel himself, carried along by an enthusiasm which was largely misplaced, accepted the government's terms and embarked on what was to be a disastrous undertaking.

As an initial step, a military and civil cadre led by the governor, Captain Stirling, established itself on the Swan River. From the first, funds were inadequate, the few settlers who accompanied Stirling had little in the way of money or resources, and the same was true of those who followed. As a result, virtually the only financial support available was £50,000 that Peel provided to bring out 300 laborers, plus livestock, from England. The lack of good soil forced the colony to spread its population thinly over a wide area and required the establishment of a communications network, for which the resources of the colonial treasury were inadequate, to market such crops as there were. The necessary labor was also lacking, and the colony endured a meager existence until 1850, when the colonists were forced to request convict labor from the British government. The British authorities complied, and between 1850 and 1868 about 10,000 convicts and an admixture of free settlers were sent to the Swan River at the British government's expense. Some £2 million were spent on the convict establishment, and the new influx of labor allowed the colony to undertake a much needed program of public works.

The Swan River colony failed, according to the colonial theorist Edward Wakefield (see Chapter 2), because it violated all the precepts of what he called "systematic colonization," and especially the vital doctrine of "sufficient price." The Swan River colony was established in the very year that Wakefield wrote his fictitious *Letter from Sydney* while languishing in Newgate Prison. In the guise of a rich emigrant to Australia who had purchased 20,000 acres for no more than two shillings an acre, he wrote:

> As my estate cost me next to nothing, so it is worth next to nothing. . . . Having fortune enough for all my wants, I proposed to get a large domain, to build a good house, to keep enough land in my own hands for pleasure-grounds, park, and game preserves; and let the rest, after erecting farm-houses in the most suitable spots. My mansion, park, preserves, and tenants were all a mere dream. I have not one of them.

It was Wakefield's conviction that the basic element for successful colonization was an adequate supply of labor. He thought that laborers arriving in a colony where land was either free or very cheap would quickly abandon their role as workers and become landowners. As a result there would never be enough labor available to allow the colony to develop and flourish. To remedy this Wakefield proposed that colonial lands should be sold at a sufficient price. He gave no specific figure. According to his formula, land should not be sold at so high a price as to put a stop to its sale altogether but its price should be high enough to prevent laborers from becoming landowners almost immediately upon their arrival. It should take them about six years, he said, to acquire sufficient funds to change their role in life. Thus the colony would always have an adequate supply of labor, for the funds derived from the sale of land would be used to pay the passage of desirable immigrants to further increase the labor force. As laborers became landowners, there would consequently always be other immigrants to replace them as wage earners. Finally, sufficient price would permit the colony to acquire more rapidly the attributes of civilization. An adequate labor supply would allow the landowner more leisure to cultivate the arts, and the high price of land would force a certain concentration of settlers, thus facilitating the development of those cultural amenities that flourish only where there is some density of population.

Wakefield's fictitious New South Wales colonist dramatized the existing situation: "We are in a barbarous condition," he wrote,

> like that of every people scattered over a territory immense in proportion to their numbers; every man is obliged to occupy himself with questions of daily bread; there is neither leisure nor reward for the investigation of abstract truth; money-getting is the universal object; taste, science, morals, manners, abstract politics, are subjects of little interest, unless they happen to bear upon the wool question; and what is more deplorable we have not any prospect of a change for the better. . . . Here we have nothing but wool, wool, wool.

The heavy emphasis on wool would eventually spell disaster for New South Wales, Wakefield thought, for overproduction would inundate the market. Wool, he concluded, was for the time being so profitable only because it required much land and little labor. It could not, however, be made the sole basis for a viable colonial economy.

Under Wakefield's influence, his followers in England formed the South Australia Company in 1834 and decided to establish a colony in South Australia along the lines suggested in the *Letter from Sydney*. Here in 1830 the explorer Charles Sturt had discovered large areas of good land. Despite lack of support from the Colonial Office, a foundation act was passed by Parliament in 1834 establishing the British province of South Australia, and in 1836 the first settlers arrived. Though the prospects were more promising than those of Swan River, South Australia also came near to disaster and had to be rescued eventually by the British government. This was not so much the fault of Wakefield's theories as of the ineffective and sporadic ways in which they were implemented. Without government backing, there was again a lack of funds, although the South Australia Company, a speculative venture, provided £320,000. Better soil and particularly the close proximity of good wheat lands gave South Australia an advantage that the Swan River colony did not possess. But a curious system of government, which provided for a governor answerable to the Colonial Office and a resident commissioner responsible to the company's Board of Commissioners in London, caused nothing but trouble. The board, which had the final authority over the colony's exchequer, used its funds neither wisely nor with sufficient dispatch to provide enough settlers to bring the land into early cultivation and production. Nor did the commissioners understand the doctrine of sufficient price. The cost of land was consequently never at the level Wakefield would have desired, and the stream of immigrants was too heavy for the colony's economy to bear.

South Australia soon followed its predecessor at Swan River into the doldrums and like it, in 1839, came under the protective wing of the British government. The colony quickly returned to life because of the additional financial resources now made available. South Australia, which contained 17,000 settlers in 1843, supported 104,000 in 1856. Improved conditions in the colony were not entirely due to the enlightened rule of the Colonial Office. Even in its distorted form, systematic colonization had brought in a better class of immigrants, for assisted passage attracted desirable settlers who might otherwise have gone to Canada, the fare to which was £5 compared with the £20 to £25 it cost to reach Australia. The cost of land in South Australia, although it was not Wakefield's sufficient price, was at least high enough to force that concentration of settlers which Wakefield considered so desirable.

It was the popularity of Wakefield's theory of systematic colonization, with its demand for a sufficient price for land, that reduced the animosity between the Emancipists and the Exclusives in New South Wales. By the early 1830s all that divided the two groups was a social barrier. Both John Macarthur and William Wentworth were prosperous and holders of large landed estates. The same was true of many of their constituents. In 1831 the British government, influenced by, but not totally understanding Wakefield's ideas, set a price of five shillings per acre on Crown land in New South Wales and throughout the Empire. This was distinctly against the interests of landholders who had acquired most of their land for nothing and held much of it without legal title. In 1838 and 1840 the British government further raised the price of land and in 1840 decided to halt the transportation of convicts to New South Wales. Such transportation had provided both Emancipists and Exclusives with cheap labor, and its prohibition resulted in the Exclusives (who had always believed that they had sufficient influence over the governor to control the future destiny of the colony) joining the Emancipists in demanding responsible government for New South Wales. Both groups were now equally convinced that they needed control of the colonial government to protect the vital interests they shared.

Whereas the British government had formerly paid no heed to Australian demands for an increased voice in the government of New South Wales because the agents of the Emancipists and the Exclusives tended to counteract each other in London, the united demand changed its attitude. In 1842 New South Wales, through a new constitution, gained representative government, though not responsible government, in the form desired by the large landholders. A high property franchise was established, so that the new settlers who had come in the 1830s, partly as a result of the semi-Wakefieldian land policy and whose interests ran counter to those of the landholders, were largely disfranchised. In the legislative council that was established the representatives of the new urban wage-earning classes were in the minority, although their constituents outnumbered the landholders.

Years of acrimonious controversy followed the establishment of the new constitution. The urban workers wanted responsible government and a democratic franchise; the landholders, who were formerly so bitterly divided among themselves, wanted a highly qualified franchise. Both sides, as was usual in such cases, claimed to be protecting the rights of Englishmen. In 1848, the landholders persuaded the British government to reinstate transportation, but when the convict ships arrived at Melbourne and Sydney, the townspeople would not allow the unwanted passengers to land. The British government was thus finally convinced that the transportation of convicts to New South Wales was no longer feasible. But the struggle over responsible government and the nature of the franchise was to continue until the discovery of gold in 1851.

The public announcement of the discovery of gold in New South Wales and Victoria, separated from New South Wales in 1850 as an independent colony, brought about a dramatic change in the life of the two colonies. Between 1851 and 1861 the population of New South Wales increased from 200,000 to 350,000, while in Victoria during the same period the population increased from 77,000 to 540,000. The Australian gold rush diluted the earlier colonizing stock to such an extent that old differences were largely obviated.

As new immigrants swarmed into the Australian colonies, the demand for increased democracy and responsible government became louder. An act of Parliament in 1850 had given each of the Australian colonies an elective legislature with a limited power of constitutional amendment. By 1855 Victoria, New South Wales, and Tasmania had, with the consent of the British government, written new consitutions with a broad democratic franchise and the implicit right of responsible government. Queensland was detached from New South Wales as a self-governing colony in 1859, and Western Australia (Swan River) achieved the same status in 1890. As for convict transportation, to which the original settlement in Australia owed its birth, it continued to Tasmania until 1852 and to Western Australia from 1850 until 1868.

Australia, like Canada in the years following the publication of the Durham *Report*, consisted of several colonies individually tied to the British Crown. And as was the case in Canada, such an arrangement proved to be an impediment to the national and economic development of the continent. But it was not until 1901 that the several Australian colonies united in federation as the Commonwealth of Australia.

Although New Zealand had started its colonial life as an administrative dependency of New South Wales, its entire history has had a quite different character. In the first place, although the aboriginal population of mainland Australia numbered, at the time of the first Europe influx, about 300,000, its existence presented no serious barrier to European settlement. The aborigines were spread thinly over a continent of almost 3 million square miles. Their culture, scarcely out of the Stone Age, was primitive and their way of life nomadic. A generally pacific, even passive, nature allowed the white colonists to sweep them aside. On the other hand, the natives of New Zealand—the Maori—although but 100,000 in number, occupied an area of only 100,000 square miles. Unlike the Australian aborigines, the Maori were organized into a highly complex society. They were settled rather than nomadic, with a definite sense of land ownership at the tribal level. These facts, plus the Maori's fierce and warlike qualities, made the settlement of New Zealand by Europeans far more difficult than the colonization of Australia had been. In the second place, white

Australia was conceived as a convict settlement, while white New Zealand owed its development, if not its birth, to Edward Gibbon Wakefield and his theory of systematic colonization.

Captain Cook had annexed New Zealand on behalf of Britain in 1769 during his first great voyage of discovery in the Pacific. But his action was studiously ignored by the British government: in 1817 the islands were referred to in Parliament as being "not within His Majesty's Dominions." Yet from about 1790 on, white men had visited and even settled in New Zealand. In 1791 efforts were made from Sydney to start a trade in New Zealand flax, and the availability of spars made from New Zealand timber and other naval stores attracted British and American sperm whalers to New Zealand waters. The first recorded European settlers were a group of sailors who spent the summer of 1792 in an area where there were no Maori. They were fortunate, for it was often a different story when deserting sailors or escaped convicts from Australia came into contact with the Maori. Some were killed and eaten, others became the tame *pakehas* (whites) of some Maori chief who might employ them as boat-builders, blacksmiths, or purveyors of arms and rum. In 1809 the entire crew of the vessel *Boyd* was massacred, although not without some justification.

The Maori did not placidly wait for western civilization to reach them. Many of them shipped out as seamen on vessels that touched the islands, to see the world for themselves. It was in this way that the Reverend Samuel Marsden, the chaplain of the convict establishment in Sydney, first met the Maori. He became convinced that he should carry the Gospel of Christ to New Zealand, and on Christmas day, 1814, with two lay associates—William Hall, a carpenter, and John King, a ropemaker—he opened the first Church of England mission on North Island, at the Bay of Islands. For some years Marsden made little progress, but in 1823 Henry Williams, an ex-naval officer who had become a clergyman, joined him with his brother William and so impressed the Maori that during the years 1823 to 1850 the few missionaries who had dedicated their lives to working in New Zealand succeeded in making considerable progress.

The Maori did not, however, change their old habits easily. Shortly after his arrival in New Zealand, Marsden had sent the Maori chief Hongi to England to help in the preparation of a Maori grammar and dictionary. During his sojourn in Britain, the seemingly benign Hongi not only sold all the presents he received, but also sold land concessions to speculators—all for cash, with which he purchased guns.

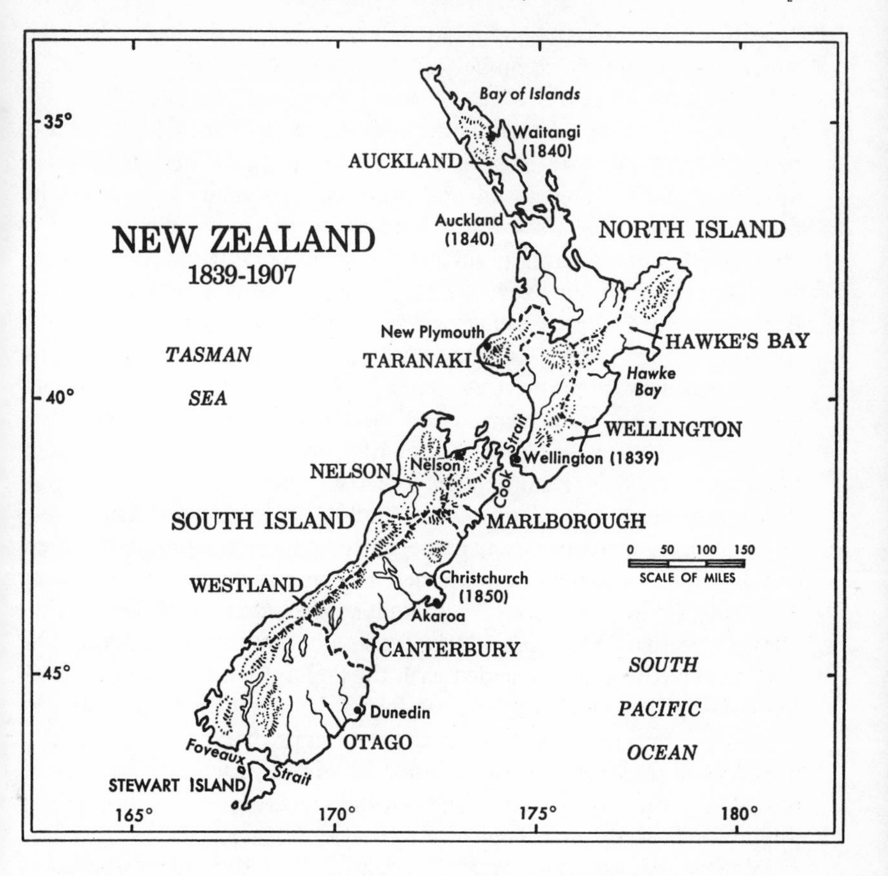

When he returned to New Zealand, Hongi completely revolutionized the art of warfare in the islands. Clad in a suit of mail allegedly given him by George IV, he devastated and conquered vast stretches of North Island, exterminating whole tribes in the process. Following Hongi's example, another chief, Te Rauparaha, started a career of conquest in South Island, with similar results. This outburst of war brought in gunrunners from Sydney, and a plague of land speculation and illicit trade swept New Zealand. A final incident of incredible barbarity forced the governor of New South Wales to intervene and send a resident, armed however with little power, to the Bay of Islands at the tip of North Island. In 1830 Te Rauparaha had hired the brig *Elizabeth* under a Captain Stewart to transport his war party on a raiding expedition. The ship's crew decoyed a rival chief and his family onto the vessel and watched as they were butchered, cooked in the vessel's galley, and served on deck to Te Rauparaha's men.

Despite the violent history of early European contact with New Zealand, the country greatly intrigued Edward Wakefield. Speaking before a Parliamentary committee in 1836, he spoke of a land "very near Australia . . . which all testimony concurs in describing as the fittest country in the world for colonizing, as the most beautiful country with the finest climate, and the most productive soil." In 1837 Wakefield formed the New Zealand Association as a noncommercial body, but the Colonial Office wanted assurance that the association would be able to bear all the costs of colonizing the islands. The association was therefore reorganized as a joint-stock company in 1839. Despite an undertaking from the Colonial Office that the new company would now receive a charter, the replacement of Lord Glenelg by Lord Normanby as colonial secretary saw the repudiation of all previous undertakings. Frustrated by the Colonial Office and spurred on by a fear of French preemption, the directors of the New Zealand Land Company determined to force the issue, and in May they sent the 400-ton vessel *Tory*, under the command of Wakefield's younger brother William, to New Zealand without authorization. The departure of the *Tory* coincided with the appointment of Captain William Hobson of the Royal Navy as British lieutenant governor of New Zealand, acting under Governor George Gipps of New South Wales. The Colonial Office had determined on this course even before the *Tory* had sailed, and it may have been the knowledge of the impending appointment that forced the vessel's hasty departure.

William Wakefield reached New Zealand in the autumn of 1839 and immediately purchased for the company a vast tract of land —about 20 million acres on either side of Cook Strait, which separates North and South Island—from Te Rauparaha and other chiefs. In that same month, Hobson at last received his instructions—to negotiate with the Maori for the recognition of the Queen's sovereignty "over the whole or any parts of those islands which they may be willing to place under Her Majesty's dominion." In addition, he was given permission to annex South Island by right of discovery.

Hobson and the British government had intervened in New Zealand at a time when a conflict between two rival philosophies in regard to the islands was reaching its most acute stage. On the one hand, the missionaries felt that New Zealand was their exclusive preserve, that it should be maintained as a home for the Maori who, guided by the missionaries, would walk in the path of righteousness. On the other hand, the New Zealand Land Company urged the settlement of New Zealand by British colonists: in the company's eyes, New Zealand was to be a white man's country. Neither the missionaries nor the settlers could consistently have made a good impression on the Maori: Wesleyans, Anglicans, and Roman Catholics fought over the souls of the Maori, and the methods by which the New Zealand Land Company acquired land were not above reproach.

Captain Hobson sighted the northern tip of North Island in January 1840 and immediately began treating with the Maori chiefs of the united tribes of New Zealand. In early February the drafting of the Treaty of Waitangi was concluded, and the first chiefs applied their marks. Forty-six chiefs indicated their assent at Waitangi itself, and during the next few months 456 more did likewise. The treaty itself was short, consisting of only three articles:

1. The signatory chiefs "cede to Her Majesty the Queen (*Te Kuini Wikitoria*) all the rights and powers of sovereignty which the said chiefs . . . exercise or possess. . . ."

2. Her Majesty "confirms and guarantees to the chiefs and tribes . . . undisputed possession of their lands . . . but the chiefs yield to Her Majesty the exclusive right of preemption."

3. Her Majesty extends her protection to the natives of New Zealand and "imparts to them all rights and privileges of British subjects."

On the southern tip of North Island William Wakefield had begun to occupy the area he claimed to have purchased and had established the town of Wellington. The first shipload of settlers arrived there two weeks before the signing of the Treaty of Waitangi and immediately voted to establish a provisional government. Hobson thought this to be high treason and declared British sovereignty over all of New Zealand on May 21, 1840. To complicate things further, a French immigrant ship was seen making its way towards South Island in the following month. Hobson consequently got the necessary signatures on the Treaty of Waitangi from the chiefs of South Island to support his action of May 21, and when the French vessel arrived at Akaroa, it found H.M.S. *Britomart* already riding at anchor. The French immigrants decided to remain under the British flag and the French government dropped any claims it might have had to New Zealand. In November 1840 New Zealand was separated from New South Wales and recognized as a separate colony.

Several more shiploads of settlers soon arrived at Wellington, and a noisy controversy ensued between the missionaries, who supported the Treaty of Waitangi and claimed that the Wakefield land purchase was illegal, and the settlers, who thought the treaty inconsequential—a "device to amuse and pacify the savages for the moment." The matter was not settled until Lord John Russell, the colonial secretary, decreed that the New Zealand Land Company's settlement had preceded the promulgation of the treaty and therefore did not breach it. To justify this decision, the company was finally granted a charter in February 1841. It was agreed that, the provisions of the Treaty of Waitangi notwithstanding, the company could occupy four acres of land in New Zealand for every pound it had spent on colonization. A subsequent investigation of the company's supposed land purchase, however, allowed it only a fraction of its original claim—clearly the victory belonged neither to the missionaries nor to the company.

As was so often the case, systematic colonization, which was a theory worked out far from the scene of actual colonization, did not work in practice as well as had been anticipated. Sufficient purchasers for company land at the established price were hard to find, and no one was ever quite sure what the price should have been in the first place. Nevertheless, as in South Australia, systematic colonization was at least a partial success, and it brought in desirable settlers, at little financial burden to the company or the Crown, though not in sufficient numbers. The system continued to operate in New Zealand until the governor arbitrarily lowered the price of land in 1853.

The New Zealand Land Company did not limit its settlements to the area around Cook Strait. Through the efforts of Edward Wakefield, subsidiary companies for the settlement of South Island were formed. A Scottish Free Church group founded a settlement in Otago in 1848, and a Church of England settlement was established and named Canterbury (later, Christchurch) in 1850. But the parent company did not survive its new children. It expired in 1850, its finances in a hopeless muddle. The New Zealand Land Company had, however, been the guiding force in the establishment of a new nation.

The pattern of early colonial society in New Zealand did not develop along the lines envisioned by Edward Wakefield. The discovery of gold on South Island in 1861 brought the usual traumatic results, and it was impossible to prevent laborers from becoming landowners since there were so few employers of labor. The large landowners were often absentee speculators, and the operators of large sheep runs had little need for labor. Consequently, by the 1890s the small farm of a few acres operated by the owner or lessee and his family became the characteristic unit of immigrant agriculture. But the colonists' existence, if not as easy or profitable as had been expected, was still in most cases better than that to which they had been accustomed in Britain.

The one quality most prominently lacking in the early New Zealand colonist's life was security. The Maori had been getting progressively more restive under British rule. They did not understand western concepts of land tenure and saw their ancestral holdings becoming the property of *pakehas*. Perhaps of greater significance was the growing fear they felt for their survival as a unique people. Like many other indigenous peoples in colonial areas, they saw a crusading religion and foreign habits and attitudes impinging on their traditional way of life.

During the 1840s strife between Maori and settlers became increasingly common. One area of conflict was at Kororareka at the Bay of Islands, where the tribesmen kept cutting down the flagpole—the symbol of British sovereignty—and where Maori–settler clashes were frequent. The turmoil continued until 1845, when Captain (later Sir) George Grey, then only thirty-three years old, was transferred from South Australia to become governor of New Zealand. Grey took immediate command and established a personal ascendancy over the Maori in January 1845 by taking their major fortress. The Maori admired bravery and ability, and they revered and trusted Grey as a consequence. He, in return, respected them. He studied the Maori language and Maori traditions and even wrote a book on Polynesian mythology. Grey's arrival presaged a period of peace. He not only defeated the tribes around the Bay of Islands, but also those in the Wellington district who followed Te Rauparaha. To avert further disturbances, he took the highly illegal step of having the old chief kidnapped and held for several months in honorable captivity on board a British vessel.

The profound influence that the missionaries had had on the Maori was made clear during the war. There were no incidents of cannibalism or of massacre of noncombatants. The tribesmen, virtually all Christian, tried to behave in what they thought was a fitting manner. Despite their admiration for Governor Grey, they complained that he had only carried their major position because he had attacked on Sunday, when most of the Maori warriors were at church!

The end of hostilities allowed Grey to devote his energies to more peaceful activities. He made a valiant, although not totally successful, attempt to solve the land question. For not only were the Maori dissatisfied, but there was also a great shortage of land for European settlement on North Island. He encouraged and supported Maori agriculture. He built schools and hospitals and rooted out corruption in the colonial administration. Finally, although he had rejected in 1846 a proposed constitution sent out by the Colonial Office, which would have given New Zealand responsible government, he did design the constitution of 1852. It provided for a remarkably democratic franchise and implied the right of responsible government which was actually achieved in 1856. Although the federal form of government established under its provisions was not practical, the constitution could be amended by a mere majority vote of the legislature. Grey left New Zealand in 1853, having guided it from the brink of disaster to responsible government and having established a tradition of benevolent state activity that was the basis of the "welfare state" which developed so early in New Zealand.

With the departure of Grey, the old Maori grievances once more came to the fore. In April 1854, just a month before the first New Zealand parliament was to meet, a gathering of Maori at Mandwapou in southern Taranaki on North Island determined to end the domination of the white man. Here, and at similar meetings, was born the Maori "king," or unity, movement which bespoke the rebirth of Maori nationalism. By 1858 a Maori king was indeed elected, with his own flag, council of state, and code of laws, although not all Maori followed him. Old and declining customs were revived. In 1860 a land dispute brought on open warfare between the king and the settlers backed by the government. Even the return of Sir George Grey as governor in 1861 failed to ameliorate the situation. In fact, an ill-considered punitive expedition from Australia exacerbated the conflict by spreading the war and driving the moderates among the Maori into the arms of the extremists. Slowly, however, European preponderance in men and arms began to tell, for there were never more than 2,000 Maori in the field at one time and against these the British could bring to bear 10,000 regulars aided by an equal number of colonists.

The king Maori made their last stand near a village called Orakau. There, in fields verdant with fruit trees and where once grain had ripened, they built their fort and challenged the British to attack. Two thousand British troops shelled 300 Maori in the fort; several times they launched unsuccessful frontal assaults. The Maori ran out of water, and their ammunition was so low that they had to resort to firing wooden bullets. General Cameron, the British commander, urged them to surrender, or at least to send out their women and children. But the women preferred to fight with the men, who defiantly shouted: "We will fight on for ever, for ever, for ever!" So saying, they opened the gates and charged the surprised British, who, in the confusion, let half the garrison escape; the other half lay dead on the field of battle.

Nevertheless, it seemed that by 1864 the war had run its course, for the main tribes of the king movement had been defeated and those who had not yet submitted were mostly in exile. But a new danger was about to appear. In 1862 Te Ua, a Maori who had fought against the Europeans, had claimed that the Angel Gabriel had appeared to him in a vision, inspiring him to found a new religion, much like that of the Taipings in China (see Chapter 5). It was a curious mixture of Old Testament morality, Christian doctrines, and Maori religious customs. Te Ua believed in the Trinity, but he revived the old Maori custom of cannibalism. His followers, known as "*Hau-Haus*" (because they felt they were impervious to bullets if they raised their right hands and shouted, "*Pai marire, hau! Hau!*"), performed their rituals near an upright pole, sometimes as high as 50 feet, with extending arms from which they hung ropes. As the Hau-Hau priests conducted services, the worshipers revolved around the mast on the ropes while the "angels of the wind" visited them. The Hau-Hau movement was an obvious attempt to return to the pristine life of Maori antiquity and to reject all things European. A government policy of land confiscation only aggravated Maori hostility. The Maori continued to fight on—and so well, according to the historian of the British army J. W. Fortescue, that British soldiers considered them, "on the whole, the grandest native enemy that [they] had ever encountered." Despite the preponderant strength of the British forces, the war dragged indecisively on.

In 1868 Grey was summarily dismissed for disobeying the Colonial Office once too often, and the British government concluded that the only way to end the war was to make the colonists bear the full responsibility for their land and native policies. In 1865 and 1866 all but one of the British regiments had been recalled, and in 1870 the last one sailed for home. As a result, the peace that finally came in

1872 was not a harsh one, for while the Maori were defeated they were not crushed. They had lost millions of acres through confiscation and their population of 55,000 in 1861 had fallen to 37,000 in 1871. Yet their doughty struggle had assured them at least some of the rights of citizenship already promised them in the Treaty of Waitangi. In 1867 Maori had been given direct representation in the general assembly of the colony, and five years later two chiefs were appointed to the upper house.

With the end of the Maori Wars, New Zealand developed rapidly. In 1870 the colony had consisted of six loosely connected provinces with a total population of 250,000. Six years later the constitution was changed so that New Zealand became a unitary state, and by 1900 it was a nation of 800,000 people living in provinces closely linked by rail, ship, road, telephone, and telegraph and in regular communication with the outside world. In the last decade of the nineteenth century New Zealand embarked on such an advanced program of democratic and humanitarian legislation that Herbert Asquith, later British prime minister, described it as "a laboratory in which political and social experiments are every day made for the information and instruction of the older countries of the world." Finally, in 1907, New Zealand achieved full dominion status.

Australia and New Zealand are two further examples of the many roads by which British settlements developed into self-governing colonies, and eventually nations, in spite of great difficulties—the one being born as a convict station, the other being faced with a resourceful and hostile indigenous population which had to be overcome and in time assimilated.

4

The Indian Mutiny: The Great Watershed in the History of British India

It was 1857, exactly one hundred years after the establishment of British dominance in Bengal. Englishmen were secure in their belief that the Empire represented the highest political and moral achievement of man. Responsible government had secured the allegiance of the colonies of white settlement, and India, the most treasured jewel in the imperial crown, basked in the warmth of an enlightened rule initiated by the reforms of the previous century.[1]

The late afternoon of Sunday, May 10, in Meerut—the huge East India Company military station 40 miles northeast of Delhi—was hot. On the surface it seemed much like any other Sunday: the sepoys (native troops) were resting in their quarters, and there was a muted bustle as the British garrison a couple of miles away prepared for church parade. Yet there was a tenseness underlying the apparent serenity. One needed to look no further back than the previous day to detect the reason, for on Saturday, May 9, 85 sepoys of the 3rd Light Cavalry—one of the finest of the East India Company's native regiments—had been degraded and put in irons at a punishment parade. Their crime had been refusal to accept, on the order of their commanding officer, a new issue of cartridges.

[1] Refer to the map of India on p. 3, Chapter 1. In present-day India the cities of Meerut and Cawnpore are called "Mirat" and "Kanpur."

The Company had begun in 1856 to distribute Enfield rifles to its troops in place of the old smooth-bore muskets, and the cartridges for the new weapon, which fitted very snugly into the barrel, had to be coated with grease to allow them to enter. Soon a rumor spread among the Indian troops that the cartridges were coated with both cow and pig fat, thus making them abhorrent to Hindus and Muslims alike. In a number of stations, British commanders had paraded their troops and assured them that the rumor was unfounded, but this did little to allay the sepoys' fears and suspicions.

In Meerut, Colonel Carmichael Smyth, the commander of the 3rd Light Cavalry, had decided to lay the rumor once and for all. He assembled his skirmishers, the pick of the regiment's troops, to show that, although the cartridges had to be torn out of their casing before being rammed into the barrel, this operation could be accomplished with the hands instead of the teeth, which was the usual method. (He had already demonstrated the proper method to the Indian havildar-major [sergeant-major] so that he could influence the Indian troops; the only result was that the havildar-major's tent was burned down.) At the parade itself, of the 90 men present, only five accepted the cartridges even after hearing their commander's explanation. The colonel, baffled by this turn of events, decided to dismiss the parade since nothing further could be done until he had consulted his superior, Major-General W. H. Hewitt, the commander of the Meerut Division.

The general, an immensely obese man who could no longer mount a horse but had to be driven about in a specially constructed buggy, was old and incompetent—typical of an army where promotion to high command came as a result of longevity, not ability. He wanted to serve out his last days of command in peace and quiet and was more annoyed at Smyth for having called the parade in the first place than he was at the insubordinate sepoys. But even with his penchant for not disturbing the *status quo*, Hewitt realized that the matter could not be ignored. He therefore ordered the convening of a court of enquiry, and his commander-in-chief in Simla subsequently determined that the 85 offenders would be tried by native court-martial.

All the members of the court, with the exception of the superintending officer, were Indian. As so many men were being tried at one time, the trial was held in a large regimental mess hall on the station. Here, commencing on May 6, the court sat for two days at a scrubbed mess table, with the defendants sitting cross-legged before it. Almost inevitably, a verdict of guilty was arrived at (by a vote of 14 to 1) and a sentence of ten years' hard labor was pronounced. The prisoners, many of whom were veterans of over 20 years' honorable service, received the news in stoic silence.

The sentence now had to be forwarded to General Hewitt for his confirmation. Although the court had recommended leniency because of the prisoners' uniformly good record, the general thought otherwise. "I would willingly attend to the recommendation of the court," he remarked,

> if I could find anything in the conduct of the prisoners that would warrant me in so doing. Their former good character has been blasted by present misbehaviour, and their having allowed themselves to be influenced by vague reports instead of attending to the advice and orders of their European superiors. . . . To the majority of the prisoners no portion of the sentence will be remitted.

Hewitt did, however, reduce by half the sentences of men who had been in the service less than five years.

The morning of Saturday, May 9, dawned gray and sultry. The British and Indian troops of the Meerut garrison—seven regiments in all—marched on to the parade ground to form three sides of a hollow square. The British troops faced each other with loaded rifles on two sides of the square, while the Indian troops, who were armed but not supplied with ammunition, occupied the third side. The prisoners stood waiting within the square, two batteries of artillery threatening in the background. In English, then in Hindustani, the sentences were read and the prisoners were stripped of their regimental accouterments, as the smiths and armorers of the horse artillery approached carrying coils of chains and leg irons.

For the next several hours, the 85 men stood in the hot dust, enduring the ignominy of being shackled in the full sight of their comrades. At last, at midday, it was done, and the prisoners were led off at an awkward shuffle. Some of them threw their boots at Colonel Smyth as they passed; some shouted "For the faith!"; others cried to their fellows, "Remember us! Remember us!" The other Indian troops were no doubt greatly disturbed, but their innate discipline and the presence of the British guns prevented any overt demonstrations of sympathy as the prisoners were marched off to their cells.

General Hewitt noted that "the majority of the prisoners seemed to feel acutely the degradation to which their folly and insubordination had brought them." Lord Canning, who was governor general throughout the coming mutiny, remarked:

> The riveting of the men's fetters on parade, occupying as it did, several hours, in the presence of many who were already ill-disposed, and many who believed in the cartridge fable, must have stung the brigade to the quick.

And so it did. The Indian troops were agitated; they were also resentful and embarrassed. During the rest of the hot day and night, they lounged uneasily in their barracks or wandered into the bazaar which separated the Indian and British lines. There they were taunted by the prostitutes: "You are cowards, not men. . . . Your brethren have been shackled and imprisoned because they would not swerve from their creed. You are not men, for if you were, you would release them." To stir the caldron of fear and rumor still further, a whisper ran through the camp that the British intended to attack the sepoys as they sat unarmed in their barracks.

The forming of the church parade in the British sector of the cantonment on that fatal Sunday afternoon only convinced the sepoys that their fears were well-founded, even though they had witnessed a similar procedure hundreds of times before. It is still not known who first voiced the resolve to free the prisoners, but in a gathering stream the Indian troopers of the 3rd Light Cavalry, mounted on their horses, approached the civil prison where their comrades were guarded by only a small detachment of sepoys. The rescue was effected in a short time and the prisoners released from their shackles.

With this first mutinous step, all inhibitions were suddenly lost—two of the three Indian regiments at Meerut broke into open revolt, to be joined later by most of the third. Cavalry and infantry, Hindu and Muslim made common cause. After murdering their British officers, they were seized by a sudden madness, seeking out all Europeans—men, women, and children—to slaughter them without pity. While the sun slowly set, British civil residents on their way to the evening service, unaware of what was happening, were shot or sabered—some as they walked, others as they rode, and still others as they drove in their carriages to enjoy the coolness of early evening. The rabble of the town poured out of the bazaar to join the mutineers, and the jails emptied as the Indian police left their posts.

In the meantime the British troops had heard the shots, and after some bungling and delays they were marched over to the Indian barracks, only to find them in flames and most of the sepoys gone. They dealt effectively with those mutineers still in the vicinity, but then, instead of proceeding elsewhere, they stood guard in the Indian lines, leaving the European quarter unprotected. There, all through the warm night, the arson, murder, and pillage continued, the bazaar and prison mob being the most enthusiastic, while the mutineers—their immediate passions sated—gathered in small groups to determine their next step. Some scattered into the countryside, but most turned their eyes southward toward the imperial city where, in theory, a Mogul emperor still ruled, and with wild enthusiasm they marched down the road to Delhi to proffer him their allegiance.

Still, the hate and violence in Meerut during these confused hours were not universal. Many Indian soldiers and domestic servants saved British families at great personal risk, and most of the sepoys on duty in the British section of the great sprawling cantonment remained loyal. They saluted their officers even as their fellows were butchering the British in the residential quarter. At the treasury, for all its manifest temptations, the sepoy guard stood firm until relieved by a British detachment.

The flame ignited at Meerut might still have been extinguished had the British acted promptly to intercept the mutineers before they reached Delhi. But this they did not do. For one thing, as we have seen, General Hewitt was both overage and incompetent. His indecisiveness was abetted by the fact that telegraphic communications with the commander-in-chief of the Bengal army, by this time moved to his summer station at Simla, had been cut, as had the wires to Delhi and Calcutta, the winter capital. On top of this, there were only three British regiments stationed between Meerut and Calcutta, a matter of one thousand miles. Meerut was thus isolated and paralyzed into inaction.

The triumphal arrival at the Mogul capital of the insurgents on the morning of May 11 was the signal for the rising of much of northern India. British garrisons, notably at Lucknow and Cawnpore, were invested, Delhi fell to the mutineers, and only the failure of the Afghans and the Sikhs to rise in support of the mutineers prevented complete disaster. The early days of the mutiny were by far the darkest for the Company's forces. But after the initial shock, superior organization and leadership enabled them slowly to reestablish their superiority. Delhi was recaptured September 20 and the Lucknow garrison finally relieved in November. The position at Cawnpore, however, had been overrun long before help could arrive. By late June 1858 the mutiny was virtually over, and an exhausted and devastated northern and central India lay at the feet of the British.

With few exceptions, the conduct of both sides during the revolt was savage, often deplorably so. Wholesale murder was the order of the day. The British destroyed entire towns, had captured Indian soldiers blown from the mouths of cannon, and murdered in cold blood the two sons of the senile emperor, Bahadur Shah. On May 13, 1857, the 3,800 Indian troops at Lahore were disarmed as a precaution against possible mutiny and placed under constant scrutiny. Nevertheless, one of their number killed the commanding officer of the 26th Native Infantry. Frightened, most of the 26th fled, those who remained behind being killed in a murderous cannonade which was directed on the regiment's lines. The next day, the fleeing sepoys arrived at the river Ravi to find themselves facing Frederic Cooper, the deputy commissioner of Amritsar, and some police. Those of the 26th who had not already been shot or drowned in attempting to cross the river were captured without much difficulty as "they evidently were possessed," Cooper later wrote, "of a sudden and insane idea that they were going to be tried by court-martial. . . ." Cooper continued to describe the subsequent events.

As fortune would have it. . . . a deep dry well was discovered within one hundred yards of the police-station, and its presence furnished a convenient solution to the one remaining difficulty which was of sanitary consideration —the disposal of the corpses of the dishonoured soldiers.

Then the executions began; Cooper resumed his narrative:

About 150 having been thus executed, one of the executioners swooned away (he was the oldest of the firing-party), and a little respite was allowed. Then proceeding, the number had arrived at two hundred and thirty-seven; when the district officer was informed that the remainder refused to come out of the bastion, where they had been imprisoned temporarily a few hours before. . . . The doors were opened, and, behold! they were nearly all dead. Unconsciously, the tragedy of Holwell's Black Hole had been re-enacted. . . . Forty-five bodies, dead from fright, exhaustion, fatigue, heat, and partial suffocation, were dragged into the light. . . .

Cooper sanctimoniously concluded:

The above account, written by the principal actor in the scene himself, might read strangely at home: a single Anglo-Saxon, supported by a section of Asiatics, undertaking so tremendous a responsibility, and coldly presiding over so memorable an execution, without the excitement of battle, or a sense of individual injury, to imbue the proceedings with the faintest hue of vindictiveness. The Governors of the Punjab are of the true English stamp and mould, and knew that England expected every man to do his duty, and that duty done, thanks them warmly for doing it.

Cooper was modestly convinced "that wisdom and heroism are still but mere dross before the manifest and wondrous interposition of Almighty God in the cause of Christianity."

This was not the only incident during the mutiny concerning a well. At Cawnpore the shoe was on the other foot, and the massacre of captured British troops and their families there serves as a monument to wanton brutality. To their credit, the sepoys present refused to have anything to do with the intended proceedings, and outside help had to be enlisted. G. O. Trevelyan, the British historian, although he was of course not an eye witness, recorded the classic description of the slaughter of the imprisoned women and children in his book *Cawnpore* (1865):

. . . The Begum [the jailer of the British] presently returned with five men, each carrying a sabre. Two were Hindoo peasants: the one thirty-five years of age, fair and tall, with long mustachios, but flat-faced and wall-eyed: the other considerably his senior, short, and of a sallow complexion. Two were butchers by calling: portly strapping fellows, both well on in life. The larger of the two was disfigured by the traces of the small-pox. They were Mahommedans, of course; as no Hindoo could adopt a trade which obliged him to spill the blood of a cow.

These four were dressed in dirty-white clothes. The fifth, likewise a Mussulman, wore the red uniform of the Maharaja's [i.e., Nana Sahib's] bodyguard, and is reported to have been the sweetheart of the Begum. He was called Survur Khan, and passed for a native of some distant province. A bystander remarked that he had hair on his hands.

The sepoys were bidden to fall on. Half-a-dozen among them advanced, and discharged their muskets through the windows at the ceiling of the apartments. Thereupon the five men entered. It was the short gloaming of Hindostan:—the hour when ladies take their evening drive. . . . Shrieks and scuffling acquainted those without that the journeymen were earning their hire. Survur Khan soon emerged with his sword broken off at the hilt. He procured another from the Nana's house, and a few minutes after appeared again on the same errand. The third blade was of better temper: or perhaps the thick of the work was already over. By the time darkness had closed in, the men came forth and locked up the house for the night. Then the screams ceased: but the groans lasted till morning.

The sun rose as usual. When he had been up nearly three hours the five repaired to the scene of their labours over-night. They were attended by a few sweepers, who proceeded to transfer the contents of the house to a dry well situated behind some trees which grew hard by. "The bodies," says one who was present throughout, "were dragged out, most of them by the hair of the head. Those who had clothes worth taking were stripped. Some of the women were alive. I cannot say how many: but three could speak. They prayed for the sake of God that an end might be put to their sufferings. I remarked one very stout woman, an half-caste, who was severely wounded in both arms, who entreated to be killed. She and two or three others were placed against the bank of the cut which bullocks go down in drawing water. The dead were first thrown in. Yes: there was a great crowd looking on: they were standing along the walls of the compound. They were principally city people and villagers. Yes: there were also sepoys. Three boys were alive. They were fair children. The eldest, I think, must have been six or seven, and the youngest five years. They were running round the well (where else could they go to?) and there was none to save them. No: none said a word, or tried to save them."

At length the smallest of them made an infantile attempt to get away. The little thing had been frightened past bearing by the murder of one of the surviving ladies. He thus attracted the observation of a native, who flung him and his companions down the well. One deponent is of the opinion that the man first took the trouble to kill the children. Others think not. The corpses of the gentlemen must have been committed to the same receptacle: for a townsman who looked over the brink fancied that there was "a Sahib uppermost." This is the history of what took place at Cawnpore, between four in the afternoon of one day and nine in the morning of another, almost under the shadow of the church-tower, and within call of the Theatre, the Assembly Rooms, and the Masonic Lodge. Long before noon on the sixteenth July there remained no living European within the circuit of the station.

Is it surprising that so much hate was engendered on both sides and that the wounds inflicted by the mutiny were never really to heal? But lessons were learned when passions cooled. William Howard Russell, the correspondent of *The Times* of London, visited Cawnpore shortly after its recapture and reflected in *My Indian Mutiny Diary:*

Among those heaps of dust and ashes, those arid mounds of bricks, those new-made trenches, I try in vain to realize what was once this station of Cawnpore. The solemn etiquette, the visits of the Brigadier and the General *en grande tenue*, the invitations to dinner, the white kid gloves, the balls, the liveries, the affectation of the *plus haut ton des hauts tons*, the millinery anxieties of the ladies, the ices, and Champagne, and supper, the golden-robed Nana Sahib moving about amid haughty stares and ill-concealed dislike. 'What the deuce does the General ask that nigger here for?' The little and big flirtations, the drives on the road—a dull, ceremonious pleasure—the faded fun of private theatricals, the exotic absurdities of the masonic revels, the marryings and givings in marriage, the little bills done by the rich merchants, the small and great pecuniary relations between the station and the bazaar, the sense of security. But one is tempted to ask if there is not some lesson and some warning given to our race in reference to India by the tremendous catastrophe of Cawnpore?

Russell was profoundly disturbed by what he saw in India. He was one of the first observers to try and analyze some of the causes of the mutiny. "How are we to prevent its recurrence?" he asked.

I am deeply impressed by the difficulty of ruling India, as it is now governed by force, exercised by a few who are obliged to employ natives as the instruments of coercion. That force is the base of our rule I have no doubt; for I see nothing else but force employed in our relations with the governed. The efforts to improve the condition of the people are made by bodies or individuals who have no connection with the Government. The action of the Government in matters of improvement is only excited by consideration of revenue. Does it, as the great instructor of the people, the exponent of our superior morality and civilization—does it observe treaties, show itself moderate, and just, and regardless of gain? Are not our courts of law condemned by ourselves? Are they not admitted to be a curse and a blight upon the country? In effect, the grave, unhappy doubt which settles on my mind is, whether India is the better for our rule, so far as regards the social conditions of the great mass of the people. We have put down widow-burning, we have sought to check infanticide; but I have travelled hundreds of miles through a country peopled with beggars and covered with wigwam villages.

British military suppression of the Indian Mutiny did not alter the fact that the entire fabric of Company rule on the subcontinent, so complacently woven over the past several decades, had violently been ripped asunder. The whole philosophy and practice of British rule in India was to be minutely scrutinized. First to go was the moribund shell of the East India Company, though it did not go down without a fight. No less a person that John Stuart Mill drew up the document that was submitted in its defense. "The Company," he pointed out, "had laid the foundations of a great Empire in India at the same period at which a succession of administrations under the control of Parliament were losing to the Crown of Great Britain another great empire on the opposite side of the Atlantic." The Company felt complete assurance that the more attention is bestowed and the more light thrown upon India and its administration, the more evident it will become that the Government in which they have borne a part had been not only one of the purest in intention, but one of the most beneficent in act, ever known among mankind.

But it was to no avail; the rule of British India was formally shifted from Company to Crown, although it must be admitted that it was more a matter of form than of substance. By an act of 1858, the post of secretary of state for India was created, with an advisory council of fifteen members.

Of greater importance was the realization by the British government that there had been something profoundly wrong with the pre-1857 philosophy of rule in India. It was evident that there had been excessive interference with the fabric of domestic Indian life and that Indians had not shared sufficiently in the ruling of their own country. In a proclamation of November 1, 1858, Queen Victoria disclaimed any desire for the acquisition of further territory in India, promised to respect "the rights, dignity, and honour" of the native princes, to uphold religious tolerance, and to make every effort to assure that "our subjects, of whatever race or creed, be freely and impartially admitted to offices in our service, the duties of which they may be qualified by their education, ability, and integrity, duly to discharge." A general amnesty and pardon were offered to those not directly implicated in the murder of British subjects, and the Crown undertook to improve the moral and material welfare of the Indian people in whose "prosperity will be our strength, in their contentment our security, and in their gratitude our best reward." This proclamation was of profound importance. It was the first imperial paper in which the British government admitted the right of an indigenous colonial population to have a part in the shaping of its own destiny. The proclamation conferred on Indians, in essence, the rights of British citizenship.

It would be absurd to ascribe the precipitation of an event as cataclysmic as the Indian Mutiny solely to cartridges supposedly coated with ritually impure fats. The story is, of course, more complicated. For one thing, a mutiny in the Indian regiments was not without precedent. From the first serious one in 1806, at Vellore in South India, mutinies had occurred with ever-increasing frequency. The Company chose to ignore these warnings, and the organization and morale of its army steadily deteriorated. The proportion of British to Indian troops was allowed to slip until, at the time of the mutiny, there were 45,322 European troops to 233,000 sepoys. Stations of importance such as Delhi and Allahabad were garrisoned solely by Indian troops. The caliber of the Company's British officers was not what it should have been. Promotion was by seniority, and ability counted for little. What able officers there were, were usually transferred from the military to the political service.

To compound these difficulties, the Company, which had formerly been very sensitive to Indian customs and traditions, had changed its attitude over the decades. More and more frequently, sepoy regiments were sent to fight beyond the bounds of India in violation of the terms of enlistment. This meant loss of caste to the soldiers, especially in the Bengal army whose troops were mainly high caste. Besides, the Company would not even offer extra allowances for such service. Thus, between 1844 and 1857, four mutinies occurred because of a lack of honesty and generosity on the part of the Company. This contravention of the terms of enlistment was legalized in 1856 by the General Service Enlistment Act, which made all recruits to the Bengal army liable for service both within and without India. Add to all this inflammable material the existence of an old prophecy that the British would be driven out of India one hundred years after the battle of Plassey (1757) and a rumor that the Crimean War, which had siphoned off many officers and artillery units from India, had resulted in a British defeat, and the ingredients for a great conflagration were present.

Discontent was not, however, limited to the army. Particularly since the passage of the India Act of 1784, the Company had done much to affront the Indian princes and landowners and the conservative upper classes in general. During the early days of Company rule, its officers had gone out of their way to be tolerant of Indian religious practices and customs. They had fired salutes on Hindu and Muslim holidays and had done their utmost to curry favor in local eyes. It was good for business, and during the eighteenth century the Company had been exclusively interested in showing a profit. Most of its servants had been self-seeking, intent on making a fortune before their return to Britain. But all this, of course, changed after the India Act of 1784. No longer were there large fortunes to be made by indulging in skulduggery. As the antislavery and missionary movement burgeoned in England, the Company came under ever-increasing attack for being so tolerant of "heathen" customs and particularly for not allowing missionaries to set foot on the subcontinent.

By the 1830s the Company's officials were "better" men than they had been in the previous century. They were more moral, more Christian, and more imbued with the necessity of improving conditions of life in India. When missionaries appeared on the scene, no longer were salutes fired on Indian religious holidays, and no longer were certain abhorrent social customs tolerated. The British Indian government had the choice of either respecting local customs, regardless of their nature, or of applying the standards of western civilization as it saw them. The latter alternative was chosen, and the result was that some practices, such as female infanticide, were prohibited.

Indians had not greatly resented the early British rulers of India. True, these men had done their best to enrich themselves at India's expense, but this had also been done by numerous non-European invaders. The next generation of British officials, however, actively interfered in Indian social and religious life, causing a resentment among Indians that outright economic exploitation alone never had, especially as these more "moral" men brought with them concepts of racial superiority which had not been present to the same extent in their predecessors. As Jawaharlal Nehru wrote in *Toward Freedom* (1941):

> There was something fascinating about the British approach to the Indian problem, even though it was singularly irritating. The calm assurance of always being in the right and of having borne a great burden worthily, faith in their racial destiny and their own brand of imperialism, contempt and anger at the unbelievers and sinners who challenged the foundations of the true faith—there was something of the religious temper about this attitude. Like the Inquisitors of old, they were bent on saving us regardless of our desires in the matter. . . .

It may seem paradoxical that the passage of humane and beneficial reforms did more to drive Indians to revolt than years of economic exploitation, but this was nonetheless the case.

Economic changes also alarmed both the great landowners and the princes. The permanent land settlement in Bengal had displaced many old landowning families, but as this deprivation had occurred long before, it was little remembered. The resumption of rent-free tenures in the 1830s, however, and the decisions of the Inam Commission of the 1850s, which resulted in the confiscation of 20,000 estates in Bombay presidency, reawakened fears that the British wished to destroy the entire structure of land tenure in India.

Of still greater significance was the elimination of a time-honored political tradition. It had always been the custom in India that ruling princes who were childless could adopt a son entitled to inherit, without prejudice, his father's dominions. Lord Dalhousie, who had become governor general in 1848, decided to override this custom in the future. He decreed that all dependent states and all those which owed their existence to the British would, when the natural line failed, be annexed by the British. This became known as the "doctrine of lapse," and of it the governor general wrote:

> The British Government in the exercise of a wise and sound policy is bound not to put aside or neglect such rightful opportunities of acquiring territory or revenue as may from time to time present themselves, whether they arise from the lapse of subordinate states by the failure of all heirs of every description whatsoever or from the failure of heirs natural where the succession can be obtained only by the sanction of the government being given to the ceremony of adoption, according to Hindu law. . . .

Between 1848 and 1854, the doctrine of lapse was invoked seven times, with the result that seven princely states came directly under British rule. The annexation of the major northern Indian state of Oudh in 1856 culminated the process, although its acquistion could not be justified even by the rather dubious doctrine of lapse.

Whatever enthusiasm the mutiny engendered in the princes of India was significantly among those who had suffered deprivation of lands or had seen their adoption of heirs not recognized by the British government. Oudh was thus one of the centers of insurgent activity. The Nana Sahib, perhaps the most important leader of the mutineers, had not been recognized as the heir of the former chief of the Maratha confederacy. The rani of Jhansi, in central India, almost the only noble figure to emerge during the mutiny, led her troops into battle and sacrificed her life because her adopted son was not permitted to succeed to the throne of Jhansi at her husband's death.

The mutiny, fortunately for the British, was largely confined to the Bengal army, not affecting the armies of the other two presidencies, Bombay and Madras; hostilities were therefore limited to northern and central India. Most of the Indian princes remained loyal to the British, while the general populace, it would seem, was on the whole indifferent.

Nevertheless, the nature of the mutiny has been a matter of dispute. Some Indian historians have attempted to interpret it as a first war of independence. Perhaps this is because nationalism seems to hunger for military success, and the Indians, although they fought nobly and well on behalf of the British, did not have the satisfaction of hurling their foreign rulers into the sea. Unlike the Scots, Indians have no Bannockburn to bolster national pride: thus the attempt to make out of the mutiny what it manifestly was not—a great national uprising against the oppressor.

One of the earliest proponents of this view, V. D. Savarkar, writing in 1909 to inspire nationalist agitation, alleged that the mutiny had long been plotted, the result of a patriotic determination to protect religion and motherland. Agents were sent out by a central authority to rouse the countryside, he claimed, in his *Indian War of Independence of 1857:*

In Bengal a messenger went to the cantonments, taking a red lotus in his hand. He would give the red lotus into the hands of the chief Indian officer in the first regiment. The chief would pass it to the nearest Sepoy. The Sepoy would pass it to the one next to him, and so the red lotus would pass from Sepoy to Sepoy through the hands of all the thousand Sepoys, and then the last Sepoy would return it back to the Revolutionary messenger. That was enough! Without a whisper or a word, the messenger would pass on like an arrow and, as soon as the next regiment was in sight, he would give the red lotus in the hands of its chief officer. In this way, the organisation, so full of poetry, became impressed with one opinion, with revolution, with blood. The red lotus was the final seal of the organisation. What a tumult of thoughts must be raging in the mind of every Sepoy when he touched the red flower! That courage which it would have been impossible for the eloquence of orators to inspire was imparted in those warlike fellows by the dumb lotus flower and by the mute eloquence of its red, red colour. . . .

Although there was certainly much dissatisfaction among Indians in the army and in the states, and some mysterious comings and goings at night, there is no sign of a coherent plot of rebellion. The distinguished historian R. C. Majumdar, originally chosen by the present Indian government to write the centenary history of the mutiny, found no evidence of either preplanning or political nationalism in the events of 1857–1858, and S. N. Sen, who finally wrote the official government study, was of a similar opinion. Sen judiciously concluded, however, that some sort of explosion was inevitable in a country where the rulers did not share the history, religion, language, or philosophy of those they governed. The real importance of the mutiny as a *national* movement, one must conclude, lies in the use it was put to by later Indian nationalists, rather than in the nature of the event itself.

The effects of the Indian Mutiny are as hard to gauge as its causes. True, it created a rift between Indians and Englishmen that was never to heal; but it also presaged the greater involvement of Indians in the affairs of their country, though not until 1935 was any form of responsible government developed—even at the provincial level—in which Indians played a major part. Posts in the civil service were made progressively more available to Indians—but they were bemused by an imperial system that would allow an Indian to be elected to the *British* Parliament (in 1892) and not allow him a part in the management of his own land. The mutiny did indeed bring about many desirable changes in British rule, but the mailed fist was always poised in the background—the proportion of British to Indian troops was raised, the artillery became an exclusive British preserve, and officers' commissions were not readily available to Indians. As for personal attitudes, which were beyond the range of legislation, hate and distrust—the legacy of the mutiny—added their problems to those older ones of social and racial distinctions. Further changes were to await a new impetus—the rise of a genuine Indian nationalism toward the end of the century and its reorientation, under the leadership of Mohandas Gandhi, in the years following World War I.

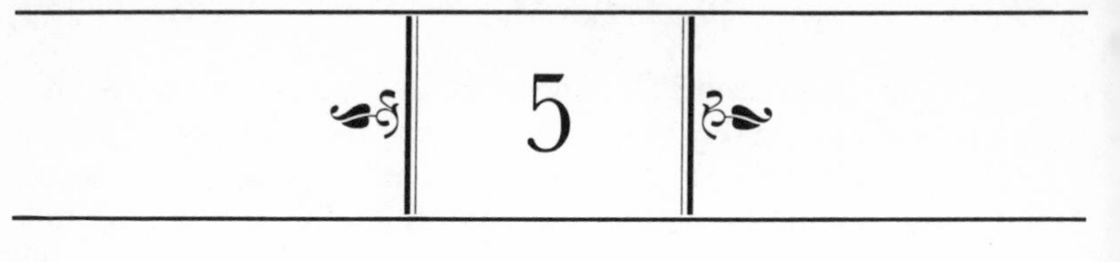

5

Imperialism and the Imperial Proconsul

WHEN LORD WILLIAM BENTINCK assumed the governor generalship of Bengal in 1828, he was ordered to avoid the acquisition of any further territory on the subcontinent. One of the directors of the East India Company, who had been instrumental in Bentinck's appointment, wrote to the new governor general:

> The expenses of [the Indian establishment] are now under consideration and I trust that they may be greatly reduced without injury to the public interests—and I would fain hope and believe that under your Lordship's administration, if Peace and Tranquillity be preserved in India, the embarrassments in which the Company's affairs are now involved will be removed and that we shall be able to render a good account of our government of India both as respects our Financial and Political administration.

Almost every governor general of India and colonial governor received similar instructions. Whitehall throughout most of the nineteenth century opposed the assumption of new imperial responsibilities—at least when they were not profitable. But this prevailing attitude did not seem to prevent new lands coming under the British flag.

There is, perhaps, some truth in the saying that the British Empire was acquired by mistake—"in a fit of absent mindedness"—and certainly its occasionally peculiar development might lend substance to this contention. The building of the first Empire was indeed inspired by the rigid precepts of mercantilism, but the later establishment of

British hegemony in South Asia and Africa was hardly the result of premeditation and prior design. Yet if no over-all imperial plan existed, a number of different factors motivated territorial expansion.

Without a doubt, the profit motive frequently made the addition of new lands to the Empire seem attractive. But not all colonies were equally lucrative, and British capital migrated to those areas offering the best investment opportunities, whether they were in the Empire or not. Thus, British investment in the United States in December 1913 amounted to £760 million compared with £379 million invested in India. This is not to say that certain very special advantages did not accrue to the British investor through the imperial connection. If nothing else, the Empire created trade patterns favoring Britain which were to persist even after the decline of the Empire itself. Furthermore, British influence in the nineteenth century reached well beyond the imperial domain into what has been termed an "informal" British Empire—an area particularly hospitable to the British financier and hence the site of heavy investment. There is considerable evidence to indicate that the British government preferred informal to formal empire and that territories were only absorbed into the latter when client governments no longer accepted British direction. Economic determinists find the hand of the financier even in the acquisition of areas that were at best marginal, such as the humid and inhospitable lands of West Africa. To them imperialism was a symptom of the final crisis stage of capitalism, when the competition for markets to absorb increasing production was at its height. Consequently, they argued, the control of markets which would have been considered worthless in previous decades became a necessity for survival.

Frequently, fear of foreign invasion and considerations of national security caused the advance of frontiers. It can be said with considerable assurance that fear, first of French, then of Russian, invasion was what chiefly influenced British Indian foreign policy throughout the nineteenth century. Later, British interest in East Africa was aroused largely by fear of German and Italian penetration into the area, which would have menaced the British position in the Sudan and Egypt. That colonization was sometimes prompted by the desire to rid the home country of surplus or unwanted population is of course well known.

A case can even be made for the humanitarian factor in imperial expansion, at least in West and South Africa, where British antislavery agitators forced the government to acquire territory in order to protect the indigenous population. Some historians have indicated that the dynamics of imperial existence required empires constantly to expand if they were not to contract—that empires could not exist in equilibrium. Perhaps, as the German-born Harvard economist Joseph Schumpeter claimed, imperialism was a social atavism, not prompted by economic reason or national interest, but purely by "the objectless disposition on the part of a state to unlimited forcible expansion"—a tendency encouraged, according to another Harvard economist, David Landes, by "the disparity of force between Europe and the rest of the world . . . [which] created the opportunity and possibility of dominion."

It has been conjectured that a law of the turbulent frontier forced the expansion of empire, for an area of order surrounded by an area of disorder had eventually, for its own protection, to conquer the area of disorder. Thus, empires would inexorably advance their frontiers until they reached some great natural barrier or the borders of another stable power. As we have said previously, the British, through the medium of the East India Company, were willing, as long as the Mogul empire was strong, to restrict their activities to trading stations such as Surat, Bombay, and Madras. With the decline of Mogul power, however, the Company was forced to raise military forces of its own and, for its own protection, to quell the anarchy in the surrounding countryside. It is interesting to note that the final northern frontiers of British India rested along the lofty natural barrier of the Himalayas, where also the great empires of China and Russia were met, but in the west, less definite geographical and political limits caused constant frontier fluctuations and frequent British interference in the affairs of Afghanistan.

One final cause of imperial expansion was individual ambition. In an age of slow communications, the "man on the spot" could frequently influence events according to his own designs, unrestrained by the wishes of the home government. Many examples of this phenomenon are to be found in the areas where the imperial power gained a footing—Cecil Rhodes in South Africa (see Chapter 6), Frederick Lugard in East and West Africa, and Sir Charles Napier in India (see Chapter 7), to mention only three—and the Colonial Office was frequently presented with a newly annexed territory it would much rather have been without.

The English economist J. A. Hobson, in his brilliant and provocative study *Imperialism* (1902), depreciated the power and influence of the "man on the spot" by declaring that the imperial proconsul was a pawn, perhaps even the unwitting pawn, of finance and financiers at home—that the expansion of the Empire was consciously decreed by a small coterie associated with the stock exchange and the great banks of England. "In view of the part which the non-economic factors of patriotism, adventure, military enterprise, political ambition, and philanthropy play in imperial expansion," Hobson wrote,

> it may appear that to impute to financiers so much power is to take a too narrowly economic view of history. And it is true that the motor-power of Imperialism is not chiefly financial: finance is rather the governor of the imperial engine, directing the energy and determining its work: it does not constitute the fuel of the engine, nor does it directly generate the power. Finance manipulates the patriotic forces which politicians, soldiers, philanthropists, and traders generate; and enthusiasm for expansion which issues from these sources, though strong and genuine, is irregular and blind; the financial interest has those qualities of concentration and clear-sighted calculation which are needed to set imperialism to work. An ambitious statesman, a frontier soldier, an over-zealous missionary, a pushing trader, may suggest or even initiate a step of imperial expansion, may assist in educating patriotic public opinion to the urgent need of some fresh advance, but the final determination rests with the financial power.

This was to some extent also Lenin's view of imperialism, and Bernard Shaw wittily presents a somewhat similar picture through the words of Napoleon in *The Man of Destiny:*

> No Englishman is too low to have scruples: no Englishman is high enough to be free from their tyranny. But every Englishman is born with a certain miraculous power that makes him master of the world. When he wants a thing, he never tells himself that he wants it. He waits patiently until there comes into his mind, no one knows how, a burning conviction that it is his moral and religious duty to conquer those who possess the thing he wants. Then he becomes irresistible. Like the aristocrat, he does what pleases him and grabs what he covets: like the shopkeeper, he pursues his purpose with the industry and steadfastness that come from strong religious conviction and deep sense of moral responsibility. He is never at a loss for an effective moral attitude. As the great champion of freedom and national independence, he conquers and annexes half the world, and calls it Colonization. When he wants a new market for his adulterated Manchester goods, he sends a missionary to teach the natives the Gospel of Peace. The natives kill the missionary: he flies to arms in defence of Christianity, fights for it; conquers for it; and takes the market as a reward from heaven. . . . There is nothing so bad or so good that you will not find an Englishman doing it; but you will never find an Englishman in the wrong. He does everything

on principle. He fights you on patriotic principles; he robs you on business principles; he enslaves you on imperial principles; he bullies you on manly principles; he supports his king on loyal principles and cuts off his king's head on republican principles. His watchword is always Duty; and he never forgets that the nation which lets its duty get on the opposite side to its interest is lost. . . .

But did the builders of the British Empire really fit this image? Were the men in the field serving the purposes of the financial power in England? The explorer H. M. Stanley (1841–1904) seemed to lend support to this contention when he declared:

> There are forty millions of people beyond the gateway to the Congo, and the cotton spinners of Manchester are waiting to clothe them. Birmingham foundries are gleaming with the red metal that will presently be made into ironwork for them and the trinkets that shall adorn those dusky bosoms, and the ministers of Christ are zealous to bring them, the poor benighted heathen, into the Christian fold.

What a happy marriage of the spiritual and the material! Many missionaries in Africa, notably David Livingstone (1813–1873), envisaged a union of commerce and Christianity—"those two pioneers of civilisation"—as the salvation of Africa. In 1857, in a speech at Cambridge, Livingstone exhorted his audience

> to direct your attention to Africa. I know that in a few years I shall be cut off in that country, which is now open; do not let it be shut again! I go back to Africa to try to make an open path for commerce and Christianity; do you carry out the work which I have begun. I leave it with you!

Yet the real ambition of Cecil Rhodes (1853–1902), almost the personification of British imperialism and high finance, was to preside over the advance of British rule into Central Africa—an enterprise that he financed himself with no personal material gain in mind.

Hobson's vision denied the proconsul of what were in fact his most characteristic qualities—independence and self-assurance: traits of the great imperial officials but not those to be expected in either the conscious or unconscious minions of the stock exchange. The proconsuls of the nineteenth century were believers in what was almost an imperial religion, and it is surprising how many of them were the sons of clergymen and adherents of dissenting sects. Like monks of some new order, they rarely married. To a large degree, they were emotionally disciples of the antislavery movement, forced by the end of slavery as a major issue in 1833 to find a new cause: for many of them, it became imperialism. Late in the century, Sir Harry Johnston (1858–1927), the "Prancing Proconsul" of Central Africa, boasted at the age of thirty-two that his only religion was the expansion of the British Empire, although he soon became more concerned with the welfare of the Queen's African subjects than with the extension of British hegemony. Sir George Goldie (1846–1925), the creator of British Nigeria, reminisced in later life:

All achievement begins with a dream. My dream, as a young child, was to colour the map red. In 1877 I left England (largely to escape from personal entanglements) to explore the interior of Nigeria. On the journey back I conceived the ambition of adding the region of the Niger to the British Empire.

Lord Lugard (1858–1945), the great British proconsul in both West and East Africa, is described by his biographer Margery Perham as having

the lasting habits of his Christian training. These merged with his more conscious standards which were those, he claimed, of an English Gentleman, derived immediately from his family, public school and army training, and ultimately, perhaps, from the code of the medieval Christian knight. It was a double sense of caste in that he felt himself to belong to a class within his nation and to a nation within Africa, both of which, he believed, had the code of *noblesse oblige*.

Men like Johnston and Lugard firmly believed that it was their prime responsibility to bring the attributes of western civilization to the less fortunate peoples of Africa. They worked with a dedication found only in the profound idealist—with an expenditure of time and energy for which no material rewards could compensate. In a letter to Rhodes in 1893, Johnston once described his life in Nyasaland:

I have done yeoman service for the British South Africa Company. As far as it was honest to go I have gone in helping them to substantiate their claims, and in the advancement of their interests. I have spared neither the risk of my own life, the abandonment of all ideas of comfort, nor the right to rest at times like other people. I do not recollect having spent one single day as a holiday during the two and a half years which I have been in Central Africa. Sundays and weekdays, mornings and evenings, I am to be found either slaving at my desk, or tearing about the country on horseback, or trudging twenty miles a day on foot, or sweltering in boats, or being horribly sea-sick on Lake Nyasa steamers. I have to carry on in my office, by myself, a most onerous correspondence in Swahili, which I have to write in the Arabic Character, in Portuguese, in French, and in English. I have had to acquire a certain mastery of Hindustani to deal with the Indian troops. I have learnt three native languages besides Swahili in order to talk straight to the people. I have undertaken grave responsibilities, and have devoted myself to the most wearisome and niggling of tasks. One day I am working out a survey which has to be of scrupulous accuracy, and another day I am doing what a few years ago I never thought I should be called upon to do—undertaking the whole responsibility of directing military operations. I have even had myself taught to fire Maxim guns and seven pounder cannon, I, who detest loud noises and have a horror of explosions.

Lugard confided in his diary: "I am never absent for an hour or so (and that but rarely) from my men. I sleep among them, walk with them on the march, and my caravan becomes my home, and the familiar faces of my men are welcome to me." Almost a century earlier Thomas Munro, a district officer in India and later a great governor of Madras, had written in a similar vein:

I go from village to village with my tent, settling the rents of the inhabitants; and this is so tedious and teasing a business that it leaves room for nothing else—for I have no hour in the day that I can call my own. At this moment while I am writing, there are a dozen people talking around me; it is now twelve o'clock and they have been coming and going since the morning. . . . One man has a long story of a debt of thirty years' standing contracted by his father. Another tells me that his brother made away with his property when he was absent during the war; and a third tells me that he cannot afford to pay his usual rent because his wife is dead, who used to do more work than his best bullock.

Or again:

From daybreak till eleven or twelve at night I am never alone except at meals and these *altogether* do not take up an hour. I am pressed on one hand by the settlement of the revenue and on the other by the investigation of murders, robberies and all the evils which have arisen from a long course of profligate and tyrannical government. Living in a tent, there is no escaping for a few hours from the crowd; there is no locking oneself up on a pretence of important business, as a man might do in a house. . . . I have no refuge but in going to bed, and that is generally so late that the sleep I have is scarcely sufficient to refresh me.

Moral dedication did not alone explain the voluntary subjugation of imperial officials to the frequently dangerous and nearly always uncomfortable life of Africa and Asia. Love of adventure, egotism, and romanticism played their part. Johnston in Central Africa fought all his battles under a large white umbrella so that the enemy would always know where he was. He dressed his Sikh constabulary in white, yellow, and black, and adorned his letter paper with the same colors, to symbolize the cooperation of Europeans, Africans, and Asians. He originated the idea of the "all-red" (i.e., British) route from the Cape to Cairo. He also had a sense of humor. Once, when it was rumored that he had supped with cannibals in the course of his duties, he answered with the following poem:

A CANNIBAL'S ODE TO HIS AUNT

Search through the crowded market,
Visit each cannibal feast,
Where will you meet
With a corpse so sweet
As that of the dear deceased?

Juicy she was and tender,
And little did we discern
The good we should reap
From the cost of her keep:
She has made us a noble return.

Beauty we scarce remember,
Virtues we soon forget,
But the taste of our Aunt Eliza
Clings, clings, to my palate yet.

But for all their talent, the proconsuls were frequently a trial to a government less enthusiastic for empire than they were. Lugard almost single-handedly prevented the abandonment of Uganda. By writing innumerable letters to *The Times* and by giving speeches from one end of England to the other, he influenced even Queen Victoria, who wrote her foreign secretary Lord Rosebery in 1892: "We must take great care what we do. The difficulties are great, doubtless, in Uganda, but the dangers of abandoning it are greater." Johnston went to great personal effort to suppress the slave trade that still flourished in Central Africa. But the Treasury opposed even the smallest expenditure, and in the long run Johnston's labors only resulted in his retirement from the colonial service in 1901 at the age of forty-three. He was too enterprising, too dedicated, too interested. He and the other proconsuls tended to disregard instructions from home and thereby often bound the authorities in London to policies they would rather have avoided.

One of the more extraordinary proconsuls of the Victorian era was Charles George Gordon (1833–1885) who was, before he died, not only to capture the imaginations of his countrymen but materially to influence the future of the British Empire. The son of a lieutenant-general and destined himself to lead a military life, he was blessed with almost boundless energy, an uncanny sense of military tactics, and a singularly charismatic personality. Religiously devout but not orthodox, being a member of the Plymouth Brethren, Gordon was a mystic and an eccentric, and in many ways an enigma. He fascinated all who met him. Lord Elton, in his biography *General Gordon* (1954), quotes several contemporary impressions of people who met Gordon; all were struck by his eyes. For example,

> the clear blue eye, which seemed to possess a magical power over all who came within its influence. It read you through and through; it made it impossible for you to tell him anything but the truth. . . . From its glance you knew at once that at any risk he would keep his promise, that you might trust him with anything and everything, and that he would stand by you if all other friends deserted you.

Another acquaintance remarked:

> What eyes they were! Keen and clear, filled with the beauty of holiness, bright with unnatural brightness, their expression one of settled feverishness, the colour blue-grey as is the sky on a bitter March morning.

Although Gordon had served with distinction in the Crimean War, it was in China that he first came to public notice. He arrived there while the Taiping Rebellion (1850–1864) was at its height. The Taipings were fanatic followers of a curious religious creed. Their leader, Hung Hsiu-ch'üan, had been exposed to the influence of American and English missionaries, and the sect he founded was based on what he had learned. He claimed to have been transported to heaven in a trance and to have been informed there that he was the younger brother of Jesus; God the Father there equipped him with a sword, a seal, and a book of celestial decrees. So armed, and possessed of divine guidance and approbation, he assumed the title of T'ien-wang, or Heavenly King, and proceeded by military action towards the establishment, in the temporal sphere, of the Great Peace, or Taiping. The creed of the T'ien-wang went as follows:

The Heavenly Father sits on the throne above.
The Heavenly Brother Christ is the next honorable, sitting on the right of the Father, excelled by no man.
By the grace of the Father and Brother we sit on the left
United as one we reign.
Disobey the Heavenly Will and you will be ground to pieces with a pestle.

Against the wretched Chinese imperial forces, the Taipings were markedly successful. In 1860 the Heavenly King threatened the European trading center of Shanghai, but the British were able to wrest a promise from him that for a period of at least one year he would not approach within 30 miles of the city. While the Anglo-French regulars could protect Shanghai itself, the Chinese merchants outside the city were far from reassured and hired an American adventurer, Frederick Ward, to organize a Chinese force against the Taipings. After an initial failure, Ward met with some success. In 1862, with the backing now of the Europeans as well as the Chinese, he took command of a new army, optimistically called "Ever-Victorious," and went on the offensive again. Ward fell mortally wounded in September, and after two successors failed to make headway, Gordon—through the miscarrying of an order from the British minister in Peking that no British officer should serve with the Ever-Victorious Army—was breveted major in March 1863, and put at the head of the irregulars—his first independent command.

Gordon immediately infused new life into his motley force. He acquired bright new uniforms for them and established an even more resplendently garbed bodyguard of 300 for himself. But more important, he disciplined the troops and through personal example turned them into a highly efficient army of irregulars. He averted several mutinies among his raw soldiers by the sheer power of his will, and in battle if his men did not leave cover when ordered, he would drag them out into the open by their pigtails and make them fire their rifles over his shoulder. He never rested, hardly ever ate. While he expected much from his troops, he was a man of broad sympathies: at his own request, his salary was cut from £3,200 per annum to £1,200—four-fifths of which he spent on medicine and other comforts for his men.

Even in the most difficult circumstances, Gordon led his troops armed only with a small rattan cane which soon became known as the "Wand of Victory." Against tremendous odds, he led the Ever-Victorious Army from one success to another, until at last, in 1864, the final victory was won and the Taiping Rebellion crushed. Characteristically, Gordon refused the vast rewards offered him by the grateful Chinese emperor, accepting only the yellow jacket and peacock feather emblematic of membership in the highest Chinese imperial order—the Mandarins of the Yellow Jacket—and two gold coins struck in his honor. This most modest of men even declined to go to Peking to receive personally the imperial thanks, and his official summary of the campaign made no mention of his own name.

Now, in early 1865, the time had come for Gordon, no longer a Chinese general but a British brevet lieutenant-colonel, to return to England. Lord Elton tells the amusing anecdote of Gordon, nearing London, tying his new suit of clothes in a bundle and towing it in the wake of the steamer on which he was traveling, so that he would be less conspicuous upon landing. But it was all in vain. He returned to find himself already a legend and for a time was forced to suffer the agony of being constantly the object of adulation. With its typical fickleness, however, the public soon forgot "Chinese" Gordon. The British government, with the same mistrust of genius it had shown in the case of Harry Johnston, virtually ignored him and would not give him a command in any of the many minor wars the nation was involved in, for the successful conduct of which Gordon's particular talents were so well suited.

Gordon's next official post took him to Gravesend, where he was entrusted with the construction of some new forts for the defense of the Thames. His duties were not too demanding and the spiritual and mystical side of his character began to develop more fully. He spent a great deal of time reading religious works and helping the poor, particularly the young boys of Gravesend. He became something of an evangelist, and many a young man was startled by the blunt question, "Do you believe in Jesus?" followed by "Then do you know that God lives in you?" For Gordon had had a "revelation"; a close friend, quoted by Elton, described the moment thus:

> . . . while dressing rather listlessly before dinner his eye fell on an opened Bible on the table and on these words: 'Whosoever confesseth that Jesus is the Son of God, God dwelleth in him and he in God.' Suddenly it flashed upon him that he had found a jewel of priceless value—he had found what alone could satisfy him, oneness with God: henceforth that was the key to

his whole after life and he wondered he had never seen it before. He wondered far more that anyone could read such words and be indifferent to them and he now tried to make them known to as many as he could. . . .

The interlude at Gravesend lasted some six years; it was followed by a tour of duty as British representative on the Danubian Commission and finally in 1874 by Gordon's appointment as governor of the equatorial provinces of the Sudan by the Egyptian khedive, Ismail Pasha. Characteristically, he would accept only one-fifth of the salary offered. Gordon served his new master tirelessly, trying to rule the Sudan (the whole of which he acquired as his charge in 1877) in an enlightened manner and suppress the still flourishing slave trade. But the surrounding corruption became too much even for him and in 1879 he resigned.

Short assignments in India, China, and South Africa—where he was promoted to major-general—occupied Gordon's time for the next few years, which were made memorable by a visit to Palestine, to satisfy his spiritual cravings. Little did he expect that events were again to call him to the Sudan.

There, in 1881, an obscure dervish had declared himself to be the "mahdi"—the expected one sent to lead a purified Islam to victory over the khedive's forces in the Sudan. In September 1882 the British reluctantly became the real rulers of Egypt by crushing a revolt against the khedive at Tel-el-Kebir. Gladstone's Liberal government was, however, most anxious to limit its new and largely unwanted imperial responsibilities; as a result, while the mahdi's revolt in the Sudan spread, the British government stayed persistently aloof and would not offer even advice to the khedive. In 1885 the situation in the Sudan became desperate; consequently, the khedive hired a retired British officer, Colonel William Hicks, to lead an Egyptian army against the mahdi and to reestablish Egyptian authority. Total disaster ensued: Hicks and his entire command were slaughtered by the mahdi's fanatical forces.

The news of this catastrophe shocked the British public and placed the government in an uncomfortable position. What was to be done? Gladstone, who had just previously announced the impending evacuation of Egypt, was faced with the prospect of the mahdi's overthrowing the puppet Egyptian government itself if the British did not act. A great clamor arose in the British press to send Gordon to put things right, and the government finally decided to bolster its popularity by yielding to the pressure. But it also decided that all the khedives' garrisons in the Sudan had to be evacuated, and it was this task Gordon was instructed to undertake. Gordon was the worst choice the government could possibly have made to carry out the order. As the British writer C. E. Carrington points out, if a crusade against Islam and the slave-traders was wanted, or a Christian martyr to bear witness and die in the mahdi's camp, then Charles Gordon would have been the man. But to ask him to lead a retreat—to be party to a surrender—was asking too much.

Controversy continues to rage over the terms of Gordon's appointment. His instructions from the cabinet were of necessity vague, as Gordon would officially be acting on behalf of the khedive. And the khedive was, of course, the creature of the British agent and consul general, Sir Evelyn Baring, whose duty it consequently became to issue Gordon's orders. The operative document is the *firman* issued after Gordon had reached Khartoum in February 1884. It appointed him governor general of the Sudan and declared that his mission was

> to carry into execution the evacuation of those territories, and to withdraw our troops, civil officers, and such of the inhabitants, together with their belongings, as may wish to leave Egypt . . . and after completing the evacuation [to] take steps for establishing an organized government for the different provinces of the Sudan.

To Gordon the second part of his instructions was the most important, and he decided that its proper implementation required his continued presence in Khartoum. He wrote in his journal: ". . . if an emissary or letter comes up here ordering me to come down, I WILL NOT OBEY IT, BUT WILL STAY HERE AND FALL WITH THE TOWN AND RUN ALL RISKS." As early as February 27, 1884, he also concluded that the mahdi would have to be "smashed up." The British government was embarrassed. Gordon had been sent to the Sudan to dissolve quietly an unwanted imperial connection. He succeeded in doing exactly the opposite and had once again become a great national hero in the bargain. While the cabinet debated its dilemma, the mahdi's hordes descended to invest Khartoum. It was March 1884.

The attention of the world was now focused on this lonely spot on the Nile. How long could Gordon hold out? Was there, perhaps, still time to extricate him? The government was in an agony of indecision, and it was not until some six months after the siege had commenced that the great popular outcry forced the sending of a relief expedition. The progress of this force was, however, discouragingly slow. On January 26, 1885, the mahdist forces broke through the defenses of Khartoum. Gordon faced his onrushing foes clad in a white uniform; he made no attempt to resist and was immediately killed by a spear thrust. His head was cut off and triumphantly displayed to the victorious dervishes. It was two days later when the lead vessels of the relief force steamed into Khartoum, to find it in the mahdi's hands.

There are many instances when the "man on the spot" forced the annexation of new areas to the British Empire by ignoring orders and acting on his own authority. Gordon accomplished this by his actions in the Sudan and their consequences—his death and the annihilation of his garrison. He forced the hand of Gladstone, who had at one time declared the mahdists to represent a legitimate movement for national freedom in the Sudan. Cries of "Avenge Gordon!" swept Britain, and Gladstone could only submit. He ordered the relief force to pacify the Sudan, but an apparent Russian move on Afghanistan delayed the venture. For many years Gordon's fate rankled in the minds of Englishmen. But the government had not forgotten the Sudan, especially in view of renewed German, French, and Italian activities in the area. In early September 1898 the forces of the khalifa, the mahdi's successor, were defeated by a British expeditionary force under General Sir Herbert (later Lord) Kitchener at Omdurman, and in 1899 the Sudan became an Anglo-Egyptian condominium. Its real conqueror had died 15 years earlier in Khartoum.

Perhaps the last in the line of great imperial figures was General Orde Wingate (1903–1944), of World War II fame, who appeared on the scene well after the great period of the Empire was over. His similarity to Gordon and others of his type was remarkable. Like Gordon, he had uncanny military acumen and was an eccentric, a mystic, and a devout but unconventional Christian. Wingate's grandfather had for a time worked with Gordon in his charitable enterprises, and Wingate himself became a member of the Plymouth Brethren. Like Gordon, he was strongly influenced by the Old Testament and fascinated by Palestine. He believed that the Jews were indeed the "chosen people," and while serving there he helped establish the Jewish military organization that was eventually to gain Israel her independence. But he also felt that "Palestine is essential to our Empire—our Empire is essential to England—England is essential to world peace." One of his associates wrote of him:

> In his upbringing, in his fundamentally religious and almost mystic temperament, as in his way of handling men of all races . . . [he] was very like his fellow countrymen and fellow pilgrims of an earlier generation, David Livingstone and General Gordon. . . . his greatness as a leader lay in qualities beyond mere intellectual grasp of war, of swift daring; it lay in a deep compelling faith.

After his premature death, Winston Churchill, then prime minister, described Wingate in the House of Commons as "a man of genius who might also have become a man of destiny."

Not only were the great imperial personalities often alike in background, character, and attitude, but Carrington has shown that the same families produced sons for the colonial service for generation after generation, families frequently closely united through marriage. Thus, the Bruce, Lambton, Grey, and Baring families, which were so connected, produced four viceroys of India, three governors general of Canada, and three secretaries of state for the colonies.

The imperial public servant of the stature of the ones we are discussing greatly ameliorated the conditions of everyday life in Africa and India, but it was often difficult for him to maintain a proper humility and avoid slipping into paternalism or, what was worse, the conviction of his own racial superiority. It is not surprising, however, that this last frequently happened; as Margery Perham remarks in her biography of Lugard:

> It would have been difficult for an Englishman of the nineties, entering Africa and seeing the nakedness, ignorance, cruelty and superstition of the people, not to believe that his race was superior and therefore justified in imposing its dominion.

Lugard adhered to the strange anthropological notions popularized by the explorer Sir Richard Burton: "I never yet saw the Negro," he wrote, "who had the dignity, and command of men, the self-respect, that the straight-haired races of Africa have." Yet when he suspected that the Royal Niger Company might be implicated in the slave trade, Lugard exploded: "Better a British administration burst up and the country lapsed to barbarism or to France than that British officers should know of these things, and tolerate them."

Rudyard Kipling in 1899 accurately reflected the prevailing attitude of the British toward the nonwhite populations of the world in his poem, "The White Man's Burden." Addressed to the United States, then in the process of suppressing the Philippine insurrection, it was both a call to duty—"bind your sons to exile to serve your captives' needs"—and an admonition indicating his reservations regarding the "lesser breeds without the law":

> *Take up the White Man's burden—*
> *The savage wars of peace—*
> *Fill full the mouth of Famine*
> *And bid the sickness cease;*
> *And when your goal is nearest*
> *The end for others sought,*
> *Watch Sloth and heathen Folly*
> *Bring all your hope to nought.*

It was when feelings of racial uniqueness and self-confidence were at their strongest that imperialism was the least attractive. Sir Francis Younghusband, the leader of the British invasion of Tibet in 1904, wrote in *The Heart of a Continent* (1896):

> No European can mix with non-Christian races without feeling his moral superiority over them. He feels, from the first contact with them, that whatever may be their relative positions from an intellectual point of view, he is stronger morally than they are. And facts show that this feeling is a true one. It is not because we are any cleverer than the natives of India, because we have more brains or bigger heads than they have, that we rule India; but because we are stronger morally than they are. Our superiority over them is not due to mere sharpness of intellect, but to that higher moral nature to which we have attained in the development of the human race.

Hopefully, feelings of moral superiority at least prevented dishonesty on the part of British colonial officials.

Of course, not all the British viewed their "race" vis-à-vis others with quite this same degree of righteous self-satisfaction. Alfred (later Lord) Milner, the British high commissioner in South Africa before, during, and after the Boer War, though not untainted by racism, manifested a proud sense of imperial mission:

> Imperialism as a political doctrine has been represented as something tawdry and superficial. In reality it has all the depth and comprehensiveness of a religious faith. Its significance is moral even more than material. It is a mistake to think of it as principally concerned with 'painting the map red.' There is quite enough painted red already. It is not a question of

a couple of hundred thousand square miles more or less. It is a question of preserving the unity of a great race, of enabling it, by maintaining that unity, to develop freely on its own line, and to continue to fulfill its distinctive mission in the world.

Milner believed in the genius of the British "race" for ruling, but he also felt that the British must share the secret of how to rule with those they governed. This sharing of the secret, he said, was "peculiar to the British Empire among Empires, and to the British nation as an Empire-building race." Joseph Chamberlain, the colonial secretary at the turn of the century, proclaimed a similar faith:

I believe in this race, the greatest governing race the world has ever seen; in this Anglo-Saxon race, so proud, tenacious, self-confident and determined, this race which neither climate nor change can degenerate, which will infallibly be the predominant force of future history and universal civilisation.

An anecdote concerning Rhodes portrays this "racial" self-confidence most clearly. One dark night, while camping out in the South African veldt, Rhodes turned towards his companion, Lord Grey, and shouted: "Wake up, Grey, wake up!" Grey asked sleepily if the tent was on fire. To which Rhodes responded, "No, no, but I just wanted to ask you, have you ever thought how lucky your are to be born an Englishman when there are so many millions who are not?"

Absolute power, if it does not corrupt absolutely, at least makes the maintenance of balance and objectivity difficult. What is remarkable, therefore, is not so much the number of bigots and fools produced by the British imperial service, but the many excellent scholars and men of broad sympathy and imagination which it developed. Sir Henry Rawlinson (1810–1895), an officer in the East India Company's army and later British minister at Teheran, became the first man to decipher cuneiform. Sir Harry Johnston was not only a wonderfully observant naturalist, but also a fine artist, a novelist of note, and one of the first great African linguists.

Sir Stamford Raffles (1781–1826), the founder of modern Singapore, was a magnificent administrator, a dedicated student of the history and art of Java, and an expert on that island's flora and fauna; the fine Malayan and Javanese ethnographical collection in the British Museum today is all that remains of Raffles' much more comprehensive collection, most of which was lost at sea. After the British seized the French-controlled Dutch East Indies during the Napoleonic wars,

Raffles was appointed lieutenant governor of Java. He had dreams of the British flag flying permanently over the island. Abhorring the cruelties of the Dutch colonists, as he observed them, he became a great champion of the Javanese people, whom he greatly admired. The Javanese, he felt,

> are neither sunk in barbarism, nor worn out by effeminacy; they have been both mistaken and misrepresented; they are neither so indolent as to refuse to labour when they feel that the fruits of it are their own, nor so ignorant as to be indifferent to the comforts and luxuries of civilised society.

Before Java was restored to the Dutch in 1816, Raffles accomplished much for the Javanese. His aim was to bestow on them "the freedom which is everywhere the boast of British subjects," and this he accomplished to a surprising degree. The cultivation of certain crops was no longer compulsory, restrictions on Javanese trading rights were removed, and the whole system of land tenure reformed. Raffles proposed nothing less than a thoroughgoing economic and social revolution, and in five years he came close to achieving it.

In other parts of the Empire throughout the eighteenth and nineteenth centuries, imperial officials from time to time appeared who were able to see their duty, untainted by their own national prejudices. Thus, Lord Northbrook, viceroy of India from 1872 to 1876, insisted on maintaining a small protective duty on goods imported into India, against the will of the home government and at a time when free trade was almost a state religion. Occasionally, one of the proconsuls was sufficiently farsighted to envisage an independent future for the component parts of the nonwhite Empire as desirable. Sir Thomas Munro, governor of Madras in the 1820s, wrote that "whenever we are obliged to resign our sovereignty we should leave the natives so far improved from their connection with us, as to be capable of maintaining a free, or at least a regular government among themselves." Mountstuart Elphinstone, Munro's counterpart at Bombay, felt that "the most desirable death for us to die should be the improvement of the natives reaching such a point as would render it impossible for a foreign nation to retain the government." Perhaps the culmination of this type of thinking was pronounced not by an imperial official, but by the novelist Anthony Trollope in his autobiographical *Australia and New Zealand* (1873), when he declared:

> We are called upon to rule [the colonies] as far as we do rule them, not for our glory, but for their happiness. If we keep them, we should keep

them—not because they add prestige to the name of Great Britain, not because they are gems in our diadem, not in order that we may boast that the sun never sets on our dependencies, but because by keeping them we may assist them in developing their own resources. And when we part with them, as part with them we shall, let us do so with neither smothered jealousy nor open hostility, but with a proud feeling that we are sending a son out into the world able to take his place among men.

If the British government remained markedly unenthusiastic about imperial adventures for much of the nineteenth century, the British people felt otherwise. Imperialism became a real force in British politics when Benjamin Disraeli declared it to be one of the three main planks of the Conservative platform in his Crystal Palace speech of June 24, 1872. But it is a curious commentary on the nature of government policy, and perhaps eloquent testimony to the power of the "man on the spot," that much more territory was added to the British Empire under the anti-imperial Gladstone than during the administration of that conscious prophet of empire Disraeli, even taking into account the much longer period that Gladstone served as prime minister.

The so-called era of prestige imperialism prompted a much greater public identification with the Empire than had previously been the case. To the industrial worker in the dreary black lands of the industrial Midlands, the thought of the British flag flying over so many remote parts of the world gave a vicarious thrill of pride and pleasure. The proconsul became a popular figure in literature, and the image created by such novelists as G. A. Henty (1832-1902) and John Buchan (1875–1940) must have had a considerable influence on generations of British schoolboys.

Henty's heroes were always boys closely associated with the great men of British history, participating with them in the important events of the time. In some 80 books, with titles such as *With Clive in India, With the Allies to Pekin, The Dash for Khartoum, With Wolfe in Canada, With Roberts to Pretoria,* and *Through the Afghan Passes,* Henty repeated this same successful formula. Most of his books opened with a letter addressed to "My dear Lads," which emphasized some homely truth. In *The Dash for Khartoum,* he exhorted his readers to "never act in haste, for repentance is sure to follow. In this case, great anxiety and unhappiness were caused through a lad acting as he believed for the best, but without consulting those who had every right to a voice in the matter." At another point he averred that "cowardice is of all vices the most contemptible," just as bravery was of all virtues the most estimable.

Henty's central characters might be poor at the outset of a tale, but poverty was not considered a detriment by the author. "I do not believe," he wrote, "that a boy is one whit less liked, or is ever taunted with his poverty, provided he is a good fellow." But most of Henty's good fellows were either the lost and unsuspecting sons of noblemen or of an aristocratic but recently impoverished line. At any rate, superior breeding nearly always showed through. Yorke Haberton, in *With Roberts to Pretoria,* was, says Henty, "a good specimen of the class by which Britain has been built up, her colonies formed, and her battlefields won—a class, in point of energy, fearlessness, the spirit of adventure, and the readiness to face and overcome all difficulties, unmatched in the world."

Regardless of their financial status Henty's heroes were always gentlemen and adventurers. They were also brave and modest. In *With the Allies to Pekin,* Rex, "if he had been in the army . . . would certainly have earned a V.C. [Victoria Cross] for the way in which he silenced those guns." But as Rex later explained it: "I don't think . . . that in an affair of this sort the risk is anything compared with that which one runs in a regular fight. These little excursions I have made have had very little risk in them—partially none. . . ." Henty was not interested in businessmen or politicians. He could never have written a novel entitled *By Wealth and Stealth, or the British Acquisition of the Suez Canal.*

Although Henty by no means denigrated nonwhite colonial peoples, he was nevertheless a firm believer in the uniqueness of the Anglo-Saxon. The raja of Tripataly in *The Tiger of Mysore* had hopes for his sons only because their grandmother was English: "I want to see that, with the white blood in your veins, you have some of the vigor and energy of Englishmen." Afghans were, although brave and independent, unruly and undisciplined; but, according to Henty,

> when led and organized by British officers there are no better soldiers in the world. . . . Guided by British advice, led by British officers, and it may be, paid by British gold, Afghanistan is likely to prove an invaluable ally to us when the day comes that Russia believes herself strong enough to move forwards towards the goal of all her hopes and efforts of the last fifty years, the conquest of India.

Although "natives" usually appeared as faithful, self-sacrificing servants or companions, Henty's heroes appreciated their qualities as fighters and worthy opponents. In *In Times of Peril*, the raja of Bithri was treated well for having been an honorable and ethical foe. Some peasants captured in the Mutiny were not put to death because "they have fought bravely for their country, and have done their duty, according to their light." No native, however, had in full the qualities which God reserved solely for Englishmen: when Perry Groves, in *At the Point of the Bayonet*, admitted to Nana that he was really English and had only disguised himself as a Maratha, the latter was not surprised:

> There are many as tall as you, but they have not your width of shoulders and strong build. Lastly, I have wondered how a young Mahratta should be endowed with so much energy and readiness, be willing to take heavy responsibilities on his shoulders and to be so full of resource.

In Henty's mind there appeared to be a scale of racial evolution with Europeans at the top, followed by Asians and Africans. He might admire the intellectual and physical powers of Indians, Chinese, and Arabs, but he rejected the possibility that they could possess the basic morality and "character," "pluck," "dash," "good-fellowship" that were so distinctly European and particularly British. Negro Africans did not have even the attributes of other non-Europeans, according to Henty. Mr. Godenough, in *By Sheer Pluck*, described them as being

> just like children. . . . They are always laughing or quarreling. They are good-natured and passionate, indolent, but will work hard for a time; clever up to a certain point, densely stupid beyond. The intelligence of an average negro is about equal to that of a European child of ten years old. A few, a very few, go beyond this, but these are exceptions, just as Shakespeare's was an exception to the ordinary intellect of an Englishman. They are fluent talkers, but their ideas are borrowed. They are absolutely without originality, absolutely without inventive power. Living among white men their imitative faculties enable them to attain a considerable amount of civilisation. Left alone to their own devices they retrograde into a state little above their native savagery.

Henty's style was, on the whole, rather flat and repetitious, and his characters were usually colorless. But he did expose his readers to a particular stereotype of the proconsul, and as he borrowed liberally from serious writers on historical and contemporary subjects, his readers did become aware of the geography of the British Empire and of the events that had made it what it was.

John Buchan, who wrote a generation after Henty, was a much

more talented and sophisticated author. Some of his stories—for example, *The Thirty-Nine Steps* and *Greenmantle*—are still classics. Buchan's heroes, though more complicated and infinitely more real and alive than Henty's, are not altogether unlike them. They are good at sports and look at even the most serious crisis as part of a game. They are always first, strongest, and wisest. Bonson Jane

> had been a noted sportsman and was still a fine polo player; his name was a household word in Europe for his work in international finance. . . . it was rumored that in the same week he had been offered the Secretaryship of State, the Presidency of an ancient University, and the control of a great industrial corporation.

Sandy Arbuthnot is "one of the two or three most intelligent people in the world," and Julius Victor is the "richest man in the world." They are offhand about and impervious to pain ("There's nothing much wrong with me. . . . A shell dropped beside me and damaged my foot. They say they shall have to cut it off. . . .") Sex does not preoccupy them; when the hero is smitten, it is because his intended "is a regular sportswoman," and he is likely to propose shyly while they are both crossing a rushing torrent. Buchan's view of Negro Africans is not much different from Henty's: they may be fearless and brave, but little else. In *Prester John*, the white hero speaks of knowing

> the meaning of the white man's duty. He has to take all risks, reckoning nothing of his life or his fortune and well content to find his reward in the fulfillment of his task. That is the difference between white and black, the gift of responsibility, the power of being in a little way a king; and so long as we know this and practice it, we will rule not in Africa alone but wherever there are dark men who live only for the day and for their own bellies.

Henty and Buchan were by no means the only novelists dealing with imperial adventures but they were probably, along with Kipling, the most influential and widely read. They heightened and touched with color the popular image of the imperial proconsul.

Despite the apparent popularity of imperialism in nineteenth-century Britain, real enthusiasm for the Empire was not to survive the Boer War which commenced in 1899. The last great imperial conflict, this time against European settlers of Dutch stock, it resulted in the British conquest and annexation of the Orange Free State and the South African Republic (the Transvaal). The Boer War captured the imagination of the world. It seemed to have been started by the British with little provocation and appeared to pit a vast and populous Empire against a small group of independent, freedom-loving folk. The Boers' fighting ability won them universal sympathy, and the revocation of civil rights, the burning of farms, and the establishment of concentration camps by the British caused revulsion both within and without Britain. The Boer War disillusioned even the most utopian, intellectual imperialists and destroyed for good the dream of an Empire dedicated to liberalism and humanitarianism.

When all is said and done, what can be concluded about British imperialism and the men who preached and practiced its philosophy in the remote parts of the world? A surprising number of imperial civil servants were selfless men, idealists dedicated to improving the lot of those they ruled on behalf of a distant monarch. That exposure to less developed lands and people should have engendered feelings of racial uniqueness and superiority is not surprising. It is unfortunate that there were not more Johnstons and fewer Younghusbands. It is also unfortunate that someone like General Reginald Dyer, in perpetrating the so-called Amritsar Massacre in 1919 (see Chapter 11), could do more harm to the imperial idea in ten minutes than many abler men could do good in their entire lifetimes. It is perhaps significant that until the mid-twentieth century the only part of the Empire where the indigenous population attained even marginal rights comparable to those of the white man was New Zealand, where the settlers were unable to defeat the Maori militarily.

It is improper, however, to judge one age by the standards of another. Imperialism was to many the hallmark of national greatness in the nineteenth century, just as the conquest of space is to others in the twentieth. The very nature of imperialism—the domination of one group over another and the promulgation of laws without the consent of the governed—limited its achievements, a fact not unknown to the imperial authorities. Thus, a democratically based independent Indian government could legislate on social matters and could outlaw untouchability, while a British Indian government could not. In one case, it was the proper function of an enlightened government; in the other, it would have been considered a gross interference with Indian religious practices and social customs, an interference which had been so highly resented even in such a seemingly noncontroversial area as compulsory inoculation for bubonic plague. A similar situation prevails in Africa. Today independent African governments can legislate against tribalism—a matter that was considered much too sensitive for British action during the colonial period.

The imperial idea was rife with contradictions. British governments preached, but never practiced, the dictum that all subjects of the Crown were equal, and Indians, for example, could never understand why they were treated as political equals in Britain, but not in India itself. As a philosophy, imperialism was largely bankrupt, but in action it was often fair, realistic, and pragmatically sound. Thus when the time came for Britain to divest herself of her Empire, the parting was usually not only bloodless but accompanied by mutual feelings of respect.

6

Cecil Rhodes: Prototype of an Imperialist

Of all the missionaries of empire, none equaled Cecil John Rhodes in dedication, intensity, or achievement. Born in 1853, the fifth of nine sons of the vicar of Bishop's Stortford, Rhodes in his early years gave little promise of his future greatness. His early ambition was to be a lawyer, and, if not that, to follow his father's footsteps in the church. "I cannot deny," he wrote his Aunt Sophy,

> for it would be hypocrisy to say otherwise, that I still above everything would be a barrister; but I agree with you it is a very precarious profession. Next to that I think a clergyman's life is nicest and therefore I shall most earnestly try to go to College, because I have fully determined to one of these two, and a College education is necessary for both. . . .

But college was not to be the immediate destination of the young Rhodes. His health was poor, and his father decided to send him to join his brother Herbert in the more salubrious climate of Natal, South Africa.[1]

The Rhodes who landed at Durban in September 1870 was not impressive in appearance. Tall, spare, and of a sallow complexion, there was little in him to attract attention or to inspire confidence. Herbert's farm lay in the Umkomaas Valley, south of Pietermaritzburg, and on it, despite numerous warnings, the two brothers tried to

[1] See the map of Africa on p. 149, Chapter 9.

grow cotton. Considering the difficulties they had to face, they did remarkably well. But the area was not really suited to the cultivation of cotton, and, within two years, first Herbert and then Cecil migrated to the newly discovered diamond fields of Griqualand West, north of the Orange and west of the Vaal rivers. Rhodes never regretted his experience on the ill-fated plantation. He learned a great deal about farming and the problems of the farmer, and for the rest of his life, he was always to feel himself one of them. He had also matured both physically and mentally and had developed determination, self-reliance, and a shrewd business sense—all of which were to stand him in good stead in the future.

The South Africa that Rhodes adopted as his own was divided between British colonies and Boer republics. There is little doubt that the British government's interest in South Africa during the early part of the nineteenth century had been limited to the Cape of Good Hope, yet British control spread over much of South Africa even before the discovery of diamonds or gold. The British had seized the Cape from the Dutch in 1806, during a period of strong missionary influence in British governing circles and the antislavery agitation of William Wilberforce. The British policy in the Cape thus came into immediate conflict with the racial philosophy of the Boers who believed in slavery and the complete subjugation of the black man, basing their views both on the Bible and the practical necessity for labor. In 1807 the slave trade was abolished in the British Empire, and the Boers were faced with a critical labor shortage. Years of friction ensued as the British authorities, encouraged by the missionaries, sought to restrain the Boers from exploiting the resident African population. In 1833 slavery itself was abolished throughout the Empire, leaving the Boer farmers and cattlemen in worse straits than before. To escape the restrictive jurisdiction of the British, thousands of Boers began trekking north from Cape Colony the next year, to settle in what became Natal, the Orange Free State, and the Transvaal. But the British, motivated at least in part by concern for the native African, followed and in 1843 annexed Natal; the entire region between the Orange and Vaal rivers was proclaimed British five years later.

There followed a struggle between conscience and financial expediency within the British government itself. The new areas, especially the Orange River Colony, were not initially remunerative and proved burdensome to maintain. Thus the British relinquished their sovereignty over all the territory beyond the Vaal River (the Transvaal) to the Boers in 1852 and two years later returned the Orange River Colony to Boer control as the Orange Free State. But the discovery of diamonds on the Orange River in 1867 ushered in a new era of bad feelings, for the area—Griqualand West—was claimed both by the Boers and the British. The decision which placed the diggings within British territory was hardly a model of disinterested arbitration, and in the years following 1867 relations between the Boer republics and the British colonies in South Africa steadily deteriorated. Rhodes was to become deeply embroiled both in the diamond business and in the political ramifications brought on by the assignment of all the diamond bearing ground to the British.

Life in the diamond fields of South Africa in the 1870s for those trying to make their fortune was physically exhausting, and, as the ground known to bear diamonds was limited, the competition for claims was ruthless. Rhodes described the diggings in a letter to his mother:

> It is like an immense number of ant-heaps covered with black ants, as thick as can be, the latter represented by human beings; when you understand there are about 600 claims on the kopje and each claim is generally split into 4, and on each bit there are about 6 blacks and whites working, it gives a total of about ten thousand working every day on a piece of ground 180 yards by 200.

When Rhodes arrived at Kimberley, the center of the diamond country, his brother Herbert, who was about to retire from the scene, had already acquired three claims. From one of these alone Rhodes could soon report a weekly income of £100. But living expenses were high: water cost threepence a bucket, meal seven to ten shillings a bushel, and firewood £3 to £4 a load. It did not take long for Rhodes's uncanny business acumen to manifest itself. Despite his youth and relative inexperience, he rarely made a mistake in a matter of business, and his position in the diamond diggings constantly improved; so much so, that by 1873, he was able to return to England to indulge his lifelong ambition of attending Oxford University. Rhodes could not yet be considered a wealthy man, but he was to become so before he finally received his degree some eight years later.

The development of Rhodes's personal philosophy, with its inherent sense of Anglo-Saxon destiny, had begun to develop long before he came to Oxford. But it was the words of John Ruskin, the art critic and antimaterialist philosopher, with their message of selfless public service based on patriotism, that confirmed intellectually what Rhodes knew intuitively. "There is a destiny now possible to us," said Ruskin,

> the highest ever set before a nation to be accepted or refused. We are still undegenerate in race; a race mingled of the best northern blood. We are not yet dissolute in temper, but still have the firmness to govern, and the grace to obey. . . . will you, youths of England, make your country again a royal throne of kings; a sceptred isle, for all the world a source of light, a centre of peace; mistress of Learning and of the Arts;—faithful guardian of great memories in the midst of irreverent and ephemeral visions;—faithful servants of time-tried principles, under temptation from fond experiments and licentious desires; and amidst the cruel and clamorous jealousies of the nations, worshipped in her strange valour, of goodwill towards men? . . .
>
> And this is what [England] must either do, or perish: she must found colonies as fast and as far as she is able, formed of her most energetic and worthiest men;—seizing every piece of fruitful waste ground she can set her foot on, and there teaching these her colonists that their chief virtue is to be fidelity to their country, and that their first aim is to be to advance the power of England by land and sea: and that, though they live on a distant plot of ground, they are no more to consider themselves therefore disfranchised from their native land, than the sailors of her fleet do, because they float on distant waves. . . . if we can get men, for little pay, to cast themselves against cannon-mouths for love of England, we may find men also who will plough and sow for her, and who will behave kindly and righteously for her, and who will bring up their children to love her, and who will gladden themselves in the brightness of her glory, more than in all the light of tropic skies. . . .
>
> You think that an impossible ideal. Be it so; refuse to accept it if you will; but see that you form your own in its stead. All that I ask of you is to have a fixed purpose of some kind for your country and yourselves; no matter how restricted, so that it be fixed and unselfish.

These passages from Ruskin's inaugural lecture at Oxford had a stunning impact on Rhodes when he read them; inspired, he now clearly realized the purpose of his life. As he pondered what Ruskin had said, Rhodes was led to conjecture on the existence of God. He concluded that while there was only a fifty percent chance of a supreme deity existing, he would support the positive assumption. If God existed, then, the proper function of man was obviously to carry out His will, which must be to develop a race who would bring peace, liberty, and justice to the world. Only the Anglo-Saxon race could be God's agent in effecting His purpose, and the proper way to implement

God's will was therefore to make the Anglo-Saxons supreme on earth. Rhodes determined to work "for the furtherance of the British Empire, for the bringing of the whole civilized world under British rule, for the recovery of the United States, for the making of the Anglo-Saxon race into one Empire."

Rhodes's initial effort to implement his newly developed philosophy took place in 1875 when he made the first draft of his will. In this he provided for the creation of a secret society to encourage

> the extension of British rule throughout the world . . . the colonization by British subjects of all lands where the means of livelihood are attainable by energy, labour, and enterprise, and especially the occupation by British settlers of the entire continent of Africa, the Holy Land, the Valley of the Euphrates, the islands of Cyprus and Candia, the whole of South America, the islands of the Pacific not heretofore possessed by Great Britain, the whole of the Malay Archipelago, the sea-board of China and Japan, the ultimate recovery of the United States of America as an integral part of the British Empire . . . colonial representation in the Imperial Parliament, which may tend to weld together the disjointed members of the Empire, and finally, the foundation of so great a power as to hereafter render wars impossible and promote the best interests of humanity.

Naïve and crude as were the provisions of this first will, they still expressed the unrefined core of Rhodes's thinking. Later drafts of the will were to be less aggressively chauvinistic but continued to express the same basic philosophy.

Rhodes was not, however, going to wait for death to implement his ideas—he was to devote his life to them. Like Gordon, he early decided that marriage would only act as an impediment to the attainment of his goals. (The only woman whose picture ever hung in Rhodes's house was an ancient stepmother of Lobengula, the Matabele king, who had once helped him.) For this same reason—to attain his goals—he wanted to acquire great wealth. When Chinese Gordon, the former leader of the Ever-Victorious Army, informed him that he had refused a whole roomful of gold offered to him by the grateful Chinese emperor, Rhodes was profoundly shocked: "I should have taken it and as many more rooms-full as they offered me," he observed. "It is no use having big ideas if you have not the cash to carry them out." As he grew older, Rhodes developed an ever-increasing obsession for money; in fact, it became difficult at times to determine whether he was more interested in the realization of his ideal or in the acquisition of the material means to make it possible. He became convinced that money could achieve anything and that every man had his price. At times the philosophy of Rhodes the financier contrasts curiously with that of Rhodes the empire-builder dedicated to the fulfillment of British racial destiny.

But Rhodes was basically a romantic dreamer. He was wont to say, when pointing on a map at the vast territories between the British possessions in South Africa and the central lakes, "All this is to be painted red; that is my dream." Or, as he expressed it in a more lyrical mood:

> As I walked, I looked up at the sky and down at the earth and I said to myself this should be British. And it came to me in that fine, exhilarating air that the British were the best race to rule the world.

Until 1880 Rhodes limited his activities largely to his multiple business enterprises. But with the formation of the De Beers Mining Company, which, under his guidance, later established a virtual monopoly in the South African diamond industry, he felt that the time had come to enter the field of politics actively. As a strong believer in *rapprochement* between the British and Afrikaner (Dutch-descended) peoples, he ran for the Cape assembly as a candidate from the predominantly Boer district of Barkly West, which elected him in 1881 and continued to do so until the end of his life.

Although Rhodes was a firm advocate of imperial expansion in Africa, he did not view the Empire as specifically centered on England. His was a broader vision of a global Anglo-Saxon confederation of equals. He detested "meddling by the Home Government"—the imposition of "the Imperial factor," as he called it—and stood strongly for "the government of South Africa by the people of South Africa with the Imperial Flag for defence."

Rhodes's first effort to advance the British flag northward via Bechuanaland, although successfully culminated in 1885, did not work out entirely to his satisfaction. Chagrined and hurt, he placed some of the blame on his still vulnerable financial position, and between 1886 and 1888 devoted most of his energies to remedying this apparent defect. He not only absorbed all his rivals in the diamond fields but established a dominant position in the newly discovered gold fields of the Transvaal. He soon had some share in every facet of South African economic life. His wealth was immense—it is estimated that his interests in De Beers alone provided an income of £200,000 annually—and so also was his power.

Rhodes put his new strength to the test in 1887 after rumors had reached him that the Portuguese and Boers in the Transvaal were negotiating a treaty with Lobengula, king of the Matabele, who controlled both Matabeleland and Mashonaland to the northeast of Bechuanaland. If this treaty were concluded it would effectively cut off British access to the north. Rhodes, thoroughly alarmed, determined to force the British high commissioner in Cape Town, Sir Hercules Robinson, to support him in an endeavor to replace the influence of the Transvaal with that of the British in Lobengula's territory. He succeeded in persuading Robinson, somewhat ruthlessly, through the sheer power of his will and personality. Rhodes later reminisced about the incident to an audience in Cape Town:

> He said to me, "But where will you stop?" and I replied, "I will stop where the country has not been claimed." Your old Governor said, "Let us look at the map," and I showed him that it was the southern border of Tanganyika. He was a little upset. I said that the Great Powers at home marked the map and did nothing: adding, "Let us try to mark the map, and we know we shall do something." "Well," said Sir Hercules Robinson, "I think you should be satisfied with the Zambesi as a boundary. (He was already getting up.) I replied, "Let us take a piece of notepaper, and let us measure from the block-house [on Table Mountain in Cape Town] to the Vaal River; that is the individual effort of the people. Now," I said, "let us measure what you have done in your temporary existence, and then we will finish by measuring up my imaginations." We took a piece of notepaper and measured the efforts of the country since the Dutch occupied and founded it. We measured what he had done in his life, and then we measured my imaginations; and his Excellency, who is no longer with us, said, "I will leave you alone."

A British agent was promptly dispatched to Lobengula's kraal. He convinced the king that the Matabele should really have no association with the Transvaal and, in early February 1888, persuaded Lobengula to sign a treaty of perpetual amity, which also bound him not to relinquish any of his territory or to sign any treaty without the sanction of the high commissioner. But the treaty was only a piece of paper. How was full advantage to be taken of its provisions? Neither the Cape nor the imperial government was willing to lift a finger to establish its control in the territories of Lobengula. Rhodes would have to depend upon his own resources.

As a first step, Rhodes sent his partner, C. D. Rudd, as his personal emissary to Lobengula, for the Matabele king was a person of considerable standing. Another visitor to his kraal has left behind a description of an audience with him, which Basil Williams quotes in his *Cecil Rhodes* (1938):

> A few minutes after I had taken my seat near his waggon a curtain was drawn aside, and the great man appeared and deliberately stepped over the front box and sat down on the board before the driver's seat. He was completely naked save for a very long piece of dark blue cloth, rolled very small and wound round his body which it in no wise concealed, and a monkey skin worn as a small apron and about the size of a Highland sporran. In person he is rather tall . . . and very stout, though by no means unwieldy. . . . His colour is a fine bronze, and he evidently takes great care of his person and is scrupulously clean. He wears the leathern ring over his forehead as a matter of course. Altogether he is a very fine-looking man, and in spite of his obesity has a most majestic carriage. Like all the Matabele warriors, who despise a stooping gait in a man, Lo Bengula walks quite erect with his head thrown somewhat back and his broad chest expanded, and as he marches along at a slow pace with his long staff in his right hand, while all the men around shout his praises, he looks his part to perfection.

Rudd, who arrived in October 1888, had to compete with a horde of other European petitioners for Lobengula's favor. But he finally prevailed and persuaded Lobengula to sign a document which granted to Rudd and his associates "exclusive power over all metals and minerals situated and contained in his kingdoms, principalities and dominions." Furthermore, as the king had "been much molested of late by divers persons seeking and desiring to obtain grants and cessions of land and mining rights in his territories," the British concessionaires were given power to exclude all such persons from the territory of the Matabele king. In return, Rudd promised to provide Lobengula with 1,000 rifles, 10,000 rounds of ammunition, and an armed steamer. He also bound himself to pay the king £100 a month.

A storm of protest arose from Rhodes's competitors when news of Rudd's success became known. Most of them Rhodes bought off, while the Exploring Company, his chief rival, was given a share in the Rudd concession. Nevertheless, Rhodes had to overcome considerable political opposition from those, who, led by the missionaries, advocated direct imperial control of Lobengula's territory. In the long run, strong pressure by Sir Hercules Robinson and other adherents of Rhodes's scheme to take advantage of the concession and the realization that Parliament would not vote the necessary funds for direct governmental action in Matabeleland and Mashonaland, converted the strong reservations of the Colonial Office into at least reluctant acquiescence. At the end of April 1889 the Exploring Company and Rhodes's group jointly applied for a charter to establish a company which was to extend the telegraph and railway northwards towards the Zambezi River, encourage immigration and colonization, promote trade and commerce, and develop minerals and other concessions under one powerful organization.

The letters patent granting a royal charter of incorporation to the British South Africa Company were signed by Queen Victoria in October 1889. The charter contained several clauses limiting the power of the company, and it guaranteed native rights and freedom of religion and trade. On the whole, however, the directors were left a free hand to develop an area that had no limits northwards. The real power was, of course, invested in Rhodes, for as one director wrote him: "Do whatever you think is right. We will support you whatever the issue."

To impress Lobengula with the might of imperial Britain, the announcement of the granting of the charter was conveyed to him with due pomp and ostentation. Through the efforts of Lord Knutsford, the secretary of state for the colonies, a contingent of Royal Horse Guards was despatched to Lobengula's kraal, and there, on a hot, dry day in January 1890, they changed from comfortable bush clothes into the burnished silver breastplates and plumed helmets of their dress uniforms. Then this unlikely contingent galloped along the dusty road to Lobengula's compound, escorting a massive coach with the royal monogram "V.R." emblazoned on its side, drawn by eight silver-caparisoned mules. Lobengula was suitably awed.

Now that the charter was granted, the next step for the company was to occupy the new territory. A band of 184 "pioneers" was organized, composed, at Rhodes's insistence, of both Boers and Englishmen. They were fully equipped at the company's expense and paid seven shillings sixpence a day. Upon arrival at their destination in Mashonaland, they were each to receive fifteen gold claims and a three-thousand-acre farm. In the last week of June 1890 the first party of pioneers, accompanied by some police detachments, left the northeastern border of Bechuanaland and entered Lobengula's territory. On the following day, they were met by a party of Matabele with a letter from Lobengula which asked: "Has the King killed any white men that an *impi* [band of warriors] is collecting on his border? Or have the white men lost anything they were looking for?" These were perfectly justifiable questions since the Rudd concession spoke only of mining and not of settlement. The Queen, when Lobengula wrote to her that "Rhodes wants to take my country by strength," replied through the new high commissioner, Sir Henry Loch: "The Queen assures LoBengula that the men assembled by the British South Africa Company were not assembled for the purpose of attacking him, but on the contrary were assembled for a peaceful object, namely searching for gold." The king was asked "to recollect that LoBengula is the friend of the Queen and the Queen wishes to maintain peace and friendship with LoBengula."

In early September the pioneers reached the site of the present city of Salisbury, where they established their settlement, and the next day, previous assurances to Lobengula notwithstanding, they raised the Union Jack and took possession of Mashonaland in the name of the Queen. Despite the dubious legality of the occupation of Mashonaland, the British government, haunted by the presence of the Germans in the west, the Portuguese in the east, and the Boers to the south, did not oppose the seizure. An Order in Council of May 9, 1891, recognized the territories occupied by the company as being "under the protection of Her Majesty" and declared that "Her Majesty has power and jurisdiction in the said territories." Lobengula had trusted the white man and been duped.

A year after the founding of Salisbury, Rhodes, who was now prime minister of the Cape Colony, was able to visit his creation himself. The first months of the settlement had not been easy, and Rhodes listened to the settlers' grievances sympathetically. He eliminated many abuses and generally aroused the loyalty and affection of the pioneers. As a young settler later wrote him: "It is quite . . . different . . . since you came, for now everyone is hopeful."

Rhodes's imagination did not, of course, limit him to the establishment of company control over the area covered by the Rudd concession. His real aim was a strip of British territory running all the way from the Cape to Cairo. Only a beginning had been made, and between 1891 and 1895, the company gained control of much of Nyasaland. But the Portuguese, who ruled in Mozambique on the east coast, also claimed the territory coveted by Rhodes, and a series of skirmishes and disputes between the company and the Portuguese ensued until an Anglo-Portuguese treaty in 1891 defined the respective spheres of the two rivals. Under the provisions of the agreement, the company gained considerable territory. The freedom of navigation on the Zambezi and Shire rivers was declared. The facilities of the port of Beira in Mozambique were made available to the company, and the Portuguese agreed to build a railroad from Beira to Salisbury, which meant that the distance to a usable port would be only 380 miles instead of the 2,000 miles to Cape Town.

How much longer the new white settlers and the Matabele would be able to live peacefully next to each other was a question that troubled both Rhodes and the other directors of the company. That Lobengula was resentful could have surprised no one. On the other hand, the settlers were not satisfied with their lot and looked longingly at the fertile highlands where the Matabele pastured their ample herds. Both Rhodes and Lobengula were anxious to avoid an open rupture. Neither one, however, was in complete control of the situation. Lobengula was the captive of his proud and bellicose warriors, while Rhodes fell victim to the ambitions of the settlers. Under the terms of the "Victoria Agreement," drawn up between the company and the settlers, the company guaranteed that should fighting break out, every pioneer combatant would be granted 6,000 acres (which the company could convert to public use by buying it back from the owner at £1 10*s*. an acre), 20 gold claims, and a share in the Matabele herds, whose capture was confidently expected. Under these combined circumstances, the hostilities which broke out in July 1893 were inevitable, as, perhaps, was the British success—in January 1894—in a war, almost totally financed by the British South Africa Company, in which the troops were equipped with artillery and Maxim guns. Lobengula did not long survive his defeat. He died a few weeks later of smallpox, a tragic victim of the clash of two irreconcilable ways of life.

Rhodes had now reached the apogee of his career. In May 1894, by an agreement with the Crown, the company took over all of Lobengula's domain as conquered territory. Virtually all administrative control over this vast area was vested in the company's board, with some supervisory functions being assigned to the secretary of state in London and the high commissioner in Cape Town. Rhodes was virtual ruler of a territory stretching from Bechuanaland to Lake Nyasa (control of Nyasaland having been obtained in 1891) and the southern tip of Lake Tanganyika. He was made a privy councilor in 1895 and attained the unusual distinction of having the new possession named after him—Rhodesia—while he still lived. In a conversation with Queen Victoria, Rhodes was asked, "What have you been doing since

I last saw you, Mr. Rhodes?" to which he answered proudly, "I have added two provinces to Your Majesty's dominions."

But much yet remained to be done. The rivalry between the Boers and the British still marred Rhodes's vision of South Africa. After he became prime minister of the Cape Colony in 1890, he devoted much of his vast energy to the healing of this rift. In the Cape itself, he worked in close alliance with Jan Hendrik Hofmeyr, the political leader of the Boer population, to help the Boer farmers. He encouraged the growth of the fruit and wine industries and actively supported improvements in animal husbandry. Rhodes felt that education would be the basis of a strong, united South Africa, and he hoped to create a great university in Cape Town, which students of both Boer and British extraction would attend.

The South Africa, united under the British flag, which Rhodes foresaw, was, of course, to be part of the envisaged empire of equals, and he undertook the radical step of communicating directly with other British-settled members of the Empire, rather than going through the medium of the British government in London. To the Canadian prime minister, Sir John Macdonald, he wrote:

> Between us we must invent some tie with our Mother Country that will prevent separation. . . . a practical one, for future generations will not be born in England. The curse is that English politicians cannot see the future.

Rhodes firmly believed in imperial reciprocity in tariff matters and perhaps best summed up his general feeling of the imperial government's role in colonial affairs when he stated in an election speech of 1898:

> We are not going to be governed from home. . . . We do everything. We pass a Bill and the Queen just puts her name to it. She never objects. . . . But what she does for us, and without our paying for it, is this: she protects us with her fleet, and when I take a new country for you she protects me from the German and the Frenchman. . . . Whenever I took a country I simply said to the Queen: "I have taken that: you must put your flag over it."

In his policy toward the native Africans Rhodes was a paternalist and, at first, not a very progressive one. A British critic was prompted to remark: "Mr. Rhodes is a very reasonable man. He only wants two things. Give him Protection and give him Slavery and he will be perfectly satisfied." The natives, Rhodes felt, were children and to extend to them the franchise would be as if "the Lord Mayor and his Corporation were to suddenly proceed to Stonehenge and finding the Druids there discuss with them municipal legislation." He believed in keeping the Africans separated from the whites, to protect them from European vices as much as for any other reason. The Glen Grey Act of 1894 partly achieved this purpose, giving Africans a limited control over their own affairs in certain specified areas which were closed to white settlement. It is a credit to Rhodes's flexibility that he was able in time to free himself from much of his racial and color prejudice and to proclaim, as his final dictum, "equal rights for all civilized men, irrespective of races, south of the Zambezi."

Rhodes's African policy could never be fully realized as long as South Africa itself remained divided between British colonies and Boer republics. While he was moving dramatically northward, Rhodes never forgot this problem so much closer to home. He understood that union would take time to achieve, and he told a Boer audience in 1891:

> It took me twenty years to amalgamate the diamond mines, that amalgamation was done by detail, step by step . . . and so your union must be done by detail, never opposing any single measure that can bring that union closer, giving up even some practical advantage for a proper union, educating your children to the fact that it is your policy and that you must have it and will have it, telling it them and teaching it them. . . . In connection with this question I may meet with opposition; but if I do I shall not abandon it.

It is a curious piece of irony that the man most passionately dedicated to South African union should have been so largely responsible for placing its peaceful attainment out of reach. Cecil Rhodes in 1895 was not the man he had been in the previous decade. His health was beginning to fail, and he was increasingly haunted by the fear that he had not long to live. He was also becoming increasingly autocratic and arrogant. He rarely listened to advice. This combination of factors and the knowledge that the Transvaal, through negotiations with the Germans and its prosperity from the gold mines, was becoming ever more independent of British influence and control, robbed Rhodes of the patience he had counseled his listeners in 1891. He himself proposed a scheme which he hoped would accomplish the new political union. The plan, in the formation of which the British colonial secretary, Joseph Chamberlain, was probably deeply implicated, was to organize and equip a revolutionary group among the large non-Boer white population of gold miners in the Transvaal. A force of British South Africa Company police was to be placed across the border in Bechuanaland to support a coup which was to overthrow the government of the Transvaal's president, Paul Kruger, and install in its stead an administration of Rhodes's choosing. From the first, this addled and dishonest plan ran into difficulties. Not enough arms were smuggled into Johannesburg, center of the Transvaal gold fields, and local support for the revolutionaries, so confidently expected, was not forthcoming. Upon being apprised of the situation, Rhodes determined to postpone the venture, but the leader of the company force on the Transvaal border, the headstrong Dr. L. S. Jameson, decided to act on his own authority, despite strong indications that the Boers knew what was afoot.

On Sunday, December 29, 1895, Jameson led his 600 men across the Transvaal border. Failure was ensured from the moment a trooper cut and buried part of a farmer's fence thinking it was the telegraph line to Pretoria, Kruger's capital. At Krugersdorp, some 20 miles from Johannesburg, Jameson was met and routed by a strong Boer contingent, and on January 2, 1896, the embarrassed invaders were forced to surrender.

For Rhodes, this bungled affair was almost the ruination of his life's work. Through his involvement, he had betrayed his Boer supporters in the Cape; he had violated the spirit of the charter of the British South Africa Company; and he had created a distrust of the British in the minds of the leaders of the two Boer republics. This distrust, combined with a certain arrogant self-confidence bred by the Transvaal's military success, made any hope of union without war, and perhaps the continuation of peace itself, illusory. Even Rhodes's closest followers were aghast. As one of them said:

> The Raid was not only wrong in its inception, but it is the deceit and treachery which accompanied it that I object to; and the Raid has put Mr. Kruger back in his old position and rehabilitated him in the civilised world. That is the pity of it, and that we have to thank Mr. Rhodes. . . . I do say, Mr. Rhodes is unworthy of the trust of the country.

Under pressure, Rhodes resigned as prime minister of the Cape and as managing director of the company. He was condemned for his misuse of these offices by committees in both the Cape and British parliaments. Rhodes was at first remorseful, but he finally decided that he was the victim of the "unctuous rectitude" of the authorities in

London. His self-confidence returned when he discovered that to the British man on the street he was more of a hero than a villian. As he said: "I found all the busmen smiling at me when I came to London; so I knew it was all right."

Rhodes retired to Rhodesia—but not for long. In March 1896 the Matabele rose in revolt. They were worsted easily enough in open battle but as a last resort retreated to the rugged Matoppo Hills from which they conducted guerrilla raids. No doubt they could eventually have been starved out, but Rhodes wanted immediate peace for the expense of continuing the hostilities was undermining the company's financial position. With a small party, he contacted the Matabele leaders and entered the hills, unarmed, to parley. As he arrived at the appointed place, Rhodes was surrounded by an overwhelming force of fully armed Matabele. But he remained calm and unruffled, and the Africans eventually laid down their weapons, allowing the conversations to commence.

Rhodes remained in the hills for two months. At first suspicious, the Matabele developed a sincere respect and admiration for him. He listened to their problems with understanding and, when all had been arranged, provided them with a million sacks of corn, at his own expense, to see them through the winter. The troubles with the Matabele never recurred, although a revolt by the Mashona in 1896–1897 also required Rhodes's intervention.

Rhodes loved the free, open life of Rhodesia. It was, after all, his country, and he invited the settlers to join in the joy of creating. "To be in this country," he told them,

> is surely a happier thing than the deadly monotony of an English country town or the still deadlier monotony of a Karroo [in the Cape Colony] village. Here at any rate you have your share in the creation of a new country. . . . You have the proud satisfaction of knowing that you are civilising a new part of the world. Those who fall in that creation fall sooner than they would in ordinary life, but their lives are better and grander.

Despite Rhodes's withdrawal from active Cape politics, he continued to hold his seat in Parliament, and from a predominantly Boer district at that. Although the Jameson raid was far from forgotten, Rhodes's great and continuing contributions to Africa and the Empire were increasingly remembered. In 1898 he was restored to the board of the company and in the following year was granted an honorary degree by his beloved Oxford.

Rhodes's days were now drawing to an end, but he remained active in the life of South Africa. He invested increasingly in new experiments in agriculture, fought for the extension of the telegraph and railways, and negotiated a new constitutional arrangement for Rhodesia. He lived to see the Anglo-Boer war, which in many ways his actions had made inevitable, and took an active part in its early stages. But his advice was not respected to the extent he demanded, and he withdrew to devote the remainder of his life to the development of Rhodesia.

Rhodes died on March 26, 1902, aged only forty-eight, and was buried in the Matoppo Hills overlooking the country whose creation he had inspired. In his will he left a lasting testimonial to his concept of empire—almost 200 scholarships at Oxford, to be extended to students from the self-governing colonies and from the United States of America (which, of course, he hoped would some day rejoin the imperial community). The choice of scholars was to be based not only on intellect, but also on character and social qualities, especially a fondness for sports. He made his purpose very clear:

> I consider that the education of young colonists at one of the universities in the United Kingdom is of great advantage to them for giving breadth to their instruction in life and manners, and for instilling in their minds the advantage to the colonies as well as to the United Kingdom of the retention of the unity of the Empire.

Through the scholarships, Rhodes wished

> to encourage and foster an appreciation of the advantages which I implicitly believe will result from the union of the English-speaking people throughout the world.

Because of him, young men from all over the world, year after year, leave their homes to study at Oxford.

Like many great men, Rhodes led a far from blameless life. There is a strange ambivalence between the loftiness of his ideals and the frequently ruthless means he used to attain them. But he was essentially unselfish. His actions were directed largely towards the fulfillment of an imperial dream which, if narrow, was yet not without its touch of nobility. And he remains to this day probably the most impressive prophet and practitioner of the imperial religion.

7

The British Acquisition of the Lower Indus Valley: A Case Study in Imperial Expansion

In order to clarify and delineate some of the factors discussed in the previous two chapters, it should prove useful to follow in detail the events leading up to the addition of a particular area to the British Empire. The lower Indus Valley in northwest India—a region known as Sind—lends itself particularly well to such an investigation, for between 1799 and 1843 British policy and activity in Sind veered from indifference to outright annexation.[1]

Sind in the eighteenth and nineteenth centuries was ruled by several princes, all members of the same family, who were known collectively as the amirs of Sind. The East India Company had maintained stations in Sind from 1635 to 1662 and from 1758 to 1775. But in 1775 the establishments were removed because of internal unrest and the decline of textile manufactures, formerly characterized as "the flower of the whole parcel and preferred before all others in their making." By the turn of the century, however, the Company's interest in Sind was rekindled, not because of improved trade prospects but because Napoleon's successful invasion of Egypt in 1798 had aroused speculation as to the possibility of a French attack on India. The East India Company, and after 1858 the Crown, was acutely sensitive to the vulnerability of the subcontinent, never realizing how ephemeral were

[1] See map of India on p. 3, Chapter 1.

the French (and later Russian) designs on its eastern empire. Consequently, during most of the nineteenth century, virtually all British diplomatic, commercial, and military machinations in the states to the west and northwest of India were directed toward the repulse of these anticipated attacks.

As Napoleon had made no secret of his ambition to lead an army across Asia Minor to India, the authorities in both England and India became convinced of the imminence of the French menace. The destruction of the young general's fleet by Nelson in the Battle of the Nile, his defeat outside Acre in Palestine, and the obvious impracticability of marching a significant force through the arid and hostile lands of southwest Asia did not diminish the determination of the Company's officers to bolster their military and diplomatic defenses in India.

Of prime importance to any defensive operation was the closing of Sind, which lay along the logical invasion route to India. Consequently, in 1800 the governor general sent an agent to Sind to reopen the Company's factory there, which was to be established "not so much with a view to commercial as to political advantages." The venture proved abortive, but matters were allowed to rest until the conclusion of the Franco-Russian accord at Tilsit in 1807 raised the specter of a combined move on India through Persia. Again the British reacted by sending emissaries to Sind, and a treaty was finally concluded in 1809 which effectively barred the lower Indus Valley to French influence. The ratification of this treaty assuaged British fears in regard to the creation of a French foothold in Sind. The realization that Napoleon, enmeshed in dynastic intrigues and unable to extricate himself from the Iberian peninsula, posed no further threat to India soon returned the affairs of Sind to their original obscurity, and the Company considered the peaceful situation to be reason "of the most forcible nature for proceeding, without unnecessary delay, to reduce our military expenses within the narrowest bounds that may be consistent with the publick security and interests."

It was not until 1820 that Sind again intruded into the thoughts of the Company's servants in India. Then they became incensed at the continuing attacks on British-protected territory by predatory tribes (the Khosas) based in Sind. As continued protests seemed unavailing, the British dispatched a contingent of troops into the tribal territory on a punitive expedition. It so happened that the amirs of Sind were finally sending a force on a similar mission at exactly the same time, and just as the Sindian troops made contact with the marauding tribes, the British arrived on the scene. Thinking that both groups of Indians were Khosas, the British attacked them, killing several Sindians as well as tribesmen.

The Indian government blithely dismissed the incident as "an unfortunate mistake, as much to be attributed to the misconduct of the Sindian commander in giving refuge to the Khosas within his camp, as to any other cause." For this reason, according to the British, "a body of Sindians was attacked on a dark night by one of our detachments and many of the troops comprising it cut to pieces." Needless to say, the rulers of Sind were more disturbed, and hostilities between them and the British were only prevented by the conclusion of another treaty under which the amirs undertook to control more adequately the actions of their unruly subjects. Sind was still considered of such little intrinsic worth that the expense of hostilities, it was thought, would far exceed any possible gain that might result from their successful conclusion. The governor general, at least in this instance, agreed with the home authorities that "no further acquisition of territory can be desirable."

Intercourse with Sind assumed a new importance when fear of Russian invasion in the late 1820s again emphasized the strategic importance of the area. In London, Lord Ellenborough, the president of the Board of Control for India, wrote: "The Directors [of the Company] are much afraid of the Russians, so am I. . . . I feel confident that we shall have to fight the Russians on the Indus." And while Sind was once more becoming vital in British eyes through the negative factor of fear, the report A *Narrative of a Visit to the Court of Scinde,* written by Dr. James Burnes as a consequence of a medical mission to Hyderabad, the capital of lower Sind, was to have an even greater influence on the determination of future British policy. In it, for the first time, the potentialities of the Indus and of Sind itself were assessed, though somewhat optimistically and inaccurately. Burnes strongly advocated British control of the region so that

> the river Indus might once more become the channel of communication and wealth between the interior of Asia and the peninsula of India; while Sinde herself . . . would rise renewed to claim a due importance in the scale of nations, and to profit by her benefits which nature has bestowed on her. . . . A single glance at the Indus will show the easy passage to the very heart of their [the amirs'] dominions, which the river offers to a maritime power.

The Indus was actually a poor avenue of communication. It was constantly silting up, and its course, impeded by sand bars and shallows, changed considerably from year to year. This fact was not realized for some time, however, and for the moment the thought of opening the Indus captured the imagination of British statesmen. Ellenborough was particularly affected. "No British flag," he wrote, "has ever floated upon the waters of this river! Please God it shall, and in triumph, to the source of all its tributary streams."

If official interest in Britain had now become directed toward the Indus Valley, so had that in India itself. With the appointment of Lord William Bentinck as governor general in 1828, the reins of government were in the hands of a Benthamite utilitarian who was not blind to the commercial possibilities of the Indus. The Company, as usual, advised the new governor general to be vigilant about costs and to avoid territorial expansion, but it was "desirous of being much better informed than we are now as to the actual state of Scind . . . particularly as to the navigation of the Main Stream of the Indus."

It was decided that as a preliminary step to the opening of the Indus, the river would have to be at least rudimentarily surveyed. Although previous attempts to do so had been frustrated by the amirs of Sind, who feared that British knowledge of the river would invite occupation, a way was found to disguise the purpose. Ranjit Singh, the Sikh ruler of the Punjab, had sent a present to George IV on the latter's coronation in 1820; the British now proposed to reciprocate by sending a gift of one dray horse and four dray mares to Ranjit Singh on behalf of the British monarch. The horses were to be accompanied by an emissary who was to "assume no ostensible character but that of an Agent deputed solely for arranging the safe passage of the horses and of presenting them to Ranjeet Singh." His real mission, of course, would be to survey the Indus and its tributary streams from its mouth to Lahore on the Ravi River and to obtain the support of the Sikhs for the British commercial schemes on the Indus. The Company hoped that both British and Indian goods could be sent up the Indus to entrepôts along its course from which they could be transshipped to the markets of Afghanistan and Persia. It was thought that in this way the British would not only undersell the Russians, but could also obtain for themselves a large portion of the trade of Central Asia.

The governor general decided to send Lieutenant (later Sir) Alexander Burnes, brother of the doctor, to lead the expedition. The destination of the presents was to be kept secret until the ships bearing them from Bombay were near the mouths of the Indus. Then letters were to be sent to the amirs of Sind "but so as to arrive too late to prevent the receipt of any answer having for its objective the prevention of the mission, until the boats shall have advanced too far to admit of being stopped." To ensure the passage of the presents by the river, a large carriage was added to the consignment and the amirs were to be told that the presents had to go by water because of their size. Burnes sailed from Bombay in late 1830 and made two attempts to land in Sind during January and February 1831. But the amirs would not let the mission proceed, using several excuses such as the presence of bandits and the lack of water in the Indus.

The amirs remained adamantly in opposition for over a month, but eventually, under pressure from Ranjit Singh in the north, they capitulated. Burnes successfully completed his mission and in the narrative of his journey wrote: "There is an uninterrupted navigation from the sea to Lahore. . . . The Indus when joined by the Punjab Rivers never shallows in the dry season to less than fifteen feet." This was quite untrue, and in the future many British attempts to develop trade through the use of the river were to come to grief. The governor general, however, was convinced "that the importance of the River Indus in a political point of view not less than as a route of commerce has not been overrated." Consequently another mission was sent to Sind to wheedle concessions from the amirs.

Treaties were signed providing for the free navigation of the Indus by the "merchants of Hindustan." But the British were still not satisfied. They wanted the establishment of a permanent British agency in Sind. Again the amirs objected, and again they were forced to concede. This time the cause of their downfall was the claim of Ranjit Singh to a considerable portion of northern Sind. The Sikhs would no doubt have annexed this region had not the British interfered on behalf of the amirs. The Sikhs retreated, but in April 1838 the British, as their price for intervening, gained the concession of an agency in Sind.

British fear of a Russian invasion through one of the northwestern states was, in the late 1830s, still the prime determinant of Indian foreign policy, and a misguided notion that the Russians were about to establish their influence in Afghanistan brought on war between Britain and Dost Mohammed, the king of Afghanistan. A former ruler of Afghanistan, long since deposed, was exhumed from retirement and declared the true king, and preparations commenced in 1838 for the invasion of Afghanistan, to place this puppet on the throne. Ranjit Singh, who had helped himself to the Khyber area of Afghanistan in 1834, was the ally of the British in this venture, and it was to satisfy him that it was decided not to use the Khyber Pass, the logical route through the mountains into Afghanistan. The only other route that could be utilized was the Bolan Pass in northern Baluchistan, and in order to reach it the British troops coming up from the south would have to traverse the possessions of the amirs of Sind. Such an action would involve a violation of an article of the treaties of 1832 which prohibited the transportation of military goods on the Indus. Through a series of trumped-up charges of Sindian "treachery," the British unilaterally abrogated the article and proceeded with their Afghan enterprise.

In the process, they forced the amirs to allow British troops to occupy certain positions and deprived them of the port of Karachi, which the Company had always coveted, by a calculated and high-handed act of aggression. When the fleet transporting the Bombay reserve force approached the city, Sindian troops fired a salute from the fortress at Manora, as was the custom in many ports (including Bombay) whenever a square-rigged vessel approached. The British commander, Admiral Sir Frederick Maitland, though aware of the custom, nonetheless claimed he had been fired on and proceeded to bombard Karachi and capture it. Upon investigation the British agent reported that not only had there been no shot in the cannon at the time it was fired, but that there was not a single ball in the fort that would fit any of the guns. The whole supply of gunpowder amounted to six pounds, which was kept in an earthen pot, and the entire garrison of 16 men, many of whom were armed only with swords, were standing outside the fort admiring the admiral's flagship, *Wellesley*, when the bombardment began. The governor of Karachi informed the British agent that, far from resisting the landing, he had orders to cooperate with the British in every way. When all this was pointed out to the governor general, his secretary replied:

The Governor-General will not call into question the correctness of the reports from the Naval Commander in Chief from which it appears no attention was paid to his pacific overtures before he felt himself compelled to resort to force, nor will his Lordship admit the denial by the Ameers or their subjects of a hostile spirit having swayed their conduct at Karachee or elsewhere.

As a final affront, the amirs of Sind were mulcted of £200,000 to help pay for the Afghan campaign on the spurious pretext that this was past tribute that they owed the "rightful ruler" of Afghanistan, their former overlord. Perhaps the amirs drew some satisfaction from watching British ineptitude and miscalculation compound their Afghan venture into a major debacle. But if this were so, they did not take advantage of the situation to increase the Company's embarrassment, although it would seem they had every justification for so doing. But there was to be no reward for their restraint; final disaster, indeed, was shortly to overtake them.

Several factors that influenced imperial expansion have already been mentioned. Among those that should now be emphasized were the difficulties caused by slow communications between London and the Empire and the responsibility—and power—that consequently fell upon the "man on the spot" which probably did more to frustrate the wishes of the East India Company and the Board of Control in London than any other single factor. At the beginning of the nineteenth century, to send and receive a reply to a letter from India to England usually took two and a half years. The utilization of the Red Sea route cut this to a year in the 1840s and occasionally to as little as three months—still an extremely long time in a period of crisis when new developments arose daily, if not hourly. Thus, the slowness of communications, and the often sporadic and inaccurate nature of the information exchanged, made the ruling of India from England both a folly and a delusion, at least before the advent of the telegraph. One of the clearest manifestations of the dilemmas inherent in this situation is the post-Afghan War history of British relations with Sind.

In October 1841 Lord Ellenborough, formerly president of the Board of Control, was appointed governor general of India. Believing in the same principles as the home authorities and determined to keep Company expenditures at a minimum, he called a halt to the further expansion of British India:

> Content with the limits nature appears to have assigned to its Empire, the Government of India will devote all of its efforts to the establishment and maintenance of general peace, to the protection of the sovereigns and chiefs, its allies, and to the prosperity and happiness of its own faithful subjects.

Ellenborough instructed the political agents in the princely states to "manifest the utmost personal consideration for the several native

Princes" to whom they were deputed and to "distinctly understand that the further extension of its dominions forms no part of the policy of the British Government." In a foreign policy memorandum, the governor general stated that he considered further expansion ill-advised, as it would endanger the stability and welfare of the state, and place an excessive strain on its finances. The Company expressed its "entire and most cordial approbation." But within a few short months, Lord Ellenborough was to speak of a British India stretching to the "chain of mountains beyond the Indus and the Himalayas as our *ultimate* boundary." He had annexed Sind and had been recalled by the East India Company. The reasons for this dramatic reversal of policy were symptomatic of the difference between viewing events from India and from England and more particularly symptomatic of the problems that could be caused by the "man on the spot."

Lord Ellenborough and Sir Charles Napier, who had been appointed commander of British troops in Sind in 1842, were in many ways alike—a fact which might have contributed to the great trust the former placed in the latter. That these two closely associated officials had common weaknesses, however, was to have a dire effect on the future of the amirs of Sind. Both men were highly unpopular in their own circles. Ellenborough, known by his contemporaries as the "Elephant," was one of the most disliked men of his day, while Napier had never succeeded in peacefully obeying any of his superiors. Both were frustrated in their ambitions: Ellenborough had been foiled in his attempt to make the Board of Control the stepping-stone to the Foreign Office, his real goal, while the megalomaniacal Napier, after achieving some distinction in the Peninsular Campaign, spent the next 30 years in the obscurity of petty commands and half pay and received his appointment to India only through the political influence of his brother William. Though both considered themselves liberal humanitarians, they were romantics—Ellenborough dreamed of leading an expedition to conquer Egypt, Napier fancied himself ruler of all Asia.

Charles Napier, of bizarre appearance, with a vast beard and matted hair, was a man of contradictions. He was capable of great generosity and small-minded parsimony, of humility and unbounded conceit. His military orders reflected both humor and justice. Worshipped by his men, he was often despised by his peers. Napier was the scion of a large and noble house—the great-great-grandson of Charles II through his liaison with Louise de Kéroualle. Napier's mother was the fascinating and beautiful Lady Sarah Lennox, who twice refused to marry George III; the great British statesman Charles James Fox was his cousin and the Duke of Richmond was his uncle.

Born in 1782, Napier grew up a proud and headstrong boy, full of dreams of military glory. Through the influence of a relative, he received a commission in the army and fought bravely and well against the French at Corunna, holding temporary command of the 50th Regiment, a responsibility he discharged with considerable skill at a difficult time. Napier was badly wounded and captured in the days following, but after his release, and the end of the war, he was promoted to lieutenant-colonel and given command of the 102nd Regiment, which was sent to Bermuda. His career now followed the byways of military service—a command in the War of 1812, two years at Farnham Military College, inspecting field officer in the Ionian Islands—but no glory, only disappointment and humiliation for a mind obsessed with visions of imperial grandeur and public acclaim. His journals are full of personal comparisons with the great men of history:

15 August, Napoleon's birthday. He too is gone and may be met with hereafter. I am at war with half of India: were it the whole I would not care! I laugh them all to scorn.

To-morrow I shall reach Sehwan where Alexander built his tower, and I shall stand where he stood, as indeed I have before, but not on the known spot. . . . How easily, were I absolute, I could conquer all these countries.

When Napier, now a major-general, landed in India he was sixty years old. If his ambitions were to be satisfied, time was short. "Charles! Charles Napier!" he wrote in his journal,

take heed of your ambition for military glory: you had scotched that snake, but this high command will, unless you are careful, give it all its vigour again. Get thee behind me Satan!

In a similar vein, he later confided to his journal,

My God! how humble I feel when I think! How exalted when I behold! I have worked my way to this great command and am grateful at having it, yet despise myself for being so gratified! . . . I despise my worldliness. Am I not past sixty? A few years must kill me; a few days may! And yet I am so weak as to care for these things! No, I do not. I pray to do what is right and just. . . . Alas! I have not the strength! . . . He who takes command loves it.

It is possible that other more practical considerations played a part in Napier's aspirations. He had never been a wealthy man, and the care of his daughters had frequently been a severe strain on his finances. Upon being congratulated by a fellow officer on his appointment to India, he had replied:

I am very rational, my wishes are only to barter a *great lack of sovereigns* in *this* country for a *lac* of rupees in that! But I am too old for military glory now. . . . If a man cannot catch glory when his knees are supple, he had better not try when they grow stiff! All I want is to catch the *rupees* for my girls, and then die like a gentleman. I suppose if I survive six years I shall do this.

Napier was indeed destined to survive; he arrived in Hyderabad, Sind, on September 25, 1842, and ominously noted that "possibly this may be the last reception they may give as independent princes to a British General!" He almost immediately set out to prove that the amirs had acted against the British interest during the Afghan War. On the basis of some very ambiguous and unimportant correspondence, the general brought charges against the amirs. "Is it possible that such a state of things can long continue?" he wrote the governor general,

A government hated by its subjects, hostile alike to the interests of the English, and of its own people; a Government of low intrigue, and above all, so constituted that it must, in a few years, fall to pieces by the vice of its own construction; will such a Government, I ask, not maintain an incessant petty hostility against us? . . . I conceive that such a state of political relations could not last, and the more powerful Government would, at no very distant period, swallow up the weaker. If this reasoning is correct, would it not be better to come to the results at once?

Ellenborough replied:

You are much more competent to decide on the spot as to the authenticity of the letters . . . than I am here, and I am prepared to abide by and support your decision. . . . If a Government were to wait in every case of suspected hostile intentions until it obtained such proof of the hostile intention, as would be sufficient to convict the person suspected in a Court of Justice, it would in most cases expose itself at once to disgrace and disaster. It is necessary to proceed upon a strong presumption of intended hostility where hesitation might seriously affect great national interests.

The Duke of Wellington informed Ellenborough that the British cabinet was dissatisfied with his having left the conduct of affairs in

Sind entirely to the discretion of Sir Charles Napier, but the governor general was charmed by the general and blind to his obvious faults. "I can assure you," he wrote to the governor of Bombay, "it is a comfort to me I cannot describe to have a man in whom I can so entirely trust!" But to trust a disgruntled yet ambitious man was a mistake. "*Mene! Mene! tekel, upharsin!*" Napier wrote, "How is it all to end? We have no right to seize Scinde, yet we shall do so, and a very advantageous, useful, humane piece of rascality it will be." And again: "My design and hope is to find excuses for acting on my own responsibility and going right before there is time to set me wrong! It is yet to be proved how I command a large force or rather a small one in the face of the enemy."

There was little time to set Napier wrong, even should Ellenborough have wanted to do so; for if the home government was fettered by the lack of up-to-date information, so was the governor general, and several weeks usually elapsed between the dispatch of a letter to Sind and the receipt of a reply. Napier took advantage of this situation. He replaced the paramount ruler of Upper Sind with a more pliable relation. He drove the amirs to distraction by attempting to force a new treaty on them, and when Ellenborough, not realizing that there were princes named Nasir Khan in both Upper and Lower Sind, deprived one of territory when he had intended to punish the other, Napier did not inform him of his mistake, although he knew the true facts of the case.

Maddened by despair and a sense of futility, the amirs of Sind finally were pressed towards armed resistance. But at the eleventh hour, it seemed Napier was to be cheated of the hostilities he so desired—the amirs gave in to all the British demands and signed a new treaty before the deadline set by Napier. But the general chose to ignore the news of this event, which was sent to him by his agent in the amirs' camp, nor did he inform Ellenborough. The amirs, noting the continued march of the general's forces despite their capitulation, marched forth to battle and inevitable defeat. Thus was Sind annexed to British India.

A wave of disbelief and anger rose in Parliament and in India House, the headquarters of the East India Company, when news of the conquest and annexation reached England. Taxed with his stupidity in confusing the two Nasir Khans, Ellenborough blandly replied:

I am unable to account satisfactorily for this error. . . . It is satisfactory to know that Sir C. Napier was aware of the error, and that the letter inaccurately addressed to Meer Nuseer Khan of Khyrpore must have been delivered to Meer Nuseer Khan of Hyderabad to whom its contents applied.

Napier had indeed sent the letter to Nasir Khan of Hyderabad, but his cousin of Khairpur nonetheless suffered the penalty and was never informed why he had lost so much territory without apparent reason. When asked about the amirs' submission to the terms of the treaty, Ellenborough denied all knowledge of the event.

The degree to which Ellenborough had strayed from his instructions and from his earlier declared policies was manifested by the tenor of communications from the Company and the Board of Control. The president of the latter body had written to Ellenborough three months before the commencement of hostilities that while he realized that views taken on the same matter might not always be identical when seen from different hemispheres, the Board of Control would earnestly press upon the governor general "to avoid as much as possible *committing* us to any course affecting territorial possessions and extension." The Board, he continued, would prefer to be "left more at liberty to form a previous decision as to what should be done, than [a] . . . judgement of what has been done." Ellenborough, for his part, complained of the lack of instructions from home and of the consequent necessity of acting on his own initiative. To which Sir Robert Peel, the prime minister, replied:

> If a Governor-General supposes that the Government at home has no responsibility for acts done in India—that in the absence of necessary information . . . that they have nothing to do but to ratify and approve, he is under a great misapprehension of our duties and our relations to him.

Gladstone later recalled that the entire cabinet had been against the annexation of Sind, and, although Ellenborough was recalled, Peel summed up much of the problem when he wrote: "Time—distance—the course of events may have so fettered our discretion that we [had] no alternative but to maintain [the] occupation of Scinde."

It might be asked why so much time has been spent on the history of the British acquisition of such a relatively minor area. But the fact remains that it is hard to find another region where so many of the varying reasons for imperial expansion presented themselves in so limited a span of time. Early contacts with Sind were confined initially to trading establishments and then to the negotiation of treaties having as their sole purpose the protection of India from invasion, first by France and then by Russia. When these fears waned, so did the British interest in the lower Indus Valley. The Khosa raids temporarily forced

Sind back onto the stage, but it was not until the two Burnes brothers had filed their reports that Sind was no longer considered an arid waste watered by a useless river, but rather the highroad to Central Asia and the key to its trade. At last the cumbersome Ganges supply line to the northwestern provinces could be replaced by a more efficient route—the Indus. That the river was not navigable was hardly considered and was not really recognized until after the annexation. Sind was to be both a major route for communication and trade and a buffer against a possible Russian attack on India. Slowly but surely British preponderance increased. At first British vessels were only tolerated on the river, and a toll was levied on all shipping. Soon the Company was there by right, and all duties were removed. Treaties in 1832, 1834, 1838, and 1839 changed the amirs from the rulers of an independent nation to princes of a client state. The Afghan War only added to their degradation. The provisions of former treaties were abrogated, their possessions were seized, and British troops marched through the Bolan Pass towards Kabul.

Despite the humiliations heaped on the amirs and the steady expansion of British influence, the absorption of Sind into British India was not desired by responsible officials either in London or Calcutta. In the final analysis, it was not calculated government policy which determined the course of Anglo-Sind relations, but rather the curious interplay between the personalities of Ellenborough and Napier. Thus, Napier's megalomania and Ellenborough's latent frustrations were able, in an era of slow communications, to carry the day against the combined weight of the East India Company and the British government.

That many of the factors which governed the East India Company's intercourse with Sind were not unique to that area perhaps goes without saying; for they reappear on continents and in places far removed from the valley of the Indus.

8

Indians in South Africa: The Imperial Philosophy on Trial

Constitutional developments within the Empire and the mechanics and motivations for imperial advance constitute only part of the story of the British imperial experience. A whole sea of problems was encountered when white men started living in areas inhabited by colored peoples, or when Indians, who were second only to the British themselves as colonists within the Empire, moved to the West Indies, British Guiana, South, Central, and East Africa, Mauritius, Burma, Ceylon, Hong Kong, Malaya, Fiji, and, for that matter, to Britain itself.

Eighteenth-century mercantilistic dogma notwithstanding, the earliest stirrings of British imperial activity were due to private initiative, not government enterprise. It was only when private companies became political as well as commercial powers that the British government felt obliged to interfere actively and was forced to develop a coherent imperial philosophy. The nineteenth century was a great era of liberal reform and growing humanitarianism in Britain, and it became increasingly difficult for the British government to maintain an ethical double standard—one for Britain and the colonies of white settlement and another for India and the Dependent Empire. The only escape from this dilemma was to establish a single code of conduct for all Englishmen serving overseas and to declare the equality of every subject of the Crown in all parts of the Empire.

Indians, particularly, had been assured that inclusion in the Empire held the promise of sharing equal rights with all other British subjects. Queen Victoria's post-Mutiny proclamation of 1858 had guaranteed this. Although the proclamation was meant to apply only to India, if an Indian moved to Britain, he assumed the same rights as any Englishman. Thus, at the turn of the century, two Indians, Dadabhai Naoroji and Sir Mancherjee Bhownaggree, served in the British Parliament (even though they still could have shared but little in the government of their own country); and Indians expected to be treated similarly in the other British possessions to which they began to immigrate in the mid-nineteenth century, largely as indentured laborers.

The introduction of Indians into South Africa was due to the discovery in the 1850s that the soil and climate of Natal were ideal for the successful cultivation of sugar.[1] The one obstacle blocking the establishment of a thriving plantation economy was a lack of labor, as few local Africans were willing laborers. The eyes of the planters consequently turned hungrily towards India, which had already come to the rescue of Mauritius, Trinidad, St. Lucia, and Grenada when they had faced a similar problem. As the Natal *Mercury* stated in April 1859: "*The fate of the Colony hangs on a Thread and that thread is Labour.*"

Natal initiated negotiations with the government of India in 1856, but it was not until 1859 that they were successfully concluded. The Calcutta authorities wanted certain definite guarantees regarding the welfare of the Queen's Indian subjects before allowing them to work in Natal. As a result, Natal Law 14 of 1859 established a "Coolie Immigration Department" which was to be the responsibility of the "coolie immigration agent." This department was to receive the monies due from employers, who were to pay three-fifths of the cost of Indian immigration. The agent was also required to keep a register of Indian immigrants and to assign them to employers. The immigrants were to complete five years of indentured service at wages of not less than ten shillings a month. Law 14 also empowered indentured Indians to purchase back the last two years of their obligation by a payment of £5, but this provision was removed in 1864. At the end of five years the immigrants became free. Ten years after their arrival, the immigrants became eligible for a paid return passage to India, although they could remain in Natal if they wished, and the governor could, at

[1] See map of Africa on p. 149, Chapter 9.

his discretion, commute the cost of the return passage into a grant of Crown land. The government of India also imposed certain regulations of its own, and its Act 23 of 1860 established standards for the feeding, clothing, and general care of the laborers, the proportion of women that had to be included in any consignment, and the method of recruitment.

Between October 12, 1860, and February 5, 1861, five vessels left the Indian ports of Madras and Calcutta for Natal, carrying 1,029 male adults, 359 women (25 percent of the total being the legal minimum until 1866 when it was raised to 50 percent[2]), and some children. Between 1863 and 1866, 2,814 more male adults disembarked in Durban.

The importation of Indian labor had an immediate effect on the economy of Natal. A lead article in the Natal *Mercury* early in 1865 stated:

> Coolie immigration after several years' experience of it is deemed more essential to our prosperity than ever. It is the vitalizing principle. It may be tested by its results. Had it not been for coolie labour, we should certainly not have had it to say that our sugar export increased from £26,000 in 1863 to £100,000 in 1864 and has prospects of greater increase before it. Had it not been for coolie labour we should not hear of coffee plantations springing up on all hands and of the prosperity of older ones being sustained through the agency of East Indian men. . . . We do not think that the white labouring population . . . need be alarmed about the fancied effects of East Indian competition. . . . His presence will rather be a benefit to European mechanics and workmen, in as much as the enlarged production and increased prosperity he will create must give wider scope for the employment of our own skilled countrymen.

Thirty years later another article in the *Mercury* declared:

> The evils attendant upon the immigration of coolies, their low standard of living and morals, the introduction by them of disease and the ever-threatening outbreak of epidemics, not to mention other serious drawbacks—are too generally appreciated to leave room for contradiction. . . .

What had occurred to cause such a radical change in the attitude of the newspaper and of the white colonists? The government and people of Natal had expected that the Indian immigrants would either return home at the end of ten years' labor, when they became eligible for a free passage, or remain in the colony solely in the capacity of laborers

[2] In 1875 the figure was stabilized at 40 percent.

or domestic servants. As General Garnet Wolseley, the administrator of Natal, wrote to the Colonial Office in 1875:

> It may be confidently expected that only a comparatively small percentage of these coolies will leave the colony even after ten years' agreement has expired. . . . they [will] not only supply the planters with labour but to a large extent furnish the colonists generally with indoor servants for whom there is a pressing want in the province.

By and large, these expectations were fulfilled by the Indians as their indentures expired, although many of them also became market gardeners to satisfy the colonists' heretofore unsatisfied demands for fresh vegetables. What had not been anticipated, however, was the influx of a small group of free Indians, mainly Muslims from Gujarat on the west coast of India, who came to Natal at their own expense to engage in commerce, and particularly in the retail business. These "passenger Indians," or "Arabs," who began arriving in the 1880s, were soon providing competition for white merchants and consequently aroused great resentment. To make matters worse, the Indian population of Natal soon outstripped the European. By 1894 there were already 43,000 Indians to 40,000 whites, not to mention some 700,000 Africans.

Even in the first years of Indian immigration, the government of India had had cause to become dissatisfied with Natal. The colony's recruiters willfully misled prospective immigrants, and Indians on the estates were frequently mistreated and did not receive adequate food, housing, or medical treatment. The coolie immigration agent, who was the officer charged with the Indians' welfare, did not have adequate power to fulfill his responsibilities. Employers fined coolies illegally for failure to work, alleged misconduct, and absence without leave; and to such an extent did they do so that the laborer frequently owed the employer money at the end of the month. Flogging was not uncommon, and an Indian who had the temerity to complain to a magistrate about conditions might expect a harsh reprisal.

Because of a severe economic depression, Natal ceased to import coolies in 1866. By 1869 the worst of the depression was over, and the planters were once more clamoring for Indian labor. Between November 1870 and March 1871, however, the first group of immigrants who had sailed to Natal ten years previously became eligible for the free return passage to India, and those who availed themselves of this opportunity carried tales of mistreatment and indifference to the officials of the government of India. Consequently, when Natal wished to obtain more Indian laborers, the government of India would not allow it.

To clear the air, a so-called "Coolie Commission" was appointed by the Natal government in 1872 to investigate the condition of Indian labor in Natal. On the whole, the two commissioners concluded that the complaints of the returning immigrants had been somewhat overdrawn. The commissioners wrote in their report:

> We are of the opinion . . . that they [the Indians] are not and never have been subject to any systematic ill-treatment and oppression by their employers. Isolated and individual cases have doubtless occurred, but under the revised supervision we have recommended even these, it is hoped, will disappear. . . . Men of steady and industrial habits have the chance of acquiring property and accumulating wealth, and it is probable that as the prosperity of the Colony advances, so in proportion will the fair prospects of these classes.

The key to this revised system of supervision was to be the "protector of Indian immigrants," whose appointment the commissioners strongly urged. He was to be "an active and efficient officer . . . [with] some experience in India or among coolies, and . . . some knowledge of Indian languages." He was to be armed with real powers and to be charged with the general supervision of all Indians in Natal. The report also made recommendations concerning medical treatment for Indians, pay and fines, and social conditions. The commissioners felt that a permanent Indian population would be of benefit to Natal and that land should be made available to Indians near Durban. "The advantages of retaining in this country a race of men of industrial habits," the Commissioners concluded, "can scarcely be doubted."

The recommendations of the report were acceptable to the British and Indian governments and were consequently implemented through Natal Laws 12 of 1872 and 19 of 1874. Immigration immediately recommenced, and between June 26, 1874, and May 1, 1875, 5,974 Indian immigrants arrived in Natal. But as the number of Indians in Natal increased, so did the pressure on the government of Natal to protect the position of the white man. As early as 1869 coolies were made subject to a curfew. In 1880–1881 several attempts to pass legislation designed to exclude qualified Indians from the parliamentary franchise were repulsed through the efforts of the governor, the Colonial Office, and the planters, who feared that the government of India might halt the flow of indentured labor. Natal clearly wanted the best of both worlds. Indian labor was considered essential for the welfare of the colony, at least by the planters, but the white settlers were not willing to tolerate a permanent Indian population and Indian business competition in return.

Not surprisingly, the chief object of dislike was the "Arab," and, from the early 1890s on, incessant attempts were made to halt the immigration of all but indentured Indians. As it was known that the British government would probably disallow all legislation which was directly discriminatory, the act "to place certain restrictions on Immigration," passed in 1897, was technically nonracial. Qualifications for entry into the colony were based on property and knowledge of a European language. As a result, most Europeans were judged eligible to enter Natal, while most Indians were not.

The Indian community in Natal was clearly in need of a champion, and in 1893 he arrived in the unlikely figure of a man, small in stature, primly dressed in European garb, who had just finished his law training in London. This man was Mohandas K. Gandhi, who was destined to spend some 21 years in South Africa and to develop there a dramatic new philosophy of revolution. Gandhi started off modestly enough, representing Indians in law suits and writing numerous petitions, memorials, and letters regarding Indian rights to officials in Natal, India, and London. But he soon became a person to be reckoned with; so much so, that on returning from a visit to India in 1896, he was attacked by a white mob in Durban and was lucky to escape with his life. Gandhi's was an unenviable task; he had to deal not only with the hostile white population and legislature of Natal, but also with governors who, though appointed by the Colonial Office, were often far from sympathetic. One such noted that the " 'Bombay Wallah' [Gandhi] has come here knowing the conditions and he can leave if he does not like them. Because we want *identured labour for agriculture*, it is not reason why we should be swamped by black matter in the wrong place—namely storekeepers etc."

The British government was not altogether clear as to what course to follow. It had the right to disallow all legislation passed by the British colonies of South Africa, regardless of their state of constitutional development. In the case of Natal, the region had become a separate Crown colony in 1856. The charter of that year had established a legislative council of four officials and 12 elected members, but considerable powers were retained by the Crown. In 1893, however, Natal was granted responsible government, and the British government consequently lost much of its control over legislation passed in the colony. The right to review and disallow acts of the legislature still remained, but imperial constitutional common law virtually prohibited its use in purely internal affairs. In practice, the Colonial Office only intervened in matters having imperial implications and, despite an official philosophy dedicated to the equality of all British subjects regardless of race, it found itself in too difficult a position to interfere with the will of a white government discriminating against nonwhite British subjects, even if that government represented only a small minority of the total population of the colony.

The government of India, which was deeply concerned with the welfare of Indians in South Africa, could not interfere with legislation passed in other colonies. But it could, and often did, call to the attention of the British government colonial laws which were considered detrimental to Indians, and it could, on its own initiative, at any time stop the emigration of Indian laborers to the rest of the Empire.

Both the British and Indian governments were intimately involved with the growing Indian problem in South Africa. For if the Empire stood for equality, any attack on a particular group of the queen's subjects by other members of the British family struck at the very roots of the imperial philosophy. When the government of Natal wished to have all Indians returned to India before their indentures expired, the Colonial Office would not approve, as it "would be such an interference with the ordinary rights of British subjects that legislation in that sense could not be sanctioned." The situation was, however, one fraught with emotional ambivalence, for it must have been difficult for Englishmen of the nineteenth century, not the most tolerant of ages, to feel in their hearts that Africans and Indians were really the equals of white men.

Joseph Chamberlain, colonial secretary in the last decade of the century, manifested some of this ambivalence when he said:

We quite sympathize with the determination of the white inhabitants of these Colonies which are in comparatively close proximity to millions and hundreds of millions of Asiatics that there shall be no influx of people alien in civilization, alien in religion, alien in customs, whose influx, moreover, would most seriously interfere with the legitimate rights of the existing labour population. An immigration of that kind must, I quite understand, in the interest of the Colonies, be prevented at all hazards, and we shall not offer any opposition to the proposals intended with that object, but we ask you also to bear in mind the traditions of the Empire which makes no distinction in favour of, or against race or colour; and to exclude, by reason of their colour, or by reason of their race, all Her Majesty's Indian subjects, or even all Asiatics, would be an act so offensive to those peoples that it would be most painful, I am quite certain, to Her Majesty to have to sanction it . . .

The British government was caught between increasingly anti-Asian white minority governments in South Africa, liberal opinion in Britain, and popular indignation in India. Frequent questions and debates occurred in the British Parliament on the subject of Indians in South Africa, and as if to underline the curious complexity of the Empire, the attack was often led by Indian M.P.'s.

Embarrassed and frustrated, the British government compromised. It insisted that the letter of any particular law be nondiscriminatory but cared little about the spirit. Thus, in 1894, when a bill making all Indians ineligible to vote in Natal parliamentary elections was read a second time in Legislative Assembly, the Colonial Office informed the government of Natal that "to assent to this measure would be to put an affront upon the people of India as no British Government could be a party to. . . ." In 1896, however, Natal was able to disfranchise for the future all Indians, regardless of qualifications, who desired to vote in parliamentary elections: the legislators merely stipulated that those "who (not being of European origin) are Natives or descendants in the male line of Natives of countries which have not hitherto possessed elective institutions," unless exempted by the governor in council, were not in future to vote in parliamentary elections. As India was not considered to have such institutions, Indians, with the exception of those already on the voters' rolls, were effectively disfranchised without ever being specifically mentioned in the legislation. The law consequently received the royal assent, as did several others which were discriminatory in nature. All Indians—men, women, and children alike—not returning to India at the end of their indenture had to pay a £3 annual tax. "Coolies" were required to register, when in a town, on the basis of belonging to an "uncivilized race"; and Indians were largely excluded from government schools and made liable to arrest if they were not in possession of a pass.

The most objectionable piece of legislation, however, was Natal Act 18 of 1897 "to amend the law relating to licenses to wholesale and retail dealers," which made all applicants for trading licenses, or the renewal of trading licenses, subject to a municipal licensing officer, who was to be appointed by the corporation. The act stipulated that all books were to be kept in English and that commercial premises should be maintained in a sanitary condition. The licensing officer was to determine whether these conditions were being met or not. Appeals were to be allowed to a board made up of municipal officers, but not to the courts of the land. The British government assented to the bill, as it contained within it nothing specifically discriminatory against Indians and because it was assured by the government of Natal that the law would be fairly administered. If the Colonial Office had scrutinized the Natal Legislative Assembly debates on the law, it would have been forced to accept what it probably already knew. "We may as well face the fact," said a leading member of the Assembly, "if the Bill passes a second reading it is no use calling it un-English or un-British because it is an indirect method of accomplishing your end, because every member of this Assembly knows full well that the object of this Bill is to get at the Asiatic trader." The municipalities, checked neither by the courts nor the colonial authorities, looked upon the law as a mandate to remove all Indians from their midst. When appeals were lodged with the licensing boards, they were nearly always laughingly dismissed, regardless of the evidence.

The government of Natal had willfully misled an all too receptive Colonial Office, a fact which was made eminently clear at a meeting attended by the government and mayors of Natal some 12 years after the passage of the act. The mayors vied with each other in telling tales of licenses denied to Indians:

During the last three years they in Maritzburg had not issued one single new license to an Asiatic and if any licenses lapse whether through insolvency or death the licenses were in no case renewed. . . . They in Durban had felt that something should be done to stop the Asiatic trade, and during the last 4 years they had reduced their licenses in Durban by one-third. . . . Mr. Dely of Utrecht said they had no Asiatic traders in their district or town and so long as they had the power they would keep them out. . . . Mr. Perkins [of Verulam] said his Board were of opinion that from this time forward no new licenses should be issued to Indians, nor should there be any transfers. . . . During the last year the Indian licenses in Verulam had been reduced by 5, and these would be further reduced as opportunity offered.

The minister of justice urged muncipalities to replace licensing officers who did not rid the town of Indians with sufficient dispatch. The prime minister remarked that it was his firm policy that no new licenses should be issued to Indians. No doubt aware of his original duplicity, he cautioned his listeners not to "blazen the fact abroad, but it was their policy nevertheless."

Although Natal was the home of the vast majority of Indian immigrants in Africa, both "Arabs" and time-expired indentured laborers began making their appearance in Cape Colony, the Orange Free State, and the Transvaal (South African Republic) by the early 1880s. The reaction in the Cape was mild compared with that in the other areas affected; but then it had been traditionally more liberal in racial matters, and very few Indians entered its precincts in any case. (There were 8,489 Indians in Cape Colony in 1904 and only 7,963 in 1921.) In 1892, however, a Franchise and Ballot Bill was introduced into the Cape legislature which stipulated that to be an eligible voter, a person must be able to write his name, address, and occupation in English. Of greater significance, the bill raised the property qualifications for the franchise from £25 to £75.

The secretary of state for the colonies, Lord Ripon, immediately received petitions of protest from both colored (persons of mixed white and Negro blood, in the British South African context) and Indian objectors. The governor, Sir Henry Loch, countered by claiming the measure was necessary, moderate, and nonracial and that it had been passed by a large majority. The Cape cabinet took the same position, but Ripon himself felt that the "legislation is contrary to the spirit and tendency of public opinion in the present day." Yet he could not properly veto a bill, technically nondiscriminatory, passed by the legislature of a self-governing colony, especially as it had already received the assent of the governor. The bill consequently was not disallowed by the British government, despite the personal reservations of the colonial secretary.

Three years later, in 1895, the Cape legislature passed an "Act to Amend and Add to the Laws Regulating the Municipal Corporation and Government of East London." This law gave the municipal authorities of East London power to require natives and Asiatics to reside in specially designated locations outside the town and also permitted the passage of municipal ordinances:

> Fixing the hours within which it shall not be lawful for natives and Asiatics to be in the streets, public places or thoroughfares . . . without a written pass or certificate . . . and for fixing such parts of streets or open spaces or pavements of the same on which natives and Asiatics may not walk or be. . . . For regulating and setting apart portions of the rivers and sea where natives and Asiatics may not bathe, and where clothes may or may not be washed.

The British government did not disallow the act. It was not considered a truly discriminatory measure in a racial sense, as its final stipulations exempted all natives and Asiatics "who are at present or may in the future become registered owners or occupiers of land within the municipality valued for municipal purposes at not less than £75." Perhaps of greater moment in the eyes of the British government was the feeling expressed by the governor, as spokesman for his ministers, that the Cape would rather secede from the British Empire than brook any interference with what it considered its domestic affairs.

The position of the British government in regard to the rights of Indians in the two Boer republics was, of course, even more complicated than it was *vis-à-vis* the British colonies in South Africa. There were very few Indians in the Orange Free State by 1890 and less than a dozen traders. Yet the government of the Free State in 1890 passed legislation forbidding the possession of land or the carrying on of trade within the republic by Indians. Merchants were given time to liquidate their businesses and compensation was accorded. The British government tried to intervene on behalf of the Indians, but to no avail, as there was no legal basis upon which to protest.

The position in the Transvaal was more complex. The British government had conceded the Transvaal its independence for the second time in April 1881. The enabling instrument was the Pretoria Convention, which also stipulated that the British government would maintain suzerainty over the republic. In 1884, a second agreement, the London Convention, was promulgated to increase the Transvaal's jurisdiction over its own affairs. No mention was made of suzerainty, and as the British government was in future years to base much of its right to protect Indians in the Transvaal on its position as suzerain, this was a matter of some importance. The Transvaal claimed that British suzerainty no longer existed from the time the London Convention replaced the Pretoria Convention. The British government took the view that the London Convention merely amended the Pretoria Convention and that those articles of the Pretoria Convention not specifically changed by the second document were still in effect. To confuse the issue further, Article 14 of the London Convention stipulated as follows:

All persons other than natives, conforming themselves to the laws of the South African Republic

(a) will have full liberty, with their families, to enter, travel, or reside in any part of the South African Republic;

(b) will be entitled to hire or possess houses, manufacturies, warehouses, shops, and premises;
(c) may carry on their commerce either in person, or by any agents whom they may think fit to employ;
(d) will not be subject in respect of their persons or property, or in respect of their commerce or industry, to any taxes, whether general or local, other than those which are or may be imposed upon citizens of the said Republic.

The Indians were by no means the only non-African British subjects in the Transvaal; indeed, with the booming gold mines, they were only a small minority, numbering about 17,000 in 1899.[3] But they were in the most difficult position. The first paragraph of Article 14 said that all persons, to be eligible for the rights stipulated, must conform themselves to the laws of the Transvaal. The republic's basic law, the *Grondwet*, clearly stated that colored persons, a designation which in the Transvaal included Indians, could not receive the same treatment as white persons and would be subject to special laws. Did the *Grondwet* take precedence over the London Convention, and did the opening lines of Article 14 thus obviate the guarantees of subsequent paragraphs as far as Indians were concerned? A long and acrimonious correspondence ensued between the British and Transvaal governments, complicated by the suzerainty issue and a general confusion as to what suzerainty actually meant in the first place.

The Colonial Office in London had always had some sympathy for the republic's desire to protect itself from the "dirty" habits of lower-class Indians and was more interested in insuring the position of the so-called higher class Indians. Consequently, when in 1885 the Transvaal legislature passed a law providing for the establishment of specified locations for Asians, the British government merely insisted that a clause be added indicating that sanitation and the public health were the rationales for establishing these sites. The significant sections of Law 3 of 1885, as amended in 1886, thus read as follows:

1. This law shall apply to the person belonging to one of the native races of Asia, including the so-called Coolies, Arabs, Malays, and Mohammedan subjects of the Turkish Empire.
2. With regard to the persons mentioned in Article 1, the following provisions shall apply:
(a) They cannot obtain the burgher right of the South African Republic.

[3] The census of 1896 shows that there were almost 34,000 white British in Johannesburg and about 5,000 Asians; the Transvaalers numbered only 6,200.

(b) They cannot be owners of fixed property in the Republic, except only in such streets, wards, and locations as the Government for purposes of sanitation shall assign to them to live in. This provision has no retrospective force.

(c) They shall, as far as those who settle in the Republic with the object of trading, etc., are concerned, be inscribed in a register to be especially kept for that purpose.

(d) The Government shall have the right, for purposes of sanitation, to assign to them certain streets, wards, and locations to live in (*terbewoning*). This provision does not apply to those who live with their employers.

After the passage of the law, Sir Hercules Robinson, the British high commissioner, informed the president of the Transvaal that

although the amended law is still a contravention of the 14th Article of the Convention of London, I shall not advise Her Majesty's Government to offer further opposition to it in view of your Honour's opinion that it is necessary for the protection of public health.

Despite the British government's acquiescence, the republic was dilatory in implementing the new law. But in time, steps were taken to put it into effect. When municipal authorities set about doing this, however, it soon became apparent that in the eyes of the Transvaal government the law demanded that Indians must not only live but also trade in locations which would be separate from the municipalities. The British government took immediate issue. It pointed out that the law referred only to locations for habitation and that Indians could continue to trade in the towns as before. Besides, the high commissioner pointed out, the context of the law implied that the locations would be "streets, wards and locations" within, rather than outside, the municipalities.

The situation was so vague and confused that both sides in 1894 decided to submit their claims, in regard to the interpretation of the law, to the arbitration of the chief justice of the Orange Free State. This dignitary decided in favor of the Transvaal, a decision which was reinforced by the similar outcome of a test case within the republic itself.

The British government nevertheless continued to intercede on behalf of the Indians in the Transvaal. Through its efforts, the publication of the order officially demanding that all Indians move to locations both for purposes of business and habitation was constantly delayed. Peripheral issues, such as the right of Indians to use sidewalks, first-class train compartments, and cabs were also debated. But in their efforts, British officials were constantly hampered by white British subjects in the Transvaal who, much as they despised the republic's government, at least agreed with its actions towards Indians. The Johannesburg *Star*, a British newspaper in the Transvaal, strongly supported the republic's Indian policy:

> Apart from the question of his loathesome habits, the coolie is not an immigrant to be encouraged. He lowers the standard of comfort, and closes the avenues to prosperity to the European trader. Economically, he is of no advantage to the country he visits—for, be it remembered that he does not settle. He accumulates money by virtue of the wretchedness in which he lives—a wretchedness constituting a terrible danger to the rest of the community—and he takes 80 per cent of that money back again to Asia. In Natal we actually have the spectacle of European trade being gradually destroyed by the impossible competition of the coolie. The Asiatic is thus a menace to the European's life, an obstacle to his commercial progress. . . .

In 1899 the Boer War intervened to prevent further developments in the Transvaal and the other affected areas. Ostensibly, the treatment of Indians in the Transvaal was one of the causes of the war. Yet if this was so, why did a British military government, unhampered by an elected legislature, make the re-promulgation of the old Transvaal legislation concerning Indians—the very law the British government had fought so hard against in the decade before the commencement of hostilities—virtually its first act upon the establishment of British control in the Transvaal? This deed was all the more regrettable in view of the loyal adherence of the Indians to the British cause throughout the war. Gandhi had organized an Indian ambulance corps for which 300 free Indians and 800 indentured laborers volunteered. The corps served with distinction, and for several days during the battle of Spion Kop, in January 1900, it evacuated the wounded under heavy fire. Throughout the siege of Ladysmith, Parbu Singh, an indentured laborer, exposed himself to enemy fire, spotting the besiegers' artillery. Later he was publicly decorated in Durban.

After the war Gandhi moved his headquarters from Durban to Johannesburg, in anticipation of a major struggle for Indian rights. He immediately founded the Transvaal British Indian Association and protested the re-enactment of Law 3. Under pressure, the British military government in the Transvaal slightly amended the original pronouncement so that Asiatics who satisfied the colonial secretary of the colony that their mode of living was in accordance with European ideas would be allowed to live, with their servants, outside locations but not to trade outside them. Businesses established before the war would be left undisturbed. But, in general, Asiatics would be required to live and trade in locations and would be prohibited from holding land elsewhere.

Despite the British government's official policy before the war, Lord Milner, as high commissioner for South Africa and governor of the Transvaal and the Orange River Colony, with jurisdiction over all conquered territories, was able to write to the secretary of state for the colonies in 1904:

> I think that to attempt to place coloured people on an equality with whites in South Africa is wholly impracticable, and that moreover, it is in principle wrong. But I also hold that when a coloured man possesses a high grade of civilization he ought to obtain what I may call "white privileges" irrespective of colour. . . . For the present, however, there is no prospect whatever of their prevailing, certainly as far as Asiatics are concerned. . . . the Asiatics are strangers forcing themselves upon a community reluctant to receive them.

So much for the equality of all British subjects. Perhaps, after all, in the years before the war, the British government had really been more interested in harassing the government of the republic than in protecting the rights of British Indian subjects within its borders.

The end was not even yet in sight, however. Ordinance 5 of 1903 attempted to regulate the entry of Indians into the Transvaal and required all Indians to register, for which a fee of £3 was charged unless an Indian had already registered in the days of the South African Republic. In 1906, four years after military government in the Transvaal had been replaced by Crown Colony status, Ordinance 29 was passed, which required the compulsory registration of all Asiatics and their identification by means of fingerprints. If any Indian failed to comply with this law, he could be fined, imprisoned, or deported from the Transvaal. Police officers could question Indians on the street or enter their homes to ask for registration documents. Indians, who were particularly sensitive about their women, found in this provision a profound threat to their way of life.

Ordinance 29 became the inspiration for Gandhi's first *satyagraha* (passive resistance) campaign. A mass meeting was held at the Imperial Theatre in Johannesburg in September 1906, and under Gandhi's leadership those in attendance swore not to obey the law which in 1907, when the Transvaal received responsible government, was reenacted by the new Transvaal parliament. Gandhi and a number of his followers kept their pledge not to register, and by the end of January 1908 there were 155 passive resisters in jail.

Jan Christian Smuts, the colonial secretary of the new Transvaal government, summoned Gandhi to his office on January 30 and, according to Gandhi, promised to repeal the "black and murderous act" if the Indians would only register voluntarily. This Gandhi agreed to do, and with some difficulty he overcame Indian opposition to this compromise. But the hated act was not repealed, and in August Gandhi called a meeting at the Hamidia Mosque in Johannesburg, where 2,000 registration certificates were burned in protest. Gandhi next led a mass march of Indians from Natal to the Transvaal in violation of the Transvaal Immigration Registration Act of 1908 and again went to prison.

What is surprising is that Gandhi throughout his troubles in South Africa maintained his belief that ultimately the British Empire stood for justice.[4] In 1906, in the midst of his travail, he interrupted his campaign in the Transvaal again to organize an Indian ambulance corps to serve in the Bambata rebellion in Zululand. Even the anti-Indian governor of Natal, Sir Henry McCallum, had been moved to offer his thanks to "Sergeant-Major Gandhi," and wrote: "I cannot allow demobilization to take place without placing on record, on behalf of the Government, my appreciation of the patriotic movement made by the Indian community of Natal in providing a bearer company for service in the field during the rebellion."

The Natal governor's gratitude was, however, largely limited to this letter, for in the years following the Boer War the difficulties of the Indians in Natal only increased. Heavy pressure was placed on the government by the municipalities to follow the example of the Transvaal in establishing special locations for Indians outside city limits. In 1907 the Indians, as "colored persons," were deprived of the municipal franchise.

The British and Indian governments strongly objected to this measure. The latter was particularly incensed and threatened to put a final stop to the emigration of indentured labor. Natal replied in 1908 by passing two bills of extreme severity, which had for their purpose the complete elimination of Indian traders in Natal. Although the British government indicated that the two measures would be disallowed, the

[4] During World War I, after he had returned to India, Gandhi recruited for the Indian Army and strongly supported the British war effort.

very fact of their passage paid eloquent testimony to the agitated state of public opinion in Natal. The planters still wanted indentured Indian labor, but the colony as a whole was unwilling to pay the price of Indian political freedom and commercial competition.

Under these circumstances, the government of India somewhat moderated its position and bargained for the welfare of the Indian population, using the threat of a termination of indentured emigration as a lever. It demanded that Indians either be allowed to maintain the municipal franchise or be granted an appeal to the Supreme Court in cases involving the issuing of licenses; for it was this lack of access to the courts that had placed Indians in such a difficult position under the terms of the Licensing Act of 1897. The Natal government chose the first alternative, and in 1909 passed the necessary legislation. Indian immigration consequently continued for two more years, ending finally in 1911 by action of the government of India.

The Boer War did nothing to improve the outlook for Indians in Cape Colony either, although the situation there was not as acute. In 1902 an immigration act was introduced into the legislature which specifically prohibited the entry of Asiatics into the Cape. In the act's final form, however, the references to Asiatics were deleted, although in practice it was still very difficult for an Indian to meet the requirements for entry into the colony. In 1906, when the Immigration Act of 1903 was amended, a member of the House of Assembly again moved a clause forbidding the entry of Asiatics into Cape Colony, but the House defeated his motion by a vote of 67 to 23.

Besides the question of immigration, the matter of Indian competition with white traders became an issue in Cape Colony as well as in Natal. In 1906 an act was passed to regulate the issuing of licenses to trade. The law provided for a licensing court to judge the fitness of applicants on the basis of honesty, ability to keep books, and so forth. The court could also refuse to renew licenses because of unsanitary conditions on the premises of the applicant. But a sufficient number of signatures in the locality involved could override the court's decision, and a storekeeper denied a license could appeal to the Supreme Court. The British government did not disallow the act, as nothing in it appeared to be to the detriment of any particular racial group. However, the Cape *Hansard*[5] of August 16, 1906, reported the words of a liberal Boer representative as follows:

[5] The term "*Hansard*" refers to the officially published volumes of parliamentary debates.

> The Attorney-General said, when the bill was introduced, that it was a bill introduced because certain people could not keep books; and another reason was that it was introduced for sanitary purposes. . . . He would ask the Imperialists who sat opposite, and who talked of British subjects having equal rights wherever they went . . . what they had to say on the point. They had now got the . . . truth. It was to keep out the Asiatics—their fellow-subjects, their brothers—(opposition laughter). . . .

When, in August 1908, the House of Assembly appointed a select committee to investigate Asian grievances, based on the working of the Immigration and General Dealers Licensing Bill, several Indian witnesses testified that, outside of Cape Town, Indians were denied licenses as general dealers or hawkers merely because they were Indians. Much of this was because European merchants, as usual, claimed that they were being driven out of business by Indians who, representing an inferior order of civilization, could undersell them by paying lower wages and living "off the smell of an oil rag." The committee found that Indians were indeed being discriminated against in some instances and recommended certain minor alterations in the working of the law.

The formation of the Union of South Africa in 1910 complicated things for the Indians still further, for now even the slight restraining influence of the British government largely disappeared. Gandhi had proceeded to England and India to express the apprehensions felt by the Indian population of South Africa about the impending union, and although his pleas had fallen mostly on deaf ears, the government of India had agreed to send Gopal Krishna Gokhale, one of the leading Indian political figures, on a journey to South Africa. Gokhale arrived in the new Union in 1912 and spent a month traveling throughout the country. He was treated with great respect wherever he went, and after an interview with General Louis Botha, the prime minister, and General Smuts, the minister of mines, defense, and interior, he claimed to have elicited from them a promise that discriminatory immigration practices would cease and that the 1908 Transvaal Immigration Registration Act and the Natal act requiring the payment of a £3 annual tax by all formerly indentured Indians choosing to remain in the province would both be repealed.

Gandhi did not believe this report, and regrettably he was right; for Smuts, after Gokhale's departure, announced in the House of Assembly that the European population in Natal would not permit the lifting of the annual £3 tax. To make matters worse, a judge of the Cape

Supreme Court, in March 1913, ruled that only Christian marriages were legal in South Africa and that rites conducted under a religion that permitted polygamous marriages were illegal—judgments that had the effect of invalidating many Indian marriages.

These two occurrences, combined with the passage of the Union Immigrants' Regulation Act of 1913, which again effectively barred the entry of Indians through the use of a language test "or on account of standard or habits of life . . . unsuited to the requirements of the Union or any particular Province thereof," brought on a major civil disobedience campaign, and in Natal some 4,000 Indian workers in the Newcastle coal mines went out on strike, as did sugar workers, waiters, cooks, washermen, and municipal employees. Soon 50,000 indentured Indians throughout South Africa were on strike and several thousand unindentured Indians in jail.

The provisions of the Immigrants' Regulation Act not only prohibited the entry of Indians into the Union but also confirmed the restrictions on the movement of Indians from one province to another. Gandhi consequently led a column of several hundred strikers and others of his adherents—2,211 souls in all—on another dramatic, but nonviolent, protest march from Natal into the Transvaal, thus purposely breaking the law. Most of the marchers were shipped back to Natal in special trains, but Gandhi and several of his closest followers were tried and sentenced to three months' hard labor.

This first massive civil disobedience campaign had a profound effect in India and Great Britain, as well as in South Africa itself, and as a consequence the Union government appointed a commission to investigate the causes of the troubles that had recently occurred and to make recommendations for the future.

The report of the commission, plus the so-called Smuts-Gandhi Agreement, which developed from a series of conversations and letters between the two protagonists, resulted in the Indian Relief Act of 1914. This act was a compromise. The £3 tax was abolished, as was all liability for arrears. Hindu, Muslim, and Parsi marriages were recognized. Those Indians domiciled in the Union whose wives and children were still in India were allowed to bring their families to South Africa, and some interprovincial movement by Indians was allowed. On the other hand, the main corpus of anti-Indian legislation remained intact. Restrictions on rights of residence, ownership of land, and trade remained largely unaltered.

Gandhi himself was, of course, not totally satisfied, but he felt that the important first step had been made and that the tide would now run in the right direction. As he prepared to depart from South Africa forever to take up his great work in India, he wrote:

> I shall hope that when the Europeans of South Africa fully appreciate the fact that now as the importation of indentured labour from India is prohibited and as the Immigrants' Regulation Act of last year has in practice all but stopped further free Indian immigration, and that my countrymen do not aspire to any political ambition, they, the Europeans, will see the justice and indeed the necessity of my countrymen being granted . . . [more] rights.

Gandhi's optimism turned out to be ill-founded. Conditions for Indians in South Africa did not improve, and the British and Indian governments were not able to influence the course of events. Changed constitutional arrangements as a result of union, the end of indentured labor as an issue, and the precedents established by the previous history of British relations with constitutionally advanced members of the Empire all precluded effective intervention.

The British government, for many reasons, had not been able to influence racial policy decisively in South Africa since about 1870, and it was vain to expect it to do so after union. Even with the best of wills, the British government might not have been able materially to improve the position of Indians in Natal or the Transvaal. Laws disallowed at the colonial level could often be effected, without interference, at the municipal level. It has always been difficult to control men's minds and prejudices through legislation, and no doubt an awareness of the futility of disallowance must have made it very easy for the British government to hide behind the façade of responsible government, which implied colonial autonomy, and to insist on form rather than substance in colonial legislation. But as Sir Mancherjee Bhownaggree told the House of Commons in 1904:

> I contend that the grant of autonomy does not carry with it the right to undermine the noblest traditions of the British Constitution and the pledges of the Crown in respect to the rights and liberties of subjects of the King belonging to other portions of his Dominions. . . . The Imperial connexion is dissolved into a figment if His Majesty's Ministers are unable to protect Indian subjects in all parts of the British dominions.

Official pronouncements by British statesmen and savants may have espoused an imperial philosophy dedicated to the equality of all British subjects. It is impossible, however, to abandon totally the standards of one's day. Sir West Ridgeway, a former provincial governor in India and later chairman of a committee sent to the Transvaal in 1906 to deal with the franchise and electoral system questions, probably represented informed British opinion quite accurately. In a long letter to *The Times* in December 1893, he disparaged

> academic imperialists at home who dream of a Utopian Empire where all citizens enjoy equal rights. This dream can never be realized; at least not for generations to come. If the Government were to make any attempt to enforce this policy, or even to support it by argument, the breakup of the Empire would follow. Our self-governing colonies—at least at this stage of their development—will not tolerate the entry of coloured races into their midst in any number. It is a question of life and death with them. Their's must be a white man's country. . . .

9

The Fashoda Incident and the Scramble for Africa

It was early July 1898, when the small huddle of boats, with its escort of one minute steamer, emerged from the desolate reaches of Lake No in the south-central Sudan, and debouched into the White Nile. This was no casual group of Sudanese traders, nor even a British expedition, but a French column of 120 Senegalese troops and seven officers and noncommissioned officers, under the command of Captain Jean Baptiste Marchand. The weary detachment had come a long way, but the journey was almost over. Some 60 miles beyond the Nile's junction with the Sobat River the French set up an encampment at Fashoda (today known as Kodok), and the stage was set for a confrontation that was to endanger the peace of Europe.[1]

Marchand had received his original instructions in February 1896. He had ordered to proceed to the White Nile and to establish French title to the Upper Nile Valley. He was, in the process, to develop friendly relations with the Mahdists (see Chapter 5, pages 82–87) and at all costs to avoid open conflict with them. A change of ministry in France resulted in the drafting of a second, broader, set of orders for Marchand. His mission was now clearly envisaged as being less military and more political in nature, its essentially anti-British char-

[1] The British press reflected the reaction in Britain to the news of Marchand's arrival at Fashoda. The French detachment was described as a band of "irregular marauders" and as the "scum of the desert." Marchand's mission was deemed a sign of "conscious antagonism" and "indubitable hostility" towards England which would have to be countered by the most vigorous means not excluding war.

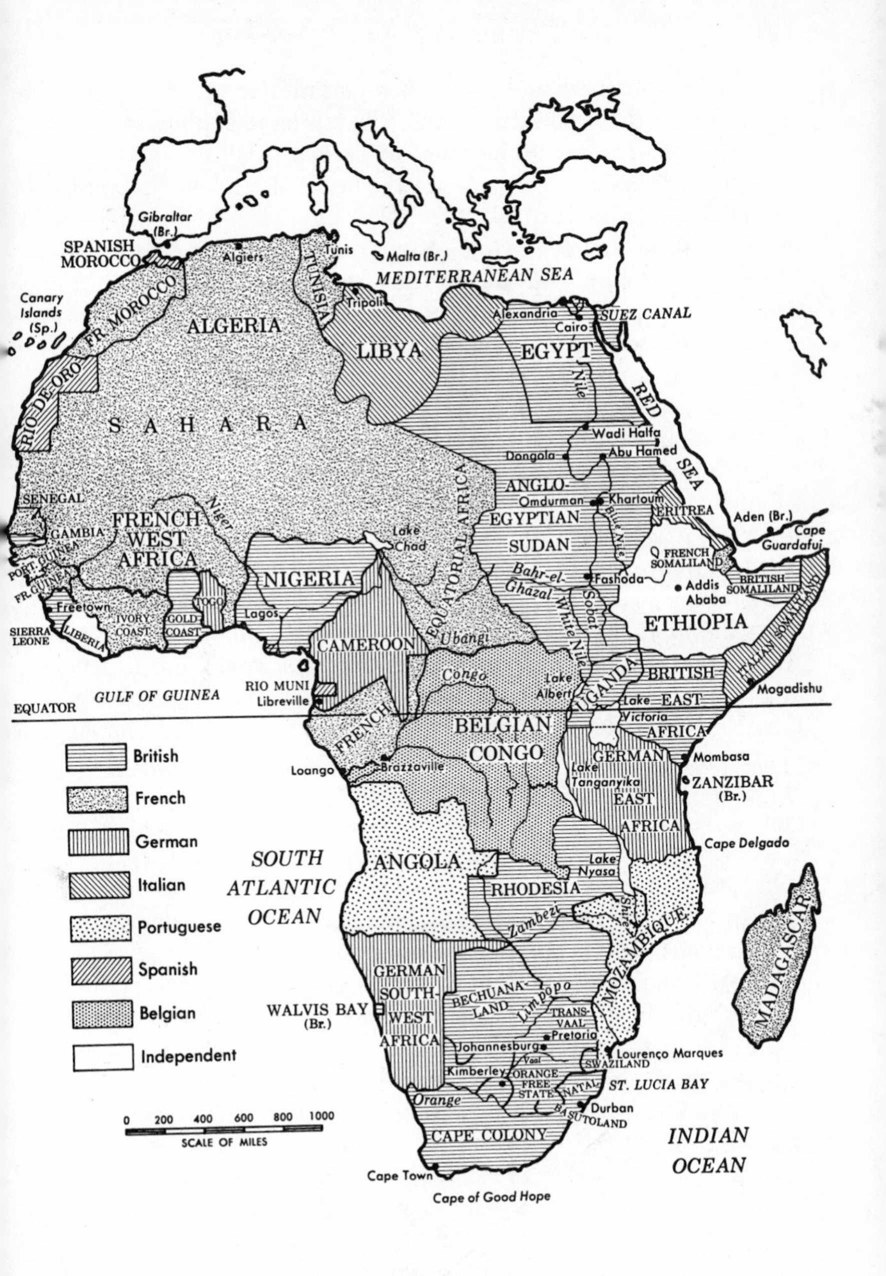

AFRICA IN 1914

acter was emphasized, and the French government's intention of gaining control of the headwaters of the Nile was more boldly stated.

That Fashoda became the point of French challenge to the British position in the Nile Valley was not the result of random chance; for as of January 1895 the British government only claimed the Nile banks as far north as Fashoda, while claiming for Egypt the territory as far south as Khartoum. Thus the country from Fashoda to Khartoum was open to claim. As a consequence, when Marchand departed from Paris, the French foreign minister, Gabriel Hanotaux, told him "Go to Fashoda. France is going to fire her pistol."

It was perhaps inevitable that the drive of British imperial power northward from Uganda would eventually collide with the east-west axis apparently being established by the French. The French had never willingly accepted their displacement by the British in Egypt. They made persistent efforts to reach the Nile from the east, through Ethiopia, and, from 1890 on, from the west, via the Ubangi country.

Marchand's road to Fashoda was a long and arduous one. He left Marseille in June 1896 and arrived at Loango, on the west coast of Africa, the next month. Here a six months' halt could not be avoided, as the tribes between Loango and Brazzaville were in revolt against their French overlords. To make matters worse, Marchand himself fell ill and almost died. Finally, the expedition set off, reaching the Congo at Brazzaville from where it started up the river in March. It was a most difficult journey. Marchand was short of transport and supplies, and it was a tribute to his courage and that of his men that they were able, after some weeks, to reach the upper Ubangi River. Here Marchand built a post at Tambura and then moved to Khogali, some 50 miles northeast, in preparation for embarking on the river Sue, the principal tributary of the Bahr-el-Ghazal branch of the Nile. The tiny steamer and the accompanying vessels were about to be launched for the final stage of the journey, when the level of the Bahr-el-Ghazal fell, delaying the expedition once more. Eventually, everything was in readiness, and the weary band of adventurers was able to proceed down river to Lake No and its appointment with history.

Once at Fashoda, the expedition went about making itself as comfortable as possible—hardly an easy task, for it had been said of Fashoda that "a more dreary or uninviting spot it is impossible to conceive." The flag of the French republic was raised with due pomp, a camp established, and even a vegetable garden planted. As a precaution, the steamer, the *Faidherbe*, was sent 250 miles back up the river to the nearest French depot for fresh supplies. Meanwhile, treaties were drawn up with the neighboring tribes, and every effort made to establish French influence in the upper reaches of the Nile Valley.

Nothing occurred to disturb the calm of Fashoda until some six weeks after Marchand's arrival. Then a group of Mahdists, followers of the Khalifa Abdulla, steaming up the Nile in one of Gordon's old ships captured by the mahdi, stumbled onto the French station and commenced firing on these unknown Europeans. Marchand successfully drove off his assailants, but his ammunition supply was left in a dangerously low state. To make matters worse, stronger opposition was on the way. On September 2, 1898, at Omdurman, the British under General Sir Herbert Kitchener finally avenged Gordon and broke the Mahdist grip on the Sudan. Five days later, the steamer *Tewfikia,* which had discovered Marchand, fell into the hands of the victorious British. Upon being questioned, the captured crew could give but a confused report about the episode at Fashoda. They knew only that they had been fired on by Europeans whose flag contained bright colors. Some enterprising British officers extracted a few of the spent bullets from the *Tewfikia*'s superstructure and found them to be nickel-covered, obviously discharged from a modern European rifle. Although his staff was thoroughly mystified by this news, Kitchener himself was not. He had already received official intimation that he might encounter the French to the south.

On September 8, the day after the *Tewfikia*'s capture, Kitchener, at the head of a flotilla of five steamers carrying a mixed force of British and Sudanese troops, started on the 500-mile journey to Fashoda. Ten days later, as the little fleet was approaching the settlement, Kitchener dispatched a letter to Marchand announcing his impending arrival. The following day he received a courteous reply. Marchand informed Kitchener that he had occupied Fashoda on behalf of the French republic on July 10, and that he had instructions from his government to claim the Bahr-el-Ghazal to the point where it met the Bahr-el-Jebel to form the White Nile, together with the country on the left bank of the river as far north as Fashoda. Marchand's was indeed an ambitious plan, depending for its implementation, as it did, upon a force of some 120 soldiers. But large tracts of African land had previously come under the sway of European powers through the efforts of smaller forces than his.

The face-to-face meeting of Kitchener and Marchand, representing the conflict of British and French ambitions in Africa, was not an altogether unforeseen happening. A year previous, Lord Salisbury, the British prime minister, had cabled to Sir Evelyn Baring, the British agent and consul-general in Cairo:

> . . . if we wait another year [before claiming the territory north of Fashoda] we may find that the French have anticipated us by setting up a French principality at Fashoda. It is, of course, as difficult to judge what is going on in the Upper Nile as it is to judge what is going on on the other side of the moon . . . but . . . if we ever get to Fashoda, the diplomatic crisis will be something to remember, and "what next" will be a very interesting question. . . .

That the crisis was not more serious was largely due to the restraint and good manners displayed by both Kitchener and Marchand. Marchand congratulated Kitchener upon his great victory at Omdurman and welcomed him to Fashoda in the name of France. Kitchener commended Marchand and his men for having successfully completed so difficult a journey but protested the occupation of Fashoda and the raising of the French flag. Marchand responded by repeating his orders, making it clear that he and his men would rather die than surrender. Kitchener then inquired whether the French would allow the flying of the Egyptian flag, and when Marchand reluctantly acquiesced, it was raised some five hundred yards to the south of the French position. Kitchener then handed Marchand a written protest against the French encroachment in the Nile Valley and, having ended the discussions with a round of whisky and soda, departed the scene, leaving behind a detachment of Sudanese troops.

In the ensuing weeks both sides behaved with remarkably sound judgment and moderation. Only in October, when Marchand left for Cairo to communicate with his government, was there any danger of a clash. Marchand's subordinate, Captain Germain, determined to follow a more aggressive policy, dispatched reconnaissance parties into the surrounding countryside and occupied the right bank of the river, even though Marchand had claimed only the left bank on behalf of the French government. The commander of the British force repeatedly protested Germain's action and was finally driven to the brink of hostilities, but Marchand returned just in time to soothe the ruffled feelings on both sides. The firing of a single shot at Fashoda might well have changed the future of Europe, but fortunately both Marchand and Kitchener realized that the problem of the Nile Valley could not be settled at this desolate spot and that the battlefields lay rather in Paris and London.

It has already been indicated that for most of the nineteenth century the British government rarely countenanced the acquisition of additional territory in Africa (see Chapters 5 and 6). In fact, the emphasis was more on disposing of already established colonies. As late as 1864 Sir Charles Adderley, the British colonial reformer, had asserted in Parliament that the four British possessions on the west coast of Africa wasted a million pounds every year. The attempt to create a "civilized" Negro community in Sierra Leone, he claimed, had failed; the Gold Coast had involved the British government in several unjustifiable wars; and the trade of Gambia and Lagos was at best negligible. The report of the Committee on West African Affairs, created on Adderley's motion, recommended the following:

> All further extension of territory or assumption of government, or new treaties offering protection to native tribes, would be inexpedient. . . . The object of our policy should be to encourage in the natives the exercise of those qualities which may render it possible for us more and more to transfer to them the administration of all the governments, with a view to our ultimate withdrawal from all, except probably Sierra Leone.

As a result of the report, Edward Cardwell, the colonial secretary, announced in 1866 that the West African establishments had been drastically reduced.

Yet during the last quarter of the century, the Union Jack was enthusiastically raised over vast new possessions in the center, the north, the east, and the west of the continent. Historians still debate what caused this great explosion of imperial zeal, but certainly the entry of France and then of Germany into the quest for colonies in Africa was of prime importance. At first, a concern for the security of already established British colonies and dependencies was manifested in London, but later it was an unreasonable enthusiasm for seeing the map painted red, rather than some other color, that developed. The incident at Fashoda proved to be the climax of the historical phenomenon popularly known as "the scramble for Africa"—the competition among the various European states for colonies in Africa.

Ever since the beginning of the nineteenth century there had been considerable interest in British intellectual circles regarding the geography of Africa. Men like Mungo Park, who attempted to discover the source of the Niger on behalf of the African Association, and Richard Burton and John Speke, who sought to solve the mystery of the Nile's source in the employ of the Royal Geographical Society, had done much to arouse public interest in the "dark continent." But it was the journeys of the missionary David Livingstone and the journalist Henry M. Stanley that brought an awareness of Africa into every British home and made British progress on the continent an object of national pride.

Between 1874 and 1877 Stanley explored the Congo basin and kept the public informed of his activities through articles in the *Daily Telegraph.* His report of a visit to the court of King Mutesa of Uganda prompted the dispatch of missionaries to that country—possibly the first step in the partition of East Africa. Meanwhile, in 1876, King Leopold II of Belgium had founded the International Association for the Exploration and Civilization of Central Africa. In 1878 he inveigled Stanley into his employ and formed a new society, the Committee for Upper Congo Studies, which, under the guise of purest philanthropy, signed treaties with chiefs in the Congo area and established a personal fief for Leopold that became a monument to all that was corrupt and cruel in imperialism.

While Stanley was laboring on behalf of King Leopold to the south of the Congo River, Pierre de Brazza was engaged in a similar venture for the French government to the north. The British observed this sudden activity with growing alarm and responded by increasing British explorations in the Niger basin and by signing a treaty in 1884 with Portugal which recognized Portuguese claims to the Congo region in preference to those of the French and Belgians. Meanwhile in North Africa, the French occupied Tunis in 1881, while the British became the dominant power in Egypt the following year.

To complicate matters further, the German chancellor Otto von Bismarck decided to take a hand in the game. He had been strongly opposed to the acquisition of colonies as being detrimental to Germany's role as arbiter of Europe. In 1884, however, partly because of domestic pressure and partly because of a desire for increased bargaining leverage, Bismarck determined to join in the scramble. The first German station in Africa was established by Karl Lüderitz at Angra Pequena in South-West Africa. Both the British and Cape governments reacted slowly, and in June 1884 Bismarck was consequently able to place all of South-West Africa (except Walvis Bay which had already been annexed by Britain) under German protection.

The Liberals, who were at that time in power in Britain, were at best reluctant imperialists, but they were slowly being goaded into a more active policy by the unwelcome activity in Africa of other nations. The antipathy of Lord Granville, the colonial secretary, however, was directed not against the Germans in South-West Africa, but against the French in West Africa, and accordingly he determined to exclude the French from the whole Niger territory. But when a British expedition arrived on the scene, it was met not by the French, but by a German force on a similar errand. The result was that the Germans established themselves in the Cameroons and Togoland, while the British acquired the southern Niger country—the Oil Rivers district—the very name of which, one prominent British anti-imperialist claimed, made him feel sick.

The growing international tension aroused by imperial rivalries, especially in the Congo basin, afforded Bismarck an excuse to convene an international conference at Berlin on the affairs of Central Africa. The conference met between November 1884 and February 1885, and the chief participants were the three major protagonists and Portugal, although 14 nations in all attended. What emerged from the proceedings was the Berlin Act. All annexations already effected were recognized. Free trade was prescribed for the Congo basin, and navigation rules were drawn up for the great rivers of Africa. Chiefly, the act created a code of conduct for those engaged in empire building on the African continent. The right of establishing a "sphere of influence" was recognized, and actual occupation, the act said, had to be "effective" to be legal. Any power assuming a protectorate was obliged to issue an official notification to this effect.

The British were the first to take advantage of the new rules. They presented to the conference evidence that the British government had negotiated treaties with the chiefs of the Niger basin and that henceforth the Niger was a British sphere within the terms stipulated by the conference. To solidify the British position, Sir George Goldie, the chairman of the National African Company, had bought out the only French company trading on the lower Niger, leaving the conference no choice but to invite Great Britain to enforce the Berlin Act on the Niger and its branches "so far as they are or will be under her sovereignty and protection." In June 1885 the British government proclaimed a protectorate over all the territory from Lagos in the west to the Cameroons in the east, and in the following year Goldie's organization, now renamed the Royal Niger Company, received a charter to administer Nigeria, which it did until January 1, 1900, when Nigeria reverted to the British Crown.

It has been estimated that 45 distinct exploring missions were roaming East, West, and Central Africa in the year following the Berlin Conference. The spectacle was not always an elevating one. In Buganda, Catholic and Protestant missionaries fought a civil war to win the territory for their versions of Christianity; the basis of the German position in East Africa was the work of three deck passengers, disguised as mechanics, who had debarked from their ship at Zanzibar in November 1884. Their leader was Dr. Karl Peters, president of the German Colonial Society, and the party was equipped with German flags and blank treaty forms which they cajoled the complaisant and naïve chiefs of East Africa into signing. Peters did not divulge the results of his mission until he had returned to Berlin, whereupon the German government proclaimed a protectorate in East Africa over what became Tanganyika (now Tanzania).

Anglo-German rivalry in East Africa was resolved by conventions concluded in 1886 and 1890. Under the provisions of these treaties, German East Africa was acknowledged to be a German colony, while a British sphere of influence in Uganda, and from there northwards to Egypt, eastwards to Somaliland, and westward to the Congo, including the watershed between the Congo and Nile rivers, was recognized by Germany.

Anglo-French rivalry was not so easily settled. A limited agreement was concluded in 1890, under the provisions of which France recognized the proclamation of a British protectorate over Zanzibar in return for a British recognition of a French protectorate over Madagascar and French influence over the western Sahara, down to Lake Chad and the British positions in Nigeria.

In 1898 this agreement was expanded and the whole Anglo-French frontier in Africa from Lake Chad to Senegal was delimited on the map. But the French still harbored resentment at the British seizure of control in Egypt and still dreamed of planting the tricolor on the banks of the Nile. The incident at Fashoda was to end the dream and to precipitate a final settlement between France and Britain in Africa. In March 1899 the two powers agreed that the watershed between the Nile and the Congo would separate their spheres of influence. Thus, neither country was to see the fulfillment of its imperial dreams in Africa at this time. The French attempt to drive a wedge across Africa from the South Atlantic to the Red Sea failed, and the British vision of an "all-red route" from the Cape to Cairo had to await the absorption of German East Africa after World War I to become a reality—but by this time the bloom was already off the imperial rose.

The last quarter of the nineteenth century, when the nations of Europe struggled to establish themselves in Africa, witnessed the greatest efflorescence of imperialist activity in the history of modern Europe. Britain, France, Germany, Portugal, Belgium, Italy, and Spain divided the great continent between them, leaving only the ancient kingdom of Ethiopia and the new republic of Liberia their independence. Perhaps nothing symbolizes better the degree to which the romance of imperialism gripped the minds of the statesmen of Europe than Marchand and his party doggedly laboring for almost two years through the jungles of Africa towards Fashoda.

10

From Empire to Commonwealth

On June 24, 1872, the leader of the Conservative party, Benjamin Disraeli, rose to his feet in London's great Crystal Palace and attacked the anti-imperial bias of Gladstone's Liberal party. He summoned his listeners to reject the Liberals' philosophy and to take pride in an Empire "which may become the source of incalculable strength to this land." Though he was no enemy of self-government for colonies of white settlement, Disraeli was convinced that

> when it was conceded, [it] ought to have been conceded as part of a great policy of Imperial consolidation. It ought to have been accompanied by an Imperial tariff, by securities for the people of England for the enjoyment of the unappropriated lands which belonged to the Sovereign as their trustee, and by a military code which should have precisely defined the means and responsibilities by which the Colonies should be defended, and by which, if necessary, this country should call for aid from the Colonies themselves. It ought, further, to have been accompanied by the institution of some representative council in the metropolis, which would have brought the Colonies into constant and continuous relations with the Home Government. All this, however, was omitted because those who advised that policy—and I believe their convictions were sincere—looked upon the Colonies of England, looked upon our connection with India, as a burden upon this country; viewing everything in a financial aspect, and totally passing by those moral and political considerations which make nations great, and by the influence of which alone men are distinguished from animals.

Disraeli concluded on a note of stentorian challenge:

> Will [you] be content to be a comfortable England, modelled and moulded upon Continental principles and meeting in due course an inevitable fate, or . . . will [you] be a great country, an Imperial country, a country where your sons, when they rise, rise to paramount positions, and obtain not merely the esteem of their countrymen, but the respect of the world?

Late Victorian England was not deaf to Disraeli's words; and the new nostalgia for empire reversed the attitude of the preceding decades and foreshadowed attempts once more to tighten the bonds between Britain and her colonies. But it was going to be difficult to convince colonial statesmen of the advantages of closer association with the mother country, even though the emotional attachment felt by the colonists towards Britain had, if anything, increased in recent years and was perhaps greater than converse feelings in Britain itself. Rather than favoring increased intimacy, the colonies were becoming ever more restive members of an Empire which, in their eyes, thwarted the growth of a conscious nationalism in the colonies, and loyalty to which implied dependence on the British Parliament.

In theory, despite the granting of responsible government, the British government maintained very real powers over legislation in the dominions.[1] The governor general was the Crown's representative in the dominions, and through him the British government made pronouncements on matters outside the competence of the dominion governments. A "triple veto" over the acts of the dominion parliaments existed. The governor general might refuse his assent to a bill passed by both houses of a dominion parliament; he might reserve it for "the signification of His Majesty's pleasure"; or the king, on the advice of his ministers in London, might disallow a piece of dominion legislation within a year of its passage. Over and beyond this, the imperial Parliament in Westminster possessed supreme power under the provisions of the Colonial Laws Validity Act of 1865, which provided for the invalidation of dominion legislation when it conflicted with an act of the imperial Parliament. Also, dominion constitutional rights were established through acts of the imperial Parliament, and the organ that had the power to create also had the power to destroy.

In most areas, these restrictions were never implemented, and what

[1] Hereafter, those areas of white settlement which had received responsible government in the nineteenth century will be referred to as dominions.

influence the Colonial Office brought to bear (which was considerable at times) was achieved through more informal means, such as conversations between the governor general and his ministers. Over the years an imperial common law developed, and as a result what seemed constitutionally possible was made impossible by custom and convention. Sir Robert Borden, the prime minister of Canada in 1917, accurately described the situation:

> It is observed that constitutional writers draw a distinction between legal powers and constitutional right. The British parliament has technically the legal power to repeal the British North America Act—taking our Dominion as an illustration. But there is no constitutional right to do so without our assent, and therefore, while there is the theory of predominance, there is not the constitutional right of predominance in practice, even at present.

The dominions, nevertheless, felt a very real sense of subservience; and the problem that the British government faced was how to bring the Empire closer together and at the same time alleviate the dominions' sense of frustration and inferiority. Fortunately, the British have never been doctrinaire politically. They have characteristically been pragmatic; consequently, it was possible for the Empire to change in form and substance without the development of intolerable stresses.

In 1887, as part of the ceremonies connected with Queen Victoria's Golden Jubilee, the British government invited 121 delegates from the dominions and Crown colonies to a meeting in London. This was the first of the Colonial Conferences, and the survival and changing nature of the Empire was largely due to the development of the Colonial Conference as an institution. After the opening meeting of the first conference, the sessions were attended only by representatives of Great Britain and the dominions, a pattern that obtained for all subsequent conferences. As a symptom of further change, it was decided in 1907 that future conferences would be called "Imperial Conferences," the first of which met in 1911. These periodic meetings, if not entirely between equals, at least tended in this direction. Each government had one vote, and the discussions usually centered on imperial defense, economic policy (including the important and, to the dominions, lucrative area of home subsidization of steamship lines, telegraph networks, and so forth), foreign affairs, and the constitution of the Empire.

From the first, ideas of imperial federation were mooted, but despite some enthusiastic support, schemes for such close association between the various members of the Empire never received much backing. In fact, at the initial conference, the colonial secretary discouraged discussion of "subjects falling within the range of what is known as Political Federation." The idea of imperial federation was not, however, to die easily, and it foundered finally, over a quarter of a century later, only because neither the dominions (with the exception of New Zealand) nor, for that matter, Great Britain itself were willing to surrender the necessary amount of individual sovereignty and because it was difficult to determine the role which vast dependencies such as India would play in any future federal structure.

Nor did much ever come of proposals for a system of preferential tariffs within the Empire. Britain remained opposed to tariffs until well after World War I, and by the 1930s, when the matter was seriously considered, the dominions had gone too far down the path towards complete independence for anything substantive to be achieved. The British government from 1887 on did encourage the development of a common defense organization for the whole Empire. But efforts in this direction were to fail for virtually the same reasons that imperial federation failed—dominion nationalism. Australia, for instance, preferred establishing its own navy to contributing to a genuinely imperial one.

Foreign policy and the imperial constitution, then, were the two chief concerns of Imperial Conferences. In matters concerning a particular dominion and not the Empire as a whole, the dominions were increasingly disputing the right of the British government to conduct their foreign affairs. Canada, as usual, was the leader in fomenting a change in the existing situation. In 1871 there had been only one Canadian among the five representatives appointed by the British government to discuss the various problems with the United States that were later settled by the Treaty of Washington; by 1897, on the joint commission appointed to settle some outstanding controversies between the two countries, there were four Canadians and one Englishman. In the Alaskan boundary arbitration with the United States in 1903, there were two Canadians, one Briton, and three Americans—and the vote of the one British representative was sufficient to decide the issue in favor of the United States. In consequence, Canadian resentment at British control of Canada's foreign policy reached a new peak, and the prime minister, Sir Wilfrid Laurier, remarked: "The difficulty as I conceive it to be, is that so long as Canada remains a dependency of the British Crown, the present powers we have are not sufficient for the maintenance of our rights." As a result of this feeling, Canada in 1907 sent representatives to Japan to discuss the treatment of Japanese nationals in Canada, with only a passing nod to the British government. On the permanent international joint commission, created in 1909 by an Anglo-American treaty, three Canadian delegates met on equal terms with three American delegates, no representatives of the British government being present.

Despite the Canadian precedent, the other dominions did not immediately follow her example, and even Canada did not establish any separate diplomatic missions for many years. On the whole, foreign policy, and especially the highest levels of foreign policy—that is, the resolution of those issues affecting the Empire as a whole—remained the exclusive preserve of the British government. It was an authority, Asquith stated to the conference of 1911, "that . . . cannot be shared." And in this view, the dominions were on the whole willing to acquiesce. They felt that if they were not consulted, they were also not responsible or likely to become involved—an impression that turned out to be quite erroneous, for it did not prevent them all from becoming embroiled in World War I.

The war was to break the dominions' complacent view that nonintervention in the formulation of imperial foreign policy implied nonresponsibility. In 1917, when the British prime minister invited the dominion prime ministers to join the five principal members of the British Cabinet in an Imperial War Cabinet, the suggestion was welcomed. This step involved no constitutional innovation but demonstrated again the flexibility of the imperial union. As W. K. Hancock states in the first volume of his invaluable *Survey of British Commonwealth Affairs* (1937), the Imperial War Cabinet was indicative "of the new principle of empire, the principle of liberty growing into equality and proving itself willing, under trial, to accept so much unity as was necessary to defend its basic values."

The role played by the dominions in the war effort, and for that matter by India as well, presaged a further recasting of the imperial framework. The dominions' contributions to the Allied cause were a sign that they had come of age as national entities in their own right. The imperial structure would have to be made to reflect the new conditions. As one example of this developing turn of events, India, which did not possess self-government, was admitted to membership in the Imperial Conference at the 1917 meeting, which recognized that a constitutional readjustment would have to follow the war. The dominions were no longer willing to leave the determination of imperial foreign policy exclusively to the British government. As a resolution of the conference stated, it would be necessary to devise "effective arrangements for continuous consultation in all important matters of common imperial concern, and for such necessary concerted action, founded on consultation, as the several governments may determine."

The British government was most receptive to the dominions' aspirations. At the close of the war, the Imperial War Cabinet moved to Paris, changing itself into the British Empire Delegation. The dominions and India participated fully with the other former combatants in the proceedings of the Peace Conference. They were members of important committees and by means of a panel system sat in turn as delegates to plenary sessions of the conference. This status was not achieved without difficulty, as the other nations were puzzled by the claim that the dominions were on the one hand independent nations and on the other hand constituent parts of another international entity —the British Empire. When it came time to sign the peace treaties, the United Kingdom delegation signed for itself and for the entire British Empire (which was not specifically mentioned), and the dominion representatives signed on behalf of their governments.

The Covenant of the League of Nations provided for a similar compromise. In the Assembly, the dominion delegates voted as separate nations, while in the Council it was the British Empire as a whole which held the permanent seat. There was some feeling that the dominions could also sit as nonpermanent members of the Council, but this matter was never put to the test.

After the war, it was again Canada that led the way in claiming the prerogatives of independent nationhood for the dominions. In 1919 the Canadian government successfully asserted the right of the Canadian parliament to ratify the peace treaties on behalf of Canada, and Canada was the first dominion to demand independent diplomatic representation in a foreign capital. On May 10, 1920, it was announced in the British and Canadian parliaments that in the future the monarch, with the advice of his Canadian ministers, would appoint a minister plenipotentiary to Washington to have exclusive control over matters dealing with Canada. Furthermore and significant of the continuing imperial connection, the Canadian minister was, in the absence of the British ambassador, to have full charge of imperial as well as Canadian affairs. The actual appointment of a Canadian minister was not made, however, until 1927, as both the Canadian government and the British Foreign Office were dubious about the implications of the second half of the arrangement.

Where Canada led, the Union of South Africa was not far behind. With its proud self-conscious Afrikaner community and the still fresh memory of the bitter Anglo-Boer War, many South Africans were concerned with the question of secession from this new Empire of autonomous nations. One political faction, led by General J.B.M. Hertzog, said South Africa had the right to secede, while the other, under the leadership of General Jan Smuts, felt it did not. Smuts stated that the legislative power of the Union was vested in its parliament, which was made up of the Assembly, the Senate, and the monarch. It was impossible for one of these parts to separate itself from the others, and the king would have no choice but to veto any law under which the Union might leave the Empire. When Andrew Bonar Law, Conservative leader of the House of Commons and future prime minister, stated in 1920 that the British government would not interfere with any dominion wishing to secede, General Smuts claimed that stipulations contained in the South African constitution itself made secession impossible:

> For secession means not only secession from the British Empire, it means also secession of Dutch-speaking from English-speaking South Africans, who made together a solemn pact at the Union. It means secession of one province of the Union from another and the break-up of the Union, which is the noblest legacy of our great statesmen, the consecration of all the sacrifices of the past. It means the secession of the natives, whose devotion to the British connexion is historical. It means the complete isolation of Dutch-speaking Africa, and in that isolation its stranglement and decay. It means the blasting of all the great hopes which have sustained our people in the past. It means that a civilised South Africa becomes a dream, and that the white people of this country has decided to commit political suicide.

As it turned out, General Hertzog and his Nationalist party were really more interested in the theoretical right to secede than in secession itself. Thus the whole debate had a rather arid, academic air to it. Not so the controversy over the South African flag: was it to remain the Union Jack or should it be a symbol more reminiscent of republican days? This seemingly petty matter aroused the deep emotional fervor implicit in the Anglo-Dutch rivalry and was to persist for many years before it was decided that both the Union Jack, to symbolize the imperial connection, and a distinctive South African flag were to be official.

The Imperial Conference to which the representatives of the dominions and India made their way in June 1921 was to have been the all-important assemblage to discuss constitutional changes—but such was not the case. It devoted itself rather to matters of imperial foreign policy, such as the allied occupation of the Ruhr, Egypt, and particularly Japan and the Pacific, for the 1921 conference blended into the Washington Naval Conference of that same year. The Washington conference brought the dominions face to face with the fact that while the British government recognized their growth into national maturity, the world as a whole felt they were merely constituent parts of the British Empire. The United States did not invite representatives from the dominions to the Washington conference. The British government responded by offering to associate with itself delegates from the dominions to form a British Empire delegation. South Africa's Smuts, however, was irate and demanded that the precedents established at Paris be followed. To this Prime Minister David Lloyd George was quite amenable, and he proposed that dominion representatives be empowered to sign on behalf of their governments any document emerging from the conference. He said the signature of every dominion would be necessary to commit the Empire as a whole. The American government fortunately tolerated this proposal, but the whole dilemma indicated that changes in imperial structure, although agreed to by Britain and the constituent parts of the Empire, did not necessarily gain acceptance by the rest of the world. Despite New Zealand's steadfast adherence to the standards of the earlier Empire, further constitutional developments would have to be effected to convince the world at large that a Commonwealth of independent nations, voluntarily cooperating in certain areas, professing similar ideals, and owing allegiance to a common ruler, had replaced the Empire of old.

Cracks were appearing in the old imperial structure with alarming speed. Ireland, particularly, preyed on the conscience of liberals both in Britain and the dominions. The continued suppression of the aspirations of Irish nationalists was not in keeping with the spirit that seemed to be guiding British policy towards the members of the imperial family. As a result, the British government was forced to conclude the Anglo-Irish treaty of 1921, at best a curious document. Under its terms, Ireland (with the exception of the six Protestant counties of Ulster) gained, as the Irish Free State, "the same constitutional status in the Community of Nations known as the British Empire as the Dominion of Canada, the Commonwealth of Australia, the Dominion of New Zealand, and the Union of South Africa. . . ." The trouble was that where the other dominions had achieved their status as a consequence of British acquiescence in their demands and were voluntary members of an Empire, the Irish had dominion status thrust upon them and found that it was short of what they desired. In their eyes, they had been forced into a community of which they wished to be no part and made to swear allegiance to a king whom they did not feel was theirs. To force a nation, through the threat of renewed war, into an organization whose very essence was voluntary participation was a grave mistake, especially as the right of secession was implied in the organization's very constitution. A curious and absurd ambivalence developed—the British insisting that the Irish Free State was part of the Empire, while the Irish government denied the existence of any imperial ties.

Several other events in the immediate postwar years convinced even the hardiest proponents of imperial solidarity that things had indeed changed. Lloyd George declared at the 1921 conference that the British Empire was "the most hopeful experiment in human organization which the world has yet seen." In the same year, he told the House of Commons that although there was in future to be a joint foreign policy for the British Empire,

> joint control means joint responsibility, and when the burden of Empire has become so vast it is well that we should have the shoulders of these young giants to help us along. It introduces a broader and calmer view into foreign policy. It restrains rash Ministers and will stimulate timorous ones. It widens the prospect.

This optimistic prognosis could not have been more wrong. In August 1922 the new Turkish leader, Mustapha Kemal (Ataturk), counterattacked the Greek forces that had fought their way into Turkey after the war and drove them into the sea. The triumph of the Turks brought them face to face with the Anglo-French positions at Chanak, in the neutral zone along the shores of the Bosporus and Dardanelles which were being patrolled by the troops of the two powers. When Kemal threatened Chanak, the French withdrew, leaving a single British infantry brigade to face the Turkish challenge. The British government determined to hold fast and cabled the dominions for support. New Zealand responded with alacrity, and within a short time 12,000 men had volunteered for duty in Turkey. The Australian government was also favorably inclined but was deterred from acting by the vehement criticism of the opposition and by the total lack of consultation that had preceded the British decision. The prime minister of Canada claimed that he had first read of the British appeal for Canadian troops in the newspapers. He and his South African counterpart demanded further information and claimed that it was the prerogative solely of their parliaments to commit their nations' armed forces. To them, there was indeed no joint responsibility when there was no evidence of joint control, and they harbored considerable doubts as to whether joint control was desirable in the first place.

When the Turkish peace treaty (which, among other things, settled the Chanak controversy) was concluded at Lausanne in 1923, the British government assumed that the dominions, despite their absence from the treaty table, would choose to accept the British position. It had again miscalculated; the dominions, led by Canada, refused to sign a treaty in the negotiation of which they had taken no part. They took note of the agreement, and finally all except Canada ratified it; but they felt that the treaty did not intimately concern them. On the other hand, when it became necessary to negotiate a treaty covering halibut fishing in the Pacific, the matter was settled in March 1923 by the Canadian and American governments without the British government taking part even though the treaty affected fishermen from other parts of the Empire.

The Imperial Conference of 1923 took cognizance of these further developments. It was recognized that the concept of joint control and joint responsibility was outmoded. The obvious alternative of separate controls and separate responsibility was adopted. No member of the Empire could by its actions commit any other members. But the dominions and Britain reminded themselves of those principles they held in common and of their responsibility to each other. They bound themselves to prior consultation on matters that might affect more than one part of the Empire.

The British government promptly forgot this new obligation in 1924 when it recognized the Soviet Union without first consulting with the dominions. In the following year, however, at Locarno, when the British government guaranteed the frontier between Germany and her neighbors to the west, the dominions were consulted, but they did not choose to associate themselves with this action. As a result, Article 9 of the treaty stated: "The present Treaty shall impose no obligation upon any of the British Dominions, or upon India, unless the Government of such Dominion, or of India, signifies its acceptance thereof." None ever did.

It was an Empire in considerable turmoil that prepared for the long-awaited constitutional conference that was to meet in London in 1926. The prophets of nationalism were in the ascendancy in most of the dominions—W. L. Mackenzie King in Canada, William Cosgrave in the Irish Free State, and General Hertzog in South Africa. Each of these men had reason to desire a change in the constitution of the Empire. General Hertzog was, of course, interested in the Union's right to secede from the Empire, and Cosgrave resented being forced to belong to a supposedly voluntary association. In the Canadian parliament of 1926, the Liberal government of Mackenzie King, which had been in power for five years, found itself in a precarious position, having lost its majority, and asked the governor general, Lord Byng, for a dissolution and new elections—a normal constitutional practice. Lord Byng refused to comply; so the Liberal government had to resign and was replaced by a Conservative government. This government was also unable to command a majority and had, in its turn, to ask for a dissolution, which the governor general this time proclaimed. In the ensuing election, the Liberals won a clear majority and returned to power determined to see that such a gross interference with Canadian constitutional practice never occurred again.

A further source of Canadian irritation concerned the Colonial Laws Validity Act of 1865. On the whole, this was a largely forgotten piece of legislation, but in 1926 the Privy Council in London invoked it and invalidated an old and hitherto unchallenged Canadian statute that forbade appeals to the judicial committee of the Privy Council in criminal cases. The basis for this decision was that the Canadian law abrogated a right conferred by an act of the imperial Parliament.

The British government had tried to keep pace with growing dominion demands for independent status within the existing framework of the Empire. In 1907 a separate Dominions Department had been established within the Colonial Office, and in 1925 the new post of secretary of state for the dominions was established. Still, there were too many matters of controversy to be resolved, and an entirely new approach was necessary.

The Imperial Conference of 1926 produced an instrument—the Balfour Report—that allowed the Empire to survive its crisis in the form of the British Commonwealth of Nations. The report was the work of a committee on interimperial relations headed by Lord Balfour, its chief author, and, as adopted by the Conference, was an imperial document ranking with the Durham Report. It provided for both diversity and unity within the Empire. The first two paragraphs of the section dealing with the status of Great Britain and the dominions in the summary of the proceedings of the 1926 Imperial Conference, contain the kernel of Balfour's work:

> The Committee are of the opinion that nothing could be gained by attempting to lay down a Constitution for the British Empire. Its widely scattered parts have very different characteristics, very different histories, and are at very different stages of evolution; while considered as a whole, it defies classification and bears no real resemblance to any other political organisation which now exists or has ever yet been tried.
>
> There is, however, one most important element in it which, from a strictly constitutional point of view, has now, as regards all vital matters, reached its full development—we refer to the group of self-governing communities composed of Great Britain and the Dominions. Their position and mutual relation may be readily defined. *They are autonomous Communities within the British Empire, equal in status, in no way subordinate one to another in any aspect of their domestic or external affairs, though united by a common allegiance to the Crown, and freely associated as members of the British Commonwealth of Nations.*

An Empire of dependent territories continued to exist, but the dominions were part of the British Commonwealth of Nations.

Several specific constitutional changes were also recommended by the conference. The Royal Titles Act should be altered to give the Irish Free State the same position, in respect to its wording, as the other dominions. The new equality of status that the dominions now enjoyed with Great Britain demanded a change in the functions of each governor general. He should in future hold "in all essential respects the same position in relation to the administration of public affairs as is held by His Majesty the King in Great Britain." The governor general was no longer to be considered the channel of communication between a dominion and the government of Great Britain when a dominion did not so wish it. The conference of 1930 added the stipulation that a governor general should be appointed by the king with the advice of his ministers in the dominion concerned. From these decisions emerged the institution of a high commissioner who would fulfill the same functions as an ambassador, only in a Commonwealth context.[2] In the area of legislation, the Imperial Confer-

[2] Not to be confused with the British ambassador to South Africa who still retains the title of British high commissioner in South Africa by virtue of his authority over the protectorates of Basutoland, Swaziland, and Bechuanaland.

ence of 1926 recommended that the dominion parliaments be declared completely sovereign. Whether appeals to the judicial committee of the Privy Council were to continue to be allowed, and under what circumstances, should be left, it was suggested, to the decision of each dominion.

The conferences of 1926 and 1930 did much to assuage the injured feelings of Hertzog and Mackenzie King. Hertzog, preoccupied with the right of secession, had felt a few months before the conference of 1926 that the necessary conditions for the preservation of the Empire as a commonwealth of free nations did not exist; however, he returned home convinced that they now did.

So far-reaching were the resolutions of the conferences of 1926 and 1930 that some of the recommendations had to be implemented by changes in British law. The Statute of Westminster, the instrument designed to effect the necessary alterations, was passed in 1931 and has been labeled as the "one great legal landmark in the history of the Commonwealth." Although it made no attempt to define either dominion status or the role of the Crown in the Commonwealth, it did try to enshrine the principle of a single indivisible Crown by stipulating that all the dominions would have to agree to any changes in the royal titles and in the succession to the throne. The Colonial Laws Validity Act was repealed, and the dominion parliaments were proclaimed sovereign and consequently empowered to repeal or amend "any existing or future act of the United Kingdom parliament . . . in so far as the same is part of the law of the dominion." The matter of appeals to the Privy Council was not mentioned in the statute, but each dominion now had the right and power to decide this issue as it saw fit. Neither was the conduct of foreign affairs, which was deemed sufficiently regulated by conventions concluded at the postwar Imperial Conferences, in any way discussed.

The Statute of Westminster included no innovations. It merely provided a legal basis for those resolutions of the Imperial Conferences of 1926 and 1930 which could not be effected by convention alone. If the Statute provided a constitution for the Commonwealth, it was in many ways a constitution of negatives, yet it is the only formal constitution the Commonwealth has. All that remained after the passage of the Statute of Westminster to hold the Commonwealth together, other than sentiment, was the Crown, which in theory was common and indivisible.

Because of a number of internal constitutional problems and

varying views of the Commonwealth connection, not all the dominion governments immediately ratified the Statute of Westminster in its entirety. Australia and New Zealand were markedly unenthusiastic about the Statute, but South Africa took full advantage of the powers conferred by it. The Irish Free State saw the Statute of Westminster as a means of declaring its complete independence from Great Britain. Where the British had formally denied that the treaty of 1921 was an international instrument, they reversed their position after 1931 in order to preserve certain concessions, such as the continued operation of naval bases in Irish ports, which the treaty had guaranteed them. The question of the Irish treaty as opposed to the Statute of Westminster placed the British government in an inherently contradictory and invidious position which was never resolved as the Free State slipped slowly into *de facto* independence.

The conventions agreed upon at the Imperial Conferences of 1926 and 1930 and the Statute of Westminster, it was assumed, completed the transformation of the Empire into a Commonwealth. But again, as was so often true in imperial history when no further developments were anticipated, this was not the case. First to come under attack was the concept of the common indivisible Crown. This time it was South Africa that set the precedent for change by deleting the words "of the United Kingdom of Great Britain and Ireland" from the oath of allegiance to be taken to the Crown, thus making it eminently clear that South Africa recognized the monarch solely in his (or her) capacity as king (or queen) of South Africa. This interpretation was similar to Canada's and became the prevailing attitude of the dominion governments towards the Crown.

The conferences of 1926 and 1930 set the pattern for relations in a Commonwealth limited to the original colonies of white settlement. But no provision was made for the Dependent Empire, and the rapid progress of the British possessions in Africa and Asia towards independence after World War II required a further adjustment in the constitution of the Commonwealth. Today the Dependent Empire has all but disappeared. What has, as a consequence, happened to the Commonwealth?

In 1947 and 1948 India, Pakistan, Ceylon, and Burma became the first British possessions to achieve independence after the war, with only Burma withdrawing from the Commonwealth. For the first time, nations with nonwhite populations and essentially non-British traditions joined the dominions in what soon became the "Commonwealth of Nations," rather than the "British Commonwealth of Nations." From 1957 on, most of the former British colonies, trust territories, and protectorates in Africa have joined the community. So have other British possessions around the world.

In mid-1965, the Commonwealth of Nations, in addition to Britain, comprised the following states (former names are in parentheses):

Commonwealth Members in Order of Their Independence

1. Canada
2. Australia
3. New Zealand
4. India
5. Pakistan
6. Ceylon
7. Ghana (Gold Coast)
8. Malaysia (Malay States, Singapore,[3] Sabah, and Sarawak)
9. Nigeria
10. Cyprus
11. Sierra Leone
12. Tanzania (Tanganyika and Zanzibar)
13. Jamaica
14. Trinidad and Tobago
15. Uganda
16. Kenya
17. Malawi (Nyasaland)
18. Malta
19. Zambia (Northern Rhodesia)
20. The Gambia

Is this new Commonwealth really a viable organization? There have been occasional attempts at policy coordination in certain spheres, some semblance of preferential trade agreements between Commonwealth members remains, and until recently the British government, if not the other members of the Commonwealth, maintained a belief in a Commonwealth citizenship which allowed the citizens of all Commonwealth countries to enter Britain freely and to assume all the rights of Englishmen.[4] Commonwealth-wide scholarship programs and sports agreements do also exist, and member states have often relied on British military and financial support in times of crisis. But these entries on the positive side of the ledger are outweighed by a tradition that forbade the discussion of intra-Commonwealth disputes (conflicts between members) and the internal affairs of any Commonwealth member, not only at the Colonial and Imperial Conferences, but at the post-1930 Commonwealth Conferences as well. If this custom was

[3] In August 1965 Singapore was "ejected" from Malaysia and became an independent state within the Commonwealth.

[4] The Commonwealth Immigrant Act of 1962 for the first time limited the ingress of Commonwealth citizens into Britain. In 1965 the Labor government published a white paper on immigration preparatory to the implementation of further controls.

unfortunate before World War II, it became more serious after 1946. The prewar Commonwealth was at least fairly homogeneous. The same cannot be said for the present one. Today the Afro-Asian members of the Commonwealth far outnumber the original constituents, and with this increase in heterogeneity, greater attention to the more serious and volatile questions of the day would be most useful. Tradition has, however, thus far triumphed. The discussions at the Commonwealth Prime Ministers' Conferences have usually been polite but substanceless, although useful meetings of subordinate officials have from time to time been held. Vital intra-Commonwealth issues—the Kashmir dispute between India and Pakistan, for example—have received, at best, only passing attention. When the 1964 Commonwealth Prime Ministers' Conference "noted with satisfaction the friendly public statements by the President of Pakistan and the Prime Minister of India and expressed [its] hopes that the problems between countries will be solved in the same friendly spirit," several members of the Indian legislature urged India's withdrawal from the Commonwealth as they resented the reference to the Indo-Pakistan disputes in this final communique issued by the Conference.

Virtually the only time that a question of major consequence was debated—the racial policies of the Union of South Africa, at the 1961 conference—it resulted in South Africa leaving the Commonwealth.

Can the Commonwealth survive in its new pattern? Members now belong to extra-Commonwealth defense organizations such as the Southeast Asia Treaty Organization (SEATO) and the Central Treaty Organization (CENTO). No semblance of a common foreign policy exists, and the former ideal of consultation before major international decisions is largely a dead letter. Even the Crown no longer stands as a unifying symbol in the same sense. An increasing number of Commonwealth states have become republics; Malaysia is a separate monarchy with an elected Malayan sovereign. Thus the British monarch no longer maintains an individual relationship with each member of the Commonwealth and is recognized only as the head of the Commonwealth by those Commonwealth nations no longer owing allegiance to the British Crown.

Can the Commonwealth now present a united front in a major crisis? Not even the former unity of sentiment and tradition continues to exist. For is it not natural for African members of the Commonwealth to have more in common with other African states than with their non-African confreres in the Commonwealth—especially as some of the Commonwealth nations have immigration laws barring or inhibiting the entry of Africans and Asians? What effect will the replacement of the present generation of British-trained and British-oriented administrators in Africa and Asia by domestically educated ones have? Will the African, Asian, and other non-European member states continue to find it useful to belong to the Commonwealth? The British attitude towards the Indo-Pakistan confrontation of autumn 1965 again roused strong demands in India for the breaking of all ties with the Commonwealth,[5] and Tanzania in September 1965 threatened to quit the organization, as did the other African Commonwealth states some three months later, should the British settlement of the Rhodesian imbroglio (see Chapter 13) not be to its satisfaction. Does the Commonwealth in fact have any substance, or is it merely a rope of sand?

The future is always hard to predict, but unless these questions can be satisfactorily answered, the days of the present Commonwealth would appear to be numbered. All that has ever really held the Commonwealth together is an emotion—a desire to belong based on a common heritage and similar traditions. This feeling is naturally most prevalent among the three original dominion members of the Commonwealth. As the memory of the British connection becomes more remote, the African and Asian Commonwealth states may prefer to cut the final link with a past not entirely savory.

Should the Commonwealth, however, return to its original membership, or survive only as a chapter in tomorrow's history books, the evolution of an Empire into a Commonwealth and finally into a multinational and multiracial community will always stand as a monument to British political pragmatism and the peaceful fulfillment of national aspirations.

[5] The week of October 3, 1965, was proclaimed "Quit the Commonwealth Week" by several dissident groups, and Prime Minister Lal Bahadur Shastri, Nehru's successor, himself accused Britain of "demolishing [India's] good will and friendship."

11

The Amritsar Massacre and the Rise of the New Indian Nationalism

In the last chapter we left India independent and a free, voluntary member of the Commonwealth. This status was not, however, achieved with ease, and it is necessary now to turn back the clock half a century to investigate the course of events. The promises set forth in Queen Victoria's post-Mutiny proclamation of 1858 had been only partially fulfilled when World War I broke out in Europe in 1914. The great subcontinent participated fully in the conflict, and the signing of the armistice in November 1918 brought a sigh of relief not only to Europe and America but to India as well.

Over a million Indian troops had fought side by side with those from other parts of the British Empire, in France, Flanders, Macedonia, Egypt, Palestine, Mesopotamia, and East Africa. India had raised three war loans and had contributed £100,000,000 to the cost of the war. Enthusiasm for and loyalty to the Empire were remarkably high. Even Gandhi believed sufficiently in the beneficence of the imperial philosophy to recruit for the Indian army. "If the Empire perishes," he said, "with it perish our cherished aspirations."

It was anticipated that India would be rewarded by the grant of responsible government, and as early as August 1917 the imperial government had declared that the attainment of responsible government by successive stages was its goal for India. The viceroy[1] and the secretary of state for India even toured India to determine how the scheme could best be implemented. Certainly there were clouds on the horizon. The overt and coercive measures used at times to raise both troops and money aroused a good deal of dissatisfaction, as did a dramatic rise in prices. Travel and import restrictions caused inconvenience, and the provisions of the Defense of India Act and the Press Act greatly encroached on personal liberty. Indians were, however, willing and eager to forget all past hardships in view of the enlightened political system that was about to emerge.

The new order of things so confidently expected did not materialize. The monsoon of 1918 failed, and there was widespread famine in the country. That, plus epidemics of influenza and other diseases, cost about 5 million lives. A new, more stringent income tax law worried the business community. But the worst blow of all was the publication in January 1919 of the draft of what became known as the Rowlatt Acts. In essence, this piece of legislation was to extend the special powers of the executive as stipulated by the Defense of India Act. It resulted from the report of the Rowlatt Committee appointed to investigate "revolutionary crime" in India. The committee found that there was considerable danger from anti-British agitation, and during 1914–1915 a number of serious disturbances had, indeed, taken place in the Punjab.[2] Most of the population, however, remained aloof from these activities. In fact, Sir Michael O'Dwyer, the lieutenant governor of the Punjab, in a speech to the Indian Legislative Council, had stated:

[The Honorable] members are doubtless familiar with the serious dangers which menaced the security of the province during the first two years of the War, the *Ghadr* conspiracy and other weak and covert movements, engineered by the King's enemies within or without India, with the object of subverting the Government, but, perhaps they are less familiar with the action, the prompt, vigorous and decisive action taken by the people of the Punjab, Muhammadans, Sikhs, and Hindus, to range themselves on the side of the law and order and to stamp out sedition and anarchy. There was no hesitation, no sitting on the fence, no mawkish sympathy with red-handed crime, no insincere apology for so-called misguided youths pursuing noble ideas, no subtle distinction between evolutionary and revolutionary patriotism.

O'Dwyer later added that "since the war began, the people of the province, so far from doing anything to embarrass the Government,

[1] The title "viceroy" was added to that of governor general in 1858.
[2] See map of India on p. 3, Chapter 1.

have rallied enthusiastically to its support." Furthermore, the Punjab government reported, the province "made a response unequalled by any other part of India to the appeal for recruits and subscribed so freely to the War Loans that the province ranked third in the list of contributors."

Yet it was at the Punjab that the Rowlatt legislation was chiefly aimed. Rowlatt Bill No. 1 stipulated, among other things, that it would be punishable by imprisonment for up to two years, or by fine, or by both, for anyone to have in his possession any seditious document, intending that the same should be published or circulated, unless he could prove that he had such a document in his possession for a lawful purpose. A seditious document was broadly defined as one which instigated, or was likely to instigate, the use of criminal force against the king, the government, or a public servant or servants. Rowlatt Bill No. 2 provided that persons could be tried by courts permitted to sit *in camera*. No appeal was to be allowed from the judgment of these tribunals, which were to consist of three persons who would hear cases without the benefit of juries or preliminary hearings. The executive was also empowered to deal with persons suspected of complicity in "anarchical or revolutionary movement" in various ways. They might be asked to execute a bond not to commit certain offenses prescribed in the act, be ordered to live only in a specific area, or to report themselves periodically to the police. Such orders would be in effect for a year and were then renewable. The act also allowed the executive to arrest and search without warrant and to confine persons so arrested, without trial, for renewable periods of a year.

To be sure, the various parts of the act did not come into operation automatically; the governor general in council had to be convinced that "in the whole or any part of British India anarchical or revolutionary movements are being promoted" before they could be put into effect. Alleged offenders were also to be protected by the investigation that was to precede any prosecution. But the investigation was again to be conducted *in camera*, and the accused might have no legal aid: "Any fact the communication of which might endanger the public safety, or the safety of an individual," would be withheld from him, and the investigating authority was not to be bound by the rules of evidence.

The outcry in India against the proposed Rowlatt Acts was immediate and universal. To make matters worse, it became known that the political reforms the British government contemplated were to fall far short of even the most modest Indian demands. Nothing approaching responsible government at the national level was to be allowed for a nation whose representatives were, as equals, deciding the fate of Europe at the conference tables of Versailles. It was under these circumstances that Gandhi and the philosophy of *satyagraha* (nonviolent resistance) first gained public notice.

Gandhi had, of course, developed the principles of *satyagraha* during his battle for Indian rights in South Africa (see Chapter 8). He explained it thus:

> The law-breaker breaks the law surreptitiously and tries to avoid the penalty; not so the civil resister. He ever obeys the laws of the State to which he belongs, not out of fear of the sanctions, but because he considers them to be good for the welfare of society. But there are some occasions, generally rare, when he considers certain laws to be so unjust as to render obedience to them a dishonour. He then openly and civilly breaks them, and quietly suffers the penalty for their breach. And in order to register his protest against the action of the law-givers, it is open to him to withdraw his co-operation from the State by disobeying such other laws whose breach does not involve moral turpitude.

The imminent Rowlatt legislation forced Gandhi into action. On March 1, 1919, he formed the Satyagraha Sabha in Bombay, whose purpose it was civilly to disobey the Rowlatt Acts if passed and such other laws as a committee of the organization might from time to time name. The Sabha was very careful in the selection of its members, and all were required to take an oath:

> Being conscientiously of opinion that the Bills known as the Indian Criminal Law (Amendment) Bill No. 1 of 1919, and No. 2 of 1919 are unjust, subversive of the principles of liberty and justice and destructive of the elementary rights of individuals on which the safety of the community as a whole and the State itself is based, we solemnly affirm that, in the event of these Bills becoming law, we shall refuse civilly to obey these laws and such other laws as a committee, to be hereafter appointed, may think fit, and we further affirm that in the struggle we will faithfully follow truth, and *refrain from violence of life, person and property.*

Lord Chelmsford, the viceroy, and E. S. Montagu, the secretary of state for India, both duly approved the Rowlatt Acts, and so the civil resistance campaign went into effect. Because of the discretionary clauses in the Acts, it was decided initially to protest against the laws affecting the sale of proscribed literature and the Press Act. The movement was to be inaugurated on April 6 by demonstrations all over

India, in which the general public was invited to join. The heart of the demonstration was to be the *hartal*, or the closing of shops and cessation of work, accompanied by fasting and attendance at religious rites and public protest meetings.

On the whole, the protests were both remarkably peaceful and very widespread. But incidents of violence did occur. Due to some confusion as to the proper date, a *satyagraha* demonstration had started in Delhi, the capital of India since 1912, on March 30, a week before the intended date. The *hartal* was almost a complete success, inasmuch as nearly all Hindu and Muslim shops closed. The vendor of refreshments in the third-class waiting room in Delhi railway station refused to close, however, and the crowd attempted to seize him. As a result, the police arrested two men, and the assemblage became incensed. During the rest of the day mob violence flared and the police fired on the crowd twice—eight persons were killed and a dozen or so wounded. The next day, a large procession accompanied the funeral cortege of those who had been killed, but no violence occurred. On April 6 the main *satyagraha* campaign commenced and progressed calmly. But the situation was destined to change with the arrest of Gandhi on April 10, while on his way to the Punjab.

The state of tension was now increasing in the Punjab. It was the center of the Muslim *Khilafat* movement of protest against British actions towards Turkey and the deposition of the caliph there. Having supplied some 400,000 troops for the army, the province was war-weary and sentitive to such inconveniences as restrictions on transportation now that the war was over. Besides, the Punjab suffered severely from the new income tax regulations, increased assessments in many regions ranging between a hundred and two hundred percent. The stocks of numerous traders in wheat had been seized under the Defense of India Act to stop speculation, and censorship of the press had been practiced with great severity. On the same day as Gandhi's arrest, two highly respected local nationalist leaders, Dr. Satyapal and Dr. Kitchlew, were arrested in Amritsar.

Until this time, however, all had been peaceful in Amritsar, as a later government report indicated:

In the great majority of towns in the Punjab there had been a *hartal* on the 6th and no disorder had followed. The Lahore papers, while interested in maintaining general excitement, had quoted the general course of the demonstration on the 6th as reflecting credit both on the character of the crowds and Government.

But news of the arrest of Gandhi compounded already existing anger at the arrest of Satyapal and Kitchlew. Shops were closed, and crowds gathered in the streets to march on the house of the deputy commissioner. The majority and minority reports of the Hunter Committee, later appointed to investigate the events in the Punjab, disagree as to the temper of the crowd, but the fact remains that it was halted at the Hall Gate Bridge before it reached the deputy commissioner's bungalow. At this point the police fired two volleys and several people were killed. The crowd, now becoming a mob, retreated into the city. Five Europeans were murdered; the town hall, the telephone exchange, two banks, and the Indian Christian Church were destroyed. A woman missionary doctor, one Miss Sherwood, was attacked and left for dead.

The peace of the tomb now descended on the city. The government forbade all demonstrations, and the funerals of the victims of the Hall Gate Bridge incident were peacefully conducted on April 11. The commissioner of the division, meanwhile, thought the situation in Amritsar sufficiently serious to turn over control to the senior military officer, "to take such steps as the military situation demanded." This did not mean martial law, and the commissioner made it clear that it was a temporary expedient to facilitate the reestablishment of civil control. The deputy commissioner published the following notice:

> The troops have orders to restore order in Amritsar and to use all the force necessary. No gatherings of persons nor processions of any sort will be allowed. All gatherings will be fired on. Any persons leaving the city in groups of more than four will be fired on. Respectable persons should keep indoors.

All third-class bookings to Amritsar were cancelled, and on the evening of April 11 Brigadier-General Reginald E. H. Dyer, the commander of the Jullunder Brigade, arrived at Amritsar to take charge of the military situation. On the next morning, he marched around the town with a strong detachment of soldiers to impress the populace and had the following proclamation drawn up, although no proper steps appear to have been taken for its publication:

> The inhabitants of Amritsar are hereby warned that if they will cause damage to any property or will commit any acts of violence in the environs of Amritsar it will be taken for granted that such acts are due to incitement in Amritsar city, and offenders will be punished according to Military Law.

All meetings and gatherings are hereby prohibited, and will be dispersed at once under Military Law.

On the morning of April 13 Dyer, accompanied by the district magistrate and a column of troops, marched through the city and, to the beating of drums, had the following proclaimed in English and Urdu:

It is hereby proclaimed, to all whom it may concern, that no person residing in the city is permitted or allowed to leave the city in his own or hired conveyance, or on foot without a pass. No person residing in Amritsar city is permitted to leave his house after eight. Any persons found in the streets after eight are liable to be shot. No procession of any kind is permitted to parade the streets in the city, or any part of the city, or outside of it, at any time. Any such processions or any gathering of four men will be looked upon and treated as an unlawful assembly and dispersed by force of arms if necessary.

Still no martial law existed, and the signatories of the minority report of the Hunter Committee pointed out that there were many important sections of the city where the proclamation was not read at all. They estimated that the total number of people who heard the proclamation could not have exceeded 10,000 in a city of more than 160,000. Besides, it was the time of the annual *Baisakhi* and cattle fairs, and villagers were streaming into town who knew little of the situation. In evidence before the Hunter Committee, the deputy superintendent of police responded to questioning as follows:

Q. You thought that it was sufficient notice for a town like Amritsar to to give of an important proclamation?
A. I did not think anything. When it was too hot to walk in the city, I took the nearest route out.
Q. You did not suggest to the General that a longer time might be given?
A. No. When we got to the Majid *mandir* the General remarked that it was getting too hot for the troops, so I took the routé to Lahgar Gate.
Q. And then this proclamation was stopped?
A. Yes.

No attempt was made to post copies of the proclamation near the Jallianwala Bagh, a large vacant enclosure, closely surrounded by buildings, which was the most likely place for public meetings.

General Dyer returned to his quarters at 12:40 P.M. and was soon informed that a meeting was planned for the Jallianwala Bagh at 4:30 P.M. He promptly marched forth with a contingent of fifty Baluchis and Gurkhas armed with rifles, fifty more Gurkhas armed only with kukris (curved knives), and two armored cars bearing machine guns. He entered the Bagh by a narrow entrance (one of the very few), leaving the armored cars outside, as they were too wide to enter. He then deployed his men to the right and left of the entrance and without hesitation ordered them to fire into the massed crowd of about 20,000 people. Ten minutes and 1,650 rounds later, 379 dead bodies (of whom 87 were villagers) littered the area, while 1,208 more persons lay wounded on the ground. No attempt was made to aid those who still lived.

Sir Michael O'Dwyer and Dyer's commanding officer approved of his action. They based their attitude on the presence of an organized conspiracy against the British, which in fact never existed. O'Dwyer told the Hunter Committee: "I have no hesitation in saying that General Dyer's action that day was the decisive factor in crushing the rebellion, the seriousness of which is only now being realized."

As two prominent British historians of India have said, the Amritsar Massacre "formed a turning point in Indo-British relations almost as important as the Mutiny." They go on to say that its far-reaching significance lay not only in the large number of people slaughtered at Amritsar, but also in the rather disturbing assumption by high-ranking British officials that Indians were an inferior race and should be treated as such. One cannot imagine a similar incident occurring in a white colony. It is interesting to note that the Hunter Committee consisted of nine members—five British and four Indian—and that, although the entire Committee was highly critical of the actions of General Dyer, the five British members all signed the majority report, which tended to justify British actions in the Punjab, while it remained for the Indian members to sign the less approving minority report.

Nehru betrayed some of the bitterness felt by Indians when he described, in *Towards Freedom* (1941), a train journey he took from Amritsar to Delhi in 1919:

> The compartment I entered was almost full, and all the berths, except one upper one, were occupied by sleeping passengers. I took the vacant upper berth. In the morning I discovered that all my fellow passengers were military officers. They conversed with each other in loud voices which I could not help overhearing. One of them was holding forth in an aggressive and triumphant tone, and soon I discovered that he was Dyer, the hero of Jallianwala Bagh, who was describing his Amritsar experiences. He pointed out how he had the whole town at his mercy and he had felt like reducing the rebellious city to a heap of ashes, but he took pity on it and refrained. He was evidently coming back from Lahore after giving his

evidence before the Hunter Committee of Inquiry. I was greatly shocked to hear his conversation and to observe his callous manner. He descended at Delhi station in pyjamas with bright pink stripes, and a dressing gown.

But really to understand the Amritsar Massacre, it is necessary, at least casually, to scrutinize some of General Dyer's subsequent statements. In the report he made on August 25, 1919, to the General Staff of the 16th Division, he wrote:

I fired and continued to fire till the crowd dispersed, and I considered that this is the least amount of firing which would produce the necessary moral and widespread effect it was my duty to produce if I was to justify my action. If more troops had been at hand the casualties would have been greater in proportion. *It was no longer a question of merely dispersing a crowd,* but one of producing a sufficient moral effect, from a military point of view, not only on those who were present, but more specially throughout the Punjab. There could be no question of undue severity.

Dyer's evidence before the Hunter Committee is of even greater interest:

Q. When you heard of the contemplated meeting at 12:40 you made up your mind that if the meeting was going to be held you would go and fire?

A. When I heard that they were coming and collecting I did not at first believe that they were coming, but if they were coming to defy my authority and really to meet after all I had done that morning, I had made up my mind that I would fire immediately in order to save the military situation. If I had delayed longer, I was liable for court-martial.

Q. Supposing the passage was sufficient to allow the armoured cars to go in, would you have opened fire with the machine guns?

A. I think, probably, yes.

Q. In that case the casualties would have been much higher?

A. Yes.

Q. I gather generally from what you put in your report that your idea in taking this action was really to strike terror? That is what you say. It was no longer a question of dispersing the crowd, but one of producing a sufficient moral effect.

A. If they disobeyed my orders, it showed that there was complete defiance of the law, and there was something much more serious behind it than I imagined, that therefore these were rebels, and I must not treat them with gloves on. They had come to fight if they defied me, and I was going to give them a lesson.

Q. I take it that your idea in taking that action was to strike terror?

A. Call it what you like. I was going to punish them. My idea from the military point of view was to make a wide impression.

Dyer wanted to strike terror not only into Amritsar, but into the whole Punjab. "I wanted to reduce their *morale*; the *morale* of the rebels." When he was asked if he continued to fire on persons lying on the ground to save themselves, he replied:

I probably selected another target. There might have been firing on the people who were still lying down, though I think there were better targets than that.

Dyer was really not at all sure of the purpose of the meeting at the time that he opened fire, and he readily admitted that there were probably many people in the crowd who had never heard his proclamation. Yet on being asked whether it would thus not have been a proper measure to ask the crowd to disperse before actually firing, Dyer answered: "No: at the time it did not occur to me. I merely felt that my orders had not been obeyed, that martial law was flouted, and that it was my duty to immediately disperse it by rifle fire." The questioning continued:

Q. What reason had you to suppose that if you had ordered the assembly to leave the Bagh they would not have done so without the necessity of your firing, continued firing for a length of time?
A. Yes: I think it quite possible that I could have dispersed them perhaps even without fire.
Q. Why did you not adopt that course?
A. I could disperse them for some time, then they would all come back and laugh at me, and I considered I would be making myself a fool.
Q. Did this aspect of the matter strike you that by doing an act of that character you were doing a great disservice to the British Raj?
A. I thought it would be doing a jolly lot of good and they would realize that they were not to be wicked.

Did Dyer make any effort to help the wounded? "No, certainly not. It was not my job."

The Amritsar Massacre was not the end of a regrettable episode; it was in some ways only the beginning. On April 15, martial law was declared in Lahore and Amritsar, subsequently being extended to other areas of the Punjab. Its promulgation allowed the more imaginative British officers to exercise their whims. In Lahore, four representatives of every ward in the city had to be present at martial law headquarters from 8:00 A.M. to 5:00 P.M. to receive and convey any orders to their respective wards. A curfew was imposed, and cars, electric lights, and fans were commandeered from the Indian population. A Lieutenant-Colonel Johnson, the officer in charge,

> thought it desirable to bring home to them all—loyal and disloyal alike—some of the inconveniences of martial law in the hope and belief that in future the weight of their influence will be wholeheartedly thrown against seditious movements likely to lead to the introduction of martial law.

Cars belonging to Indians were given to Europeans "to teach [Indians] a lesson." It was made unlawful for two persons to walk abreast, and owners of property on which martial law notices were affixed were made responsible for their preservation. The property owners so selected were those "suspected to be not very loyal."

One of the martial law notices in Lahore was stuck on the wall of Sanatan Dharm College, from where it was subsequently torn. Colonel Johnson consequently ordered the students and professors of the college arrested and marched in the hot sun the three miles to the fort, where they were interned for 30 hours. When asked, "Do you think it a reasonable order to make?" the colonel replied, "Quite. I would do it again. It was one of the few brain-waves I had." When an anti-British poster was found on the wall of Dayal Singh College, Colonel Johnson determined upon even more drastic action against the students of seven of Lahore's colleges. Over a thousand students were forced to attend roll call four times a day, which involved walking a total distance of 16 miles in the sweltering heat. Some were arbitrarily expelled or had their stipends stopped. Colonel Johnson believed in punishing all for the guilt of some and in dealing harshly even with "suspected sedition."

In Amritsar, General Dyer was still in charge. On April 19, he decreed that Indians wishing to pass along the street where Miss Sherwood, the medical missionary, had been attacked, would have to crawl. Dyer explained:

> The order meant that the street should be regarded as holy ground, and that, to mark this fact, no one was to traverse it except in a manner in which a place of special sanctity might naturally in the East be traversed.

General Dyer erected a triangle for flogging in the street, and six prisoners accused of having assaulted Miss Sherwood were flogged there before the case had even been tried. Floggings were common throughout the martial law area, as were student and teacher roll calls. In many places Indians had to close their umbrellas, alight from their carriages or horses, and salaam, sometimes by touching their foreheads to the ground, when any European officer passed. At Sheikhupura the British civilian officer in charge wanted to erect a "repentance house" to allow Indians to do penance for their black deeds of April 1919.

There were, of course, some serious disorders, but even in these cases one cannot help but feel that the methods employed for dealing with them were inappropriate—promiscuous firings on unidentified groups of persons from armored cars and armored trains, bombings and machine-gunnings from planes. One of the pilots was questioned by the Hunter Committee:

Q. You fired machine guns into the village and threw bombs on those people who took shelter in the houses, but there were other innocent people in those houses?

A. I could not discriminate between innocent and other people who were, I think, doing damage or were going to do damage.

Q. What I mean, Captain, is this. When you threw the bombs on them they began to run away. Was not your object really accomplished?

A. No.

Q. What was the further need of machine-gunning and killing them? Your object was to disperse the crowds that had assembled and were attempting to proceed to Gujranwala. The throwing of bombs must have resulted in some casualties. Was there any further need of firing of machine guns?

A. Yes, to do more damage.

Q. But then the object seemed to be to hit or kill more people in that crowd, although they had begun to disperse and were running away after the bombs had been thrown at them?

A. I was trying to do this in their own interests. If I killed a few people, they would not gather and come to Gujranwala to do damage.

Q. Do I take it then, although by the first throwing of bombs they began to disperse and run away, you still machine-gunned them in order to prevent the possibility of their reassembling, the idea being to produce a sort of moral effect on them?

A. Yes. Quite right.

The progress of the crisis in the Punjab must have been a profound shock to many Indians. It proved to them that British attitudes had changed little since the Mutiny of 1857, and that whatever progressive legislation might say, in the eyes of most Englishmen the Indian was an inferior person. Queen Victoria's proclamation of 1858 appeared to be a sham.

General Dyer was at first promoted, and when disciplinary action was finally taken against him many months later, the beneficial effects of even this belated act of justice were vitiated by the raising of a large sum of money, by public subscription in India and England, and its presentation to General Dyer, along with a sword inscribed to the "Saviour of the Punjab." To make matters worse, the press, many members of the House of Commons, a large majority of the House of Lords, and even a prominent judge rallied to Dyer's defense. Clearly, a double standard of behavior still existed.

These postwar events also served to change the course of the Indian nationalist movement. As Philip Mason, a former British administrator in India, remarked: "The whole situation had changed. Government had been carried on with the consent—usually apathetic and halfhearted, but still consent—of the governed. That consent was now changed to active mistrust." Both wings of the Indian National Congress[3]—the Liberals who believed in change by constitutional means and the Activists who preached direct action—were to be swept aside by the disillusionment engendered by the Amritsar Massacre, the Rowlatt Acts, and the Government of India Act[4] which became law in December 1919. Into this vacuum stepped the enigmatic figure of Gandhi. At this time Gandhi was looked upon in India with a combination of respect for his actions in South Africa and contempt for his rather curious political methods. Nehru wrote of his first meeting with Gandhi in 1916: "All of us admired him for his herioc fight in South Africa, but he seemed very distant and different and unpolitical to many of us young men."

Gandhi chief assets were complete honesty and absolute moral

[3] The Indian National Congress, organized in 1885, was the core of the Indian independence movement. In its early years, all Indian nationalists, whether Hindu or Muslim, tended to belong. In time the Muslim League, which was founded in 1906, came to represent the separate and distinct interests of the Muslims of India, while the Congress, although claiming to be secular, was associated in the minds of most people, with Hindu India. Many prominent Muslims, however, continued to be members of the Congress. As Indians gained an ever increasing role in the administration of their country, the Indian National Congress and the Muslim League became the two chief political parties.

[4] The Government of India Act of 1919, popularly known as the Montagu-Chelmsford Act, did little to increase the role of Indians in government at the national level and limited itself to establishing "dyarchy," or the division of responsibility in the provinces. The less important aspects of provincial administration —the "transferred subjects"—were placed under the jurisdiction of ministers appointed by the governor from the elected Indian members of the provincial legislative council. The more vital functions of government—the "reserved subjects" —essentially remained in the hands of the governor.

impeccability. When the first *satyagraha* campaign was apparently progressing successfully in April 1919, Gandhi terminated it prematurely, appalled by the violence it engendered. In his *Autobiography: The Story of My Experiments with Truth* (1957) he even called his decision to start the demonstrations in the first place a "Himalayan" blunder:

> A satyagrahi obeys the laws of society intelligently and of his own free will, because he considers it to be his sacred duty to do so. It is only when a person has thus obeyed the laws of society scrupulously that he is in a position to judge as to which particular rules are good and just and which unjust and iniquitous. Only then does the right accrue to him of civil disobedience of certain laws in well-defined circumstances. My error lay in my failure to observe the necessary limitation. I had called on the people to launch upon civil disobedience before they had thus qualified themselves for it, and this mistake seemed to me of Himalayan magnitude.

Gandhi again confounded his followers by calling off a second campaign of noncooperation—the boycotting of all things British—this prompted by the Punjab crisis, because he felt that the Government of India Act was at least a step in the right direction. But the British did not choose to flesh out the bare bones of the Montagu-Chelmsford reforms as Gandhi anticipated, and he returned to civil disobedience. In February 1922 a limited experiment was launched at Bardoli near Bombay. Once more, violence obtruded and Gandhi again stopped the campaign. He declared:

> Let the opponent glory in our humiliation or so-called defeat. It is better to be charged with cowardice and weakness than to be guilty of denial of our oath and to sin against God. It is a million times better to *appear* untrue before the world than to be untrue to ourselves.

These apparent fits and starts of policy, if not of purpose, rather than discouraging his followers, merely solidified their support, and by 1922 Gandhi had established a complete ascendancy over the minds and hearts of his countrymen. However, Gandhi, having temporarily foresworn civil disobedience, was for the time being weaponless, and the government arrested him for preaching sedition. He was found guilty and sentenced to six years' imprisonment. But as he was not in good health, it was thought wise to release him after he had served two years.

So began a cycle of civil disobedience campaigns and prison terms punctuated by fasts. For the next decade, Indian domestic affairs were almost always at the flash point, and racial antipathy, if anything, increased. But the die was cast, as many enlightened Englishmen began to realize. The appointment of the Indian Statutory Commission (better known as the Simon Commission) in 1927 resulted in a series of Round Table Conferences and finally in the Government of India Act of 1935. This piece of legislation established responsible government at the provincial level and dyarchy at the center. It was an enactment that would have been warmly welcomed in 1919 but was considered quite inadequate by the Indian nationalists of the mid-1930s. Nevertheless, it did give Indians invaluable experience in administration which stood them in good stead when independence came. The Government of India Act also provided for the creation of an Indian Federation if a sufficient number of the princely states acquiesced, but, unfortunately, this scheme never came into operation.

The last episode of the story which began in 1600 will be detailed in the next chapter. At this point, let it suffice to say that when India finally achieved independence in the late summer of 1947, it owed much to a coherent and dedicated nationalist movement that received its baptism of fire in the traumatic days of April 1919.

12

End of an Empire: The Partition of India

As the last British troops slowly marched through the Gateway of India on the wharf of Bombay to their waiting transports, over two centuries of British rule in India came to a close. India had been an empire in itself, the most treasured jewel in the imperial crown, and the solemn proclamation of the independence of India and Pakistan on August 15, 1947, more than any other single event, dramatized the end of an era—the collapse of the imperial edifice.

The viceroy's declaration of war on Germany in 1939 on behalf of India, because it was accomplished solely through his fiat and without consultation with Indian politicians, had driven a permanent wedge between the government and the Indian National Congress. The viceroy, Lord Linlithgow, tried to assuage the Congress's injured feelings by announcing that dominion status was Britain's constitutional goal for India, once the war was over. He was, moreover, willing to form immediately an advisory council representing all elements of Indian opinion to advise him on the conduct of the war. The Congress rejected these proposals, demanding the granting of full responsibility without delay as its price for cooperating in the war effort. The viceroy found it impossible to acquiesce in this demand, and those Congress ministries in control of provincial governments[1] resigned in October

[1] The Government of India Act of 1935 had provided for responsible government in the provinces of India. In the provincial elections held in February 1937, the Congress secured clear majorities in 5 of the 11 provinces. In Bombay it was

1939—an event celebrated by the Muslim League, which had been becoming increasingly more disenchanted with the predominantly Hindu Congress, as "the day of deliverance."

The disastrous early phases of World War II caused a temporary mellowing of the Congress's attitude for, as Gandhi himself said, "We do not seek our independence out of British ruin." The Congress offered its cooperation to the British government if even a provisional national government were set up. To this more optimistic atmosphere, the viceroy responded with the so-called "August offer" of August 8, 1940. He would not agree to the creation of a Congress-controlled national government because he claimed that the Muslims, or, as he put it, "large and powerful elements in India's national life," would strongly oppose such a scheme. He did, however, repeat in greater detail his previous offer. He was willing, as soon as the war was over, to allow a constitution to be drafted for India by a representative body, and at once to nominate additional members to the viceroy's Executive Council and appoint a "War Advisory Council" to be made up of representatives of British India and the Indian states.

Hopes for Indian cooperation, however, faded again as the Congress turned down the "August offer" and in October 1940 launched a civil disobedience campaign which resulted in the incarceration of some 14,000 members of the Congress by May 1941. The Muslim League took advantage of the situation to develop a united and coherent political organization and for the first time, under the leadership of Mohammed Ali Jinnah, started actively to espouse the idea of a separate Muslim state of Pakistan.

With the entry of Japan into the war at the end of 1941 and the rapid advance of Japanese forces into Southeast Asia, the British government decided to make another approach to both the Hindu and Muslim leaders of the Indian nationalist movement. On March 8, 1942, Rangoon, the capital of Burma, fell, and a few days later the British prime minister announced that Sir Stafford Cripps, the leader of the House of Commons and a member of the War Cabinet, would lead a mission to India to present a dramatic new offer.

Much of what Cripps had to say was a repetition of previous proposals, only stated in more concise terms. India was to become a

---

able to form a ministry with the help of some sympathetic non-Congress members. In the North-West Frontier Province a pro-Congress Muslim group won control. In Bengal a Muslim coalition took office, while in the Punjab the noncommunal Unionist party organized the government. See map of India on p. 3, Chapter 1.

dominion at the end of the war, and to effect this end a constituent assembly, to be elected by the provincial legislatures, would proceed to negotiate a treaty with the British government. The right of secession from the Commonwealth was to be guaranteed. The Indian princely states would be free to join the new dominion, and to allay Muslim fears it was stipulated that any province could choose not to be bound by the new constitution and "to retain its present constitutional position, provision being made for its subsequent accession if it so desires." Neither the Congress nor the Muslim League was willing to accept the Cripps offer, the former remaining adamant in its demand for the immediate granting of dominion rights.

The failure of the Cripps mission ended the last hope of official Indian cooperation in the conduct of the war. The Congress's decision to reject the offer was not easily arrived at, but once committed to noncooperation, the organization decided to pursue this policy actively. A "Quit India" drive was set in motion, and on August 8, 1942, the All-India Congress Committee resolved to start a mass civil disobedience campaign unless the British turned over control of affairs to an Indian government immediately. The viceroy, with the approval of his Executive Council, moved swiftly. On the morning of August 9, Gandhi and the other Congress leaders were arrested, and the Congress was declared an illegal body. It is estimated that in all 60,000 people were arrested in the last five months of 1942, during which time a serious but short outbreak of violence claimed some 900 lives. To make matters worse, Subhas Chandra Bose, a former Congress president, fled India and organized an "Indian National Army" in Malaya which, in conjunction with the Japanese, advanced on the borders of India in 1943.

In general, though, the arrest of the Congress leaders broke the back of any plans for mass agitation. The Indian National Army turned out to be at worst a minor nuisance, while the Muslim League devoted most of its efforts to increasing its strength for the struggle that lay ahead. It should also not be forgotten that over two million Indian soldiers—the largest volunteer army in history—served with distinction wherever British forces were engaged.

By May 1944 the Japanese threat to India had passed, and Gandhi was released from detention for reasons of health. He immediately entered into a series of conversations with Jinnah, but these talks proved abortive. Lord Wavell, who had replaced Lord Linlithgow as viceroy in October 1943, realized that the question of India's future could be put off no longer. In March 1945 Wavell flew to London for consultations and returned with instructions that in future all members of his council, with the exception of himself and the commander-in-chief of the army in India, should be Indians selected from the political parties on the basis of Hindu-Muslim parity. Wavell consequently called a conference at Simla at the end of June 1945 to determine the membership of the council, but unfortunately the conference broke down when the Congress and the Muslim League could come to no agreement.

The war was now drawing to a close, and in the British general election of July 1945 the Labor party come to power. The Labor government decided on a fresh approach to the Indian situation. New elections were ordered for the central and provincial councils, as was the reconstitution of the viceroy's Executive Council. Of greater importance, it was determined that a constituent assembly should be summoned as soon as possible.

The elections were held in December 1945 for both general seats and those reserved for minorities. The Congress swept virtually all the general seats, and the Muslim League, except in the North-West Frontier Province, was similarly successful in respect to those reserved for Muslims. By this time, of course, the goal of independence no longer constituted an issue; the British were in no position to maintain their hold on India, even if they had so desired. The question now was what form the new India would take after the departure of the British.

In January 1946 a Parliamentary delegation visited India, and in March, almost four years to the day after his previous journey, Sir Stafford Cripps led a cabinet mission to assist the viceroy in arriving at an equitable method for drawing up an Indian constitution and for forming a broadly representative Executive Council. The mission's task was at best a difficult one, as it required the cooperation of both the League, which insisted that India was really two nations, and the Congress, which was equally sure that it was not. After numerous consultations with all concerned, the cabinet mission, rejecting the Muslim League's plan for partition, came up with the proposal that India should have a union government, competent only in the areas of defense, communications, and foreign affairs; the various provincial governments were to be at liberty to form themselves into regional groupings with governments empowered to deal with such nonunion matters as the provinces did not wish to arrogate to themselves. It was envisaged that the provinces would join either Hindu or Muslim groupings, depending on the religion of the majority of the population. The provinces were to retain all residual sovereignty. The princely states were to be included in the cabinet mission's scheme on terms negotiated with them individually.

Both the Congress and the League accepted these proposals as the basis for further discussion, and the mission consequently refined its suggestions more carefully. It proposed a constituent assembly to be elected by the members of the provincial legislatures. This assembly was to be divided into three sections—Section A representing provinces with Hindu majorities; Section B representing the predominantly Muslim provinces of the Punjab, Sind, and the North-West Frontier Province; and Section C representing Bengal and Assam, both with small Muslim majorities. Each of these three sections was to draw up a constitution for the provinces included within it and was also to decide whether a regional government should be formed and, if so, with what powers. A province could opt out of a group by a vote of its legislature, but it could only do so after the new constitutions had come into effect. It was anticipated that a second constituent assembly would be convened later to write the union constitution.

It was now up to the Indian political parties. Despite the mission's rejection of his plans for Pakistan, Jinnah nonetheless convinced the Muslim League on June 6 to pass a resolution accepting the new constitutional scheme and agreeing to participate in the constituent assembly, although it was hoped that the proposed arrangements "would ultimately result in the establishment of complete sovereign Pakistan." Nothing, however, was heard from the Congress regarding the new constitutional scheme, and as time began to run out, the viceroy determined to proceed without further delay with the establishment of an interim government of 14 persons: six Hindus—members of the Congress; five Muslims—members of the Muslim League; one Sikh, one Parsi, and one Indian Christian. No noticeably hostile reaction emanated from either side, and for the first time in many months there seemed some hope of preserving the unity of India. A cartoon in the *Hindustan Times* showed the cabinet mission preparing to depart, and the caption read: "All's well that ends well."

But the optimism was premature. Gandhi insisted that as the Congress was nonsectarian, one of the Muslims in the interim government would have to be a Congress member, especially as the former Congress president, Abul Kalam Azad, was a Muslim. Since the acceptance of this proposal would have cut the Muslim League's representation to four, Jinnah was, of course, deeply incensed and offered to form a government made up entirely of League members. The viceroy could accept the proposal of neither Gandhi nor Jinnah, with the result that the interim government, in the form envisaged by the viceroy, could not be appointed. What hope now remained was based on the somewhat equivocal acceptance of the mission's constitutional proposals which had finally been passed by the Congress.

The whole delicate structure, however, was soon to collapse in ruins. At a press conference on July 10, the official leader of the Congress, Jawaharlal Nehru, proceeded to clarify the Congress's position on the constitutional proposals. He stated that the Congress had "agreed to go into the Constituent Assembly and have agreed to nothing else . . . we have committed ourselves to no single matter to anybody." In regard to the vital grouping plan, Nehru felt "the big probability is that . . . there will be no grouping." In other words, the Congress was completely repudiating its acceptance of the constitutional proposals and totally rejecting the cabinet mission's formula. The Muslim League, as a consequence, withdrew its previous acceptance of the cabinet mission's constitutional plan, vowed to boycott any interim government, and determined on a program of "direct action" for the establishment of Pakistan, to be launched at an appropriate time. "This day," Jinnah ominously declared, "we bid goodbye to constitutional methods."

The situation in July 1946 now stood in much the same position as it had before the cabinet mission's arrival—neither plans for future constitutional development nor an interim government existed. Consequently, the viceroy decided to do the best he could under the circumstances, and on August 6 he wrote to Nehru, recently elected Congress president, inviting him to form an interim government. This Nehru was willing to do. But before the government could even be announced, the Muslim League, on August 16, declared "Direct Action Day," with the result that bloody rioting broke out in Calcutta, during which at least 5,000 people were killed and 15,000 injured. The disorders soon spread to predominantly Muslim East Bengal and to the Hindu-majority province of Bihar, where rumors and lurid reports in local newspapers precipitated the massacre of several thousand Muslims.

The viceroy was certain that the only way to stanch the ever-increasing flow of blood was to convince the Muslim League to join the interim government and the constituent assembly. Jinnah reluctantly agreed to both points. But not much was really accomplished. In the interim government, the two parties tended to work on parallel lines rather than together, and when the constituent assembly was finally summoned for December 9, Jinnah ordered the Muslim League representatives not to attend. In a final desperate bid to save the situation, the leaders of the Congress and the League and Baldev Singh, the Sikh representative, were invited to confer with Prime Minister Clement Attlee in London. But it was too late; and the Congress, on the threat of leaving the government itself, demanded the resignation of the League members of the interim government unless the League adhered to its promise to send representatives to the constituent assembly. Faced with this deadlock, Prime Minister Attlee determined to act on his own initiative. On February 20, 1947, he announced to the House of Commons that it was His Majesty's government's "definite intention to take the necessary steps to effect the transference of power to responsible Indian hands by a date not later than June 1948." It would have to be determined

> to whom the powers of the Central Government in British India should be handed over on the due date, whether as a whole to some form of Central Government for British India, or in some areas to the existing Provincial Governments, or in such other way as may seem most reasonable and in the best interests of the Indian people.

Coincident with the British government's enunciation of this new policy, Viscount Mountbatten replaced Lord Wavell as viceroy. Mountbatten arrived in New Delhi on March 22 with instructions to preserve the unity of India as outlined in the cabinet mission's proposals. If by October he were to determine that this was not feasible, he was to investigate other approaches to the problem of the transfer of power. Mountbatten soon concluded that any agreement between the Congress and the League on the establishment of a single government was impossible. Matters had already gone too far. Jinnah realized that time, or the lack of it, was on his side. "The Muslim League," he said, "will not yield an inch in its demands for Pakistan," and his adamant rejection of all alternatives was to prove decisive.

There was no time for a leisurely approach; the Congress and Muslim members of the interim government devoted most of their energies to working actively against each other. Unbridled communal violence had erupted in the Punjab and the North-West Frontier Province. In many parts of the country, all semblance of law and order had disappeared. Mountbatten, seeing the true nature of the situation, decided on the partition of India as the only practical course of action. As the British government was no longer in a position to guarantee the maintenance of peace, Mountbatten also concluded that the date for the transfer of power would have to be moved up from June 1948, and the date of August 15, 1947, was finally announced. This meant that only a few short weeks remained to settle all the details of a very complex procedure.

In a broadcast of June 3, the viceroy revealed "the method by which power will be transferred from British to Indian hands." India was to be divided into the dominions of India and Pakistan, the provinces of the Punjab and Bengal were to be bifurcated, and a boundary commission was to determine where the frontiers were to lie. A referendum was to decide the fate of the North-West Frontier Province. None of the protagonists were totally satisfied by this decision. The Congress in principle opposed partition. Jinnah wanted all of Bengal and the Punjab within Pakistan, while the Sikhs were faced with the division of their homeland in the Punjab. Yet it was generally realized that no other alternative existed, and with remarkable accord the discussions on the implementation of partition commenced.

No one seemed to anticipate any real trouble, let alone the nightmare that in fact lay ahead. The various actors in the unfolding drama busily prepared for the impending day of independence. As a first step, the Indian Independence Bill was introduced into the British Parliament on July 4 and received the Royal Assent on July 18. Next, a "Partition Committee," consisting of two Congress representatives and two delegates from the Muslim League, with Lord Mountbatten acting as chairman, was established. The committee was to continue its deliberations even after August 15, and the problems it faced were almost limitless for all the administrative paraphernalia of a nation long united had to be divided. The splitting of the armed forces was particularly sad, involving as it did the destruction of a coherent military tradition which had persisted for many generations. As Baldev Singh, the defense minister in the interim government, said:

> Rarely in peacetime has a fighting force suffered such vicissitudes during so short a period as the Indian Army during the days of its partition. Following the decision to partition the country, the Army had to be divided and reconstitution, which began immediately, meant the breakup of battalions, regiments, installations, training institutions, etc.

The allotting of administrative personnel, fiscal assets, and official records, and a myriad of similar questions, posed problems of staggering complexity. Of greatest moment, however, was the matter of territorial division and the drawing of frontiers. To effect this task, two boundary commissions—one for the Punjab and one for Bengal and Assam—were appointed, with Sir Cyril Radcliffe as chairman of both. What emerged from his efforts was the so-called Radcliffe Award, which was not announcd until two days after independence. As might have been anticipated, neither of the parties concerned was happy with the provisions of the award. Hindu newspapers characterized it as arbitrary and unjust, while the Muslim press was similarly outraged by what it considered the award's anti-Muslim bias. Nevertheless, both sides agreed to abide by its terms, at least for the time being.

Meanwhile, the intercommunal antipathies in the Punjab had been growing in intensity, and Mountbatten found it necessary to call a special meeting of the Partition Committee to deal with it. He persuaded both sides to declare their respect for the rights of minorities in the Punjab, and a special Punjab "boundary force" of 50,000 men, under the command of a British general with both an Indian and a Pakistani subordinate, was created to see that no violence occurred during the change in administration.

It is hard to imagine the difficulties the viceroy had to face in conducting negotiations between two such hostile groups and dissimilar leaders—Jinnah always ready to take offense and Gandhi, although never an official member of the Congress team, yet a key factor in the discussions, frequently obstructing progress by his own curious habits and firm views. Nevertheless, on August 7, when there were still seven days left on Mountbatten's specially designed calendar indicating the time remaining until the transfer of power, Jinnah was able to leave India forever to become president of the Pakistan constituent assembly meeting in Karachi, the new nation's capital. On August 13 Mountbatten also flew to Karachi, and on the next day he addressed the assembly, exhorting its members to be tolerant of the minorities within the new state and reminding them of the example set in this regard by an earlier Muslim, the Emperor Akbar. "Akbar's tradition has not always been consistently followed by the British or Indians, but I pray for the world's sake that we will hold fast, in the years to come, to the principles that this great ruler taught us."

As the viceroy returned to New Delhi that same day, leaving Jinnah to be governor general of the new dominion, he noticed several large fires ominously illuminating the Punjab countryside.

Where the atmosphere in Karachi had been rather restrained, the exact opposite was true in New Delhi. It had been arranged that the Indian constituent assembly would convene late on the night of August 14 so that India could attain its independence at the first dawning of the new day. As the final moments of British rule in India were passing, Nehru eloquently addressed the assembly:

> Long years ago we made a tryst with destiny, and now the time comes when we shall redeem our pledge, not wholly or in full measure, but very substantially. At the stroke of the midnight hour, when the world sleeps, India will awake to life and freedom. A moment comes, which comes but rarely in history, when we step out from the old to the new, when an age ends, and when the soul of a nation, long suppressed, finds utterance. It is fitting that at this solemn moment we take the pledge of dedication to the service of India and her people and to the still larger cause of humanity.

Lord Mountbatten was then asked to serve as independent India's first governor general, while Nehru became the new nation's prime minister.

Friday, August 15, 1947, was a day of high emotion and uninhibited enthusiasm in New Delhi. At precisely 8:30 a.m., a fanfare of trumpets heralded the entrance of Earl Mountbatten of Burma,[2] the governor general of free India, into the great Durbar Hall. He repeated the oath of office after the chief justice of India, Dr. Kania, and the ministers of the first cabinet were then sworn in. Next, the large bronze doors at the end of the hall were opened, and the band played "God Save the King," followed by the Indian national anthem, "Jana Gana Mana."

The whole assemblage then proceeded to the Council House where Mountbatten was to address the assembly. Vast crowds shouting "Jai Hind!" ("India forever!") and "Mountbatten ki jai!" ("Long live Mountbatten!") blocked the route, and the official party made its way only with the greatest of difficulty. Once arrived, Mountbatten paid eloquent tribute to all those who had worked so hard for so many weeks to make the events of that day possible. Gandhi he described as the architect of India's freedom through nonviolence and Nehru as a leader of courage and vision, under whose enlightened guidance India would "attain a position of strength and influence and take her rightful place in the comity of nations." As for himself, Mountbatten declared: "From today I am your constitutional Governor-General and I would ask you to regard me as one of yourselves, devoted wholly to the

[2] Mountbatten was created an earl on August 14.

furtherance of India's interests." In reply, Rajendra Prasad, on behalf of the Indian government, declared that

> while our achievement is in no small measure due to our own sufferings and sacrifices, it is also the result of world forces and events and, last though not least, it is the consummation and fulfillment of the historic tradition and democratic ideals of the British race. . . . The period of domination of Britain over India ends today, and our relationship with Britain is henceforward going to rest on a basis of equality, of mutual goodwill and mutual profit.

After lunch, Lord and Lady Mountbatten attended a party for 5,000 school children, to whom they distributed gifts. Later in the afternoon, the Indian flag was unfurled in a special ceremony so congested that Mountbatten, when leaving the scene, had to rescue twelve persons, including four women, a child, a press photographer, and Nehru himself, who perched on the hood of the state coach. As this curious entourage made its way through New Delhi, one spectator noticed that a rainbow matching the saffron, white, and green colors of the Indian flag, had appeared in the sky—surely a most happy omen.

But the independence of the states of the Indian subcontinent, apparently so auspiciously launched, was to be marred by a chapter of horrors with few parallels in history. Within a few short months both Gandhi and Jinnah were dead—Gandhi assassinated, Jinnah from natural causes—and several million Hindus and Muslims had either been slain or displaced. Prompted largely by mutual fear, riots erupted first between the Sikhs and the Muslims in the border area of the Punjab. Terror-stricken refugees streamed from one side of the border to the other. Stabbing, shooting, and looting became the order of the day. It was not unusual for trains packed with refugees to arrive at their destinations with no one left alive. The lives of the aged, of women and children, were equally forfeit if they encountered others than their coreligionists. The Punjab boundary force, so hopefully organized, was of little use as many of its members were also infected by communal animus. Even had all the troops been reliable, they were not present in sufficient numbers to cope with the magnitude of the situation. Rich and poor alike were driven from their homes in the largest population transfer ever recorded. Those that survived were in a miserable condition; most had seen their homes destroyed and their loved ones hacked to pieces before their eyes.

As Hindu and Sikh refugees from the Punjab streamed into Delhi, tension mounted in the capital itself. Rumors of a Muslim plot to overthrow the Indian government began to spread, and people suddenly remembered that Delhi had, after all, been the capital of the Mogul empire and the seat of Muslim power and culture in the north of India. Hindu fears that the Muslims were arming were aggravated by the fact that most of the ammunition dealers in New Delhi were Muslims. On August 21 there was an explosion in the quarters of a Muslim science student who was thought to be making a bomb. A few days later the first stabbing was reported, and on August 25 a fight, which quickly spread, broke out between a Muslim and a Hindu worker at Birla Mills.

Until this moment the local authorities had managed to maintain control, but they had few steady troops at hand. On the morning of September 4 a bomb exploded in a Hindu section of the city, and from that moment the knifings, robbing, and arson increased to such an extent that the local authorities were no longer able to contain the situation. Soon firearms came into play, and the incidence of casualties went up. As usual, most of the victims were women and children, the old and infirm. It was not until more troops were available and a high level government emergency committee was formed that any semblance of order was restored. But the trouble kept spreading, and soon many of the districts adjoining New Delhi, as well as much of the United Provinces and the Eastern Punjab, were alight.

This is not to say that everyone behaved uniformly badly. There were frequent cases of both Hindus and Muslims risking their lives to save neighbors who were of a different faith. Superhuman efforts to save the situation were made by many, and especially by Gandhi, whom Mountbatten described as "the one-man boundary force who kept the peace while a 50,000-strong force was swamped by riots." The magnitude of the problem unleashed by religious passion can best be attested to by stark numerical facts: from August 1947 to the middle of 1948, within a period of ten months, at least half a million people had lost their lives, an estimated seven and a half million non-Muslims had left Pakistan for India, and some five and a half million Muslims had moved in the opposite direction.

A final moment of dark tragedy occurred on January 30, 1948. Gandhi, devoting virtually all his energies to the dampening of communal ardor, found the prayer meetings he held daily in the garden of Birla House in New Delhi particularly effective. Here he was not loath to read the *Koran* to the assembled throng nor to ask each Hindu and Sikh present to bring at least one Muslim to the next meeting. On the fatal day, there was present in the crowd a fanatic named Nathuram Godse. As Gandhi approached the wooden platform from which he was to conduct the services, Godse stepped forward and shot the Mahatma three times. Gandhi died almost instantly.

It is ironical that Godse was a Hindu, not a Muslim, and that he killed Gandhi because he resented the Mahatma's tolerance towards Muslims. As Godse later stated at his trial:

> I sat brooding intensely on the atrocities perpetrated on Hinduism and its dark and deadly future if left to face Islam outside and Gandhi inside . . . and I decided all of a sudden to take the extreme step against Gandhi.

Gandhi's assassination and the bereavement felt by all Indians, Hindu and Muslim alike, helped to shock people back to reason. Slowly the communal hatred of the postpartition period abated, the refugees were absorbed, and the ravished fields replanted. But other problems, notably conflicting claims to Kashmir, arose to prevent the development of any cordiality between India and Pakistan. It is unfortunate, in retrospect, that the British could not have left one of their greatest achievements—a united India—to their successors.

India's imperial experience was, of course, not a wholly negative one, even from the Indian point of view. India and Pakistan decided to remain members of the Commonwealth and both states owe much to their colonial heritage. Yet the verdict of history may well be that the greatest contribution the British made in two hundred-odd years of association with the subcontinent was the manner in which they dispassionately effected the transfer of power and peacefully made their departure.

13

The Legacy of British Imperialism

THE ESTABLISHMENT of colonies in areas with large indigenous populations always placed the imperial power, even if it were liberal and enlightened, in an untenable position. Morally, it is hard to justify imperialism, and it was difficult for colonial authorities to interfere with even the most obnoxious local customs and traditions without being accused of intolerance and excessive authoritarianism. Thus, some of the more enlightened British actions in India, such as the elimination of *sati* (self-immolation of widows), caused the greatest indignation. A British Indian government could never legislate against untouchability, while the government of an independent India was able to do so without difficulty. Nationalists in all the colonies constantly railed against the Preventative Detention Act,[1] yet in nearly all cases, when these colonies went their own way, the Preventative Detention Act was retained and usually made more stringent. Before 1947 the Indian National Congress was dedicated to the creation of separate language provinces in India. After independence, when the Linguistic Provinces Commission met, its report reflected the same opposition to language states that the British had previously manifested:

Face to face with the centuries-old India of narrow loyalties, petty jealousies and ignorant prejudices engaged in mortal conflict, we were simply

[1] An enactment common to most British colonies which allowed the government to detain persons for varying lengths of time without normal judicial process.

horrified to see how thin was the ice upon which we were skating. Some of the ablest men in the country came before us and confidently and emphatically stated that language in this country stood for and represented culture, race, history, individuality, and finally a sub-nation.

British colonial administrators were often more right than wrong and frequently knew better what would benefit the lands they governed than the local populace itself. Paternalism, however, is always resented, and colonial peoples wanted to do for themselves that which was done on their behalf by rulers of a different race and from an alien cultural background. This is not to say that former colonies abandoned institutions and legal codes established by the colonial administration. The Indian government did not revive *sati* nor repeal most of the laws enacted before independence, and the legal systems, legislatures, and administrative machinery of virtually all former colonies is still based on those inherited from the British.

British imperialism was an historical phenomenon. Essentially it no longer exists. Yet a connection with the imperial past is maintained not only through the sharing of similar institutions by Britain and her former colonies, but also through the Commonwealth and the existence of certain vestigial problems. In the Commonwealth context, the British government continues to offer considerable economic and technical assistance to its former possessions. It is perhaps ironical that it was not until the dying days of the Empire that the British taxpayer started contributing towards the welfare of the colonies. Before World War II, colonies were expected to bear virtually all the costs of their own administration, except in cases of dire calamity. The construction of schools and hospitals, the salaries of officials—all came from the colonial revenues; and given the poverty of most of the Dependent Empire, progress and development were as a consequence agonizingly slow.

In 1940, however, Parliament passed the first substantive Colonial Development and Welfare Act which provided £5 million a year for "any purpose likely to promote the development or the resources of any colony or the welfare of its people." In 1945 a similar act was passed which greatly increased the funds available, and further legislation along the same lines was implemented from time to time. To be sure, many mistakes were made in the initial use of these moneys, but the passage of the Colonial Development and Welfare Acts was symptomatic of a greater maturity and a new sense of responsibility among British statesmen. It is to their credit that they in no way tried to scuttle their colonies, that they spent some time preparing their charges for independence, and that they did not terminate their association with former colonies. Between 1957 and 1962, for example, the British government poured £481 million in aid into the Commonwealth and what remained of the Empire. It became startlingly clear at the Commonwealth Prime Ministers' Conference of July 1964 that one of the main factors keeping the newly independent nations of Asia and Africa in the Commonwealth was the willingness of Britain and the dominions to maintain and increase extensive programs of economic and technical assistance for their less fortunate Commonwealth partners.

The Prime Ministers' Conference of 1964 also reminded the world that the British government was embarrassed by the continued existence of at least one exceedingly complicated colonial dilemma—Southern Rhodesia. The problems in that colony are reminders of the major crisis that has faced the British government in the postwar years of imperial readjustment. Virtually all the major British possessions in Asia and Africa achieved independence without difficulty and in a spirit of mutual good will. This peaceful transfer of power was facilitated by the fact that Englishmen were, in most cases, merely birds of passage who did not settle permanently in British overseas dependencies. In a few cases, however—notably South Africa, Kenya, and Southern Rhodesia—a significant number of Britons or other Europeans had sunk roots and established homes, schools, business enterprises—in fact, a whole way of life. Many of their families had lived in Africa for several generations, and they were used to maintaining complete political power over vastly larger indigenous populations. Somehow the legitimate aspirations of the Africans to guide their own destinies had to be reconciled with the interests of these small European populations who were entrenched politically and had great financial stakes in the countries involved.

The Union of South Africa, which had been granted full responsible government in 1910, was the only member of the Commonwealth in which the white settlers were outnumbered—by about five to one—by the indigenous population, yet had complete political control. Of the some three million whites, about two thirds were Afrikaner[2] rather than British. Sternly fundamentalist by religion and implacably convinced of white superiority over the Negro, the post-World War II Afrikaner governments officially adopted a policy of strict *apartheid* (racial segregation) in the Union, to the consternation of her fellows in the Commonwealth. Only reluctantly wedded to British constitu-

[2] In modern usage the term "Afrikaner" is preferred to "Boer."

tional usages and chafing under the mounting criticism, South Africa informed the 1960 Commonwealth Prime Ministers' Conference of her intention to become a republic and to apply for membership in the Commonwealth.[3] In ensuing discussion the criticism of South Africa's racial policy became so heated that South Africa's prime minister, Dr. Hendrik Verwoerd, withdrew his country's application. Thus, on becoming a republic on May 31, 1961, South Africa left the Commonwealth and ceased to be a uniquely British or Commonwealth problem.

In Kenya the situation was less exacerbated though it was difficult enough. The white population, mainly British by stock and tradition, had settled as farmers, appropriating, under the protection of the British Crown, the best land of the local tribes. After World War II the swift growth of Kenya's African nationalist movement forced a most difficult decision on the Colonial Office. To its credit, it decided in favor of the African population, over the wishes of most (but not all) of the white settlers. Consequently, in 1963 Kenya received its independence as an African-governed dominion, and the next year became a republic within the Commonwealth. Today, only Southern Rhodesia stands poised on the edge of disaster with the problems inherited from the imperial past still unresolved.

As we have learned in Chapter 6, Rhodesia came under the British flag through the efforts of Cecil Rhodes and his British South Africa Company. After World War I the company was forced to surrender its charter, and in 1923 that part of Rhodesia north of the Zambezi River became the British protectorate of Northern Rhodesia, while the area south of the river chose in a plebiscite to become a self-governing colony—Southern Rhodesia—rather than a part of the Union of South Africa.

The constitutional arrangement in the Rhodesias remained virtually unchanged until September 1953, when the creation of the Federation of Rhodesia and Nyasaland, comprising the self-governing colony of Southern Rhodesia and the protectorates of Northern Rhodesia and Nyasaland, added a unique new entity to an Empire and Commonwealth already noted for the constitutional diversity of its components.[4] Federation was a triumph for the white settlers of British

[3] When Commonwealth members change their relationship to the British Crown by becoming republics, it has become customary for them to reapply for membership in the Commonwealth in their new status.

[4] The Federation would only become permanently established after a constitutional review conference to be held within ten years.

Central Africa, the great majority of whom lived in Southern Rhodesia: it increased the power of the white settlers, some 300,000 of whom could now dominate more than eight million Africans, and seemed to assure the future transfer of almost all remaining power from London to Salisbury, the Federation's capital in Southern Rhodesia, even though Britain remained the protecting power in Northern Rhodesia and Nyasaland.

That virtually all Africans in the three areas were opposed to fedration is beyond dispute. Yet the British government persisted in its support of the scheme, depending on the African Affairs Board in Salisbury to protect African rights through its power to reserve for review laws which the board considered detrimental to the welfare of the African population. The Africans and their supporters, however, were aware not only that the African Affairs Board was made up of members of a legislature which, although it contained some Africans, was predominantly white, but also that since the time when Southern Rhodesia became a self-governing colony, the British government, though possessing the power to review and reject discriminatory legislation, had never once done so.

It was not until 1957 that the true implications of federation began to manifest themselves. In that year the Federation government decided to move towards the resolution of several issues that it still considered outstanding. In April Sir Roy Welensky, a Southern Rhodesian and prime minister of the Federation, arrived in London for talks with the British government. In the course of these negotiations, Welensky gained four concessions from a Conservative government strongly committed to the success of the Federation: (1) Britain would relinquish the right to initiate legislation which would be effective in the Federation; (2) all Federation civil servants, including British Colonial Office personnel in the two protectorates, were eventually to be "locally based"; (3) the constitutional review, required as a necessary precursor for the final establishment of the Federation, was to be held no later than 1960, although this date was well in advance of that originally scheduled; and (4) the review conference would "consider a programme for the attainment of such statutes as would enable the Federation to become eligible for full membership of the Commonwealth."[5]

Immediately after Welensky's return from London, a Constitution

[5] The Federation was not considered a member of the Commonwealth, although its prime minister often attended meetings as a courtesy.

Amendment Bill was introduced into the federal assembly, where it was passed by the necessary two-thirds majority and later by the territorial legislatures. In 1958 a Federal Electoral Bill was similarly approved. The effect of these two enactments was to enlarge the federal assembly from 36 to 59, to divide the eligible voters into an upper ("A") and lower ("B") election roll based on property and educational qualifications, and to vest the power to elect 44 of the members of the enlarged assembly exclusively in the voters of the upper roll. To make matters worse, the election of the African members of the assembly was placed more directly into the hands of the Europeans: the two rolls were to be combined for the election of two-thirds of the African delegation, and the "A" roll voters (virtually all Europeans) far outnumbered those on the "B" roll. (Nor was eligibility for the "B" roll easy for Africans, for an annual income of £150 and literacy in English were required.[6])

The Constitution Amendment and Federal Electoral Acts were found too discriminatory even by the moribund African Affairs Board, which declared itself against both measures and used its power to reserve the legislation for review by the British government. The hollowness of the revered safeguards for African rights was clearly proved when the British Parliament, on the advice of the federal government, assented to both acts.

Simultaneous with these changes in the federal constitution was an attempt by Garfield Todd, the prime minister of Southern Rhodesia, to liberalize slightly the qualifications necessary for Africans to be admitted to the common voters' roll of that colony.[7] His very modest proposal, in its original form, was to enfranchise those few Africans who had had ten years' education and had worked in responsible posts as teachers and agricultural administrators. In its final version, Todd's bill was watered down considerably, but it was still too liberal for the white population of Southern Rhodesia, and Garfield Todd was removed from office by the members of his own party.

The events of 1957 and 1958 finally convinced Africans that they could expect justice neither from the federal government nor from the British authorities in London. Disturbances consequently erupted in

[6] As of 1960 there were 91,664 voters on the "A" roll, 1,697 of whom were Africans; on the "B" roll there were 4,877 Africans and 169 Europeans. The 1961 constitution of Southern Rhodesia is similar in form.

[7] Each constituent part of the Federation maintained its own identity and had its own governor, though there was also a governor general of the Federation. Southern Rhodesia retained its own legislature and voters roll.

Nyasaland in March 1959. The governor declared a state of emergency, white troops were flown in from Salisbury, and 52 persons, all Africans, were killed, while 1,332 Africans were detained without trial. The federal government, the governor of Nyasaland, and Alan Lennox-Boyd, the secretary of state for the colonies, all claimed that there was a well-laid plot to murder the white population in Nyasaland.

The result of the Nyasaland outbreaks dramatically wrested the political initiative in the Federation from its white leaders. When, in April 1957, Welensky had returned from London he felt assured of the rapid advance of the Federation to dominion status and virtual independence. In February 1959, just before the start of the unrest in Nyasaland, Julian Amery, a junior minister in the Colonial Office, rose in the House of Commons to answer a questioner desiring to know whether Britain still stood by her guarantee to the African peoples of Northern Rhodesia and Nyasaland. Amery replied: "Her Majesty's Government have never departed from their pledges given at the time Federation was introduced." In July, Prime Minister Harold Macmillan himself answered a similar question in a different vein:

> We want to make it abundantly clear that the purpose of our policy is, as soon as possible and as rapidly as possible, to move towards self-government in Northern Rhodesia and Nyasaland. . . . The British government will certainly not withdraw its protection. When all the units are agreed that British government protection is no longer needed then—and only then—can the whole Federation go forward to independence.

It was in this same month that a commisssion of inquiry, headed by Sir Patrick Devlin and appointed to investigate the situation in Nyasaland, issued its report. The commission felt that the federal government had wilfully misled the British authorities as to developments in Central Africa, in order to achieve dominion status at the constitutional review conference scheduled for 1960. The commission described Nyasaland as "being in some ways a police state" and went on to deny categorically that African opposition to the Federation was limited to a few extremists, as its government claimed:

> The [Federal] government's view [is] that these nationalist aspirations are the thoughts of only a small minority of political Africans, mainly of self-seekers who think their prospects of office will be worse under Federation; and that the great majority of the people are indifferent to the issue. We have not found this to be so. . . . It was generally acknowledged that

the opposition to Federation was there, that it was deeply rooted and almost universally held.

Of greatest importance, the commission found that there was no evidence of a murder plot against the white population ever having been conceived in Nyasaland, the Colonial Office's solemn statements to the contrary notwithstanding.

The Devlin Report caused an uproar in both London and Salisbury. Lennox-Boyd formally rejected the report on behalf of the Conservative government whose supporters included many peers with heavy investments in Central Africa and many "Blimpish" backbenchers who considered any alteration in the political balance in Central Africa treasonable. The 1959 general election, however, permitted Macmillan to rid himself of Lennox-Boyd and to replace him with Iain Macleod.

Macleod, with Macmillan's backing, made it clear to the federal government in Salisbury that London was going to take a greater interest in Central Africa and that a commission would be appointed to investigate the situation and thus provide an objective report upon which the constitutional review conference could base its deliberations. Welensky was allowed to recommend for appointment the 13 Federation members of the commission, and the British government matched his list with 13 appointments of its own. The commission, headed by Lord Monckton, a former Conservative cabinet minister and a prominent member of the English bar, began its work in the Federation in February 1960.

The Monckton Report, which appeared in October, recommended African majority rule in the north and the right of secession from the Federation for all its constituent parts. Howls of frustration and rage emanated from Salisbury and from certain elements in the Conservative party in Britain, but Macleod was determined to reverse the pre-1957 trend, at least in those territories of the Federation that were still British protectorates; in the summer of 1960, even before the Monckton Report had appeared, he had chaired a conference in London on the future of Nyasaland. The constitutional formula which emerged provided for a majority of African members in the Nyasaland legislature.

Northern Rhodesia presented a more complicated problem. Each revision of the territory's constitution had given greater power to the settlers. As a result, Kenneth Kaunda, the African Nationalist leader, urged his followers to boycott the election held in 1959 under the so-called Lennox-Boyd Constitution, because of its "racialist unfairness." When the African boycott threatened to take a violent turn, the governor banned Kaunda's party, the Zambia Congress, and interned Kaunda and several of his followers. But, as in Nyasaland, the new British attitude manifested itself in 1961–1962 when a new colonial secretary, Reginald Maudling, developed a constitution for Northern Rhodesia which, although extremely complicated in its franchise provisions, nevertheless made it possible for Africans to gain a majority in the legislature, which they did in the subsequent elections. By late 1963, then, it was manifestly clear that Nyasaland and Northern Rhodesia were going to be independent African states and that the Federation had collapsed.[8]

The only problem that remained, then, was Southern Rhodesia (or Rhodesia, as it became after Northern Rhodesia became Zambia), and here the British government does not have the power to influence events that it had in the two northern territories. Rhodesia, with a white population of about 220,000 of a total of more than four million, not only retained the status of a self-governing colony but had as well the unique advantage of controlling its own armed forces. In Kenya, which also had a significant white population, the British government was able to dictate a constitution establishing African control largely because Kenya, as a Crown Colony, had no military forces of its own which were independent of control from London.

This is not to say that the British government placed all the pressure on the Rhodesian government that it could. Rhodesia in 1965 was indeed a self-governing colony which to all intents and purposes had responsible government, and, by constitutional tradition, the right of the British government to interfere in its internal affairs was strictly circumscribed. The rest of the world, however, is not impressed with the niceties of imperial constitutional development, and one cannot help but feel that Westminster has too often hidden behind the casuistry of constitutional practice to avoid affronting the white settlers and those Englishmen at home with strong emotional attachments to Rhodesia or with large investments in this last outpost of Empire. It was this pusillanimous attitude that forced the noted colonial administrator Sir Hugh Foot (now Lord Caradon) to resign in 1962 the post he held on behalf of the British government in the United Nations.

[8] Nyasaland became independent as Malawi in July 1964 and Northern Rhodesia became the independent Republic of Zambia in October 1964; both are full members of the Commonwealth.

Since 1960, in Rhodesia itself, the government has moved steadily to the right. In August 1962 two measures of extreme severity were passed—the amendments to the Unlawful Organizations Act and the Law and Order (Maintenance) Act, which resulted in the virtual banning of all African political activity. In the elections of 1963 the government of Sir Edgar Whitehead was replaced by an even more conservative one headed at first by Winston Field and later by Ian Smith—a decision that was reaffirmed with near unanimity by the white voters in May 1965. Threats of U.D.I. (unilateral declaration of independence) became ever more persistent, and on November 11, 1965, Prime Minister Smith announced the fatal step. It must consequently be concluded that, despite some slight opposition from liberal white elements, the government seems determined to force Rhodesia into the isolation and state of world opprobrium heretofore reserved exclusively for Portugal and the Republic of South Africa.[9]

Whether the situation in Rhodesia can be rationalized without recourse to violence is not clear. One can only hope so. But that an African majority government will in time be established is evident, although the role that the British government (even a Labor government) can play in bringing this situation about is hard to determine. When the imperial dilemma in Rhodesia is finally solved, however, it will essentially mark the end of one of the most dramatic manifestations of the postwar world—the liquidation of the British Empire.

[9] Two countries with which Prime Minister Ian Smith's Rhodesian Front government has been becoming increasingly more intimate. The prime minister strongly favors a military alliance with South Africa, and in September 1965, Rhodesia established quasi-independent diplomatic relations with Portugal, over strong British objections.

Additional Reading

It is not the author's intention to offer below a comprehensive list of works dealing with the history of the British Empire. Only a few books which may be of particular interest to the reader are mentioned in conjunction with the various subject areas covered in the book. For general reference purposes, the first three volumes of the *Cambridge History of the British Empire* are recommended.

Chapter 1. Robert Clive, Warren Hastings, and the Changing British Attitude Toward India

A. M. Davies. *Clive of Plassey* (New York, 1939)

Keith Feiling. *Warren Hastings* (New York, 1954)

Holden Furber. *John Company at Work* (Cambridge, Mass., 1948)

Penderel Moon. *Warren Hastings and British India* (New York, 1949)*

Philip Woodruff [Mason]. *The Men Who Ruled India*, vol. 1: *The Founders* (New York, 1954)*

Chapter 2. The Durham Report and the Establishment of Responsible Government in Canada

J. G. Lambton, Earl of Durham. *The Durham Report*, abr. version with introduction and notes by Sir Reginald Coupland (New York, 1945)

Chester New. *Lord Durham: A Biography of John George Lambton, First Earl of Durham* (New York, 1929)

* Available in paperback.

Chapter 3. COLONIZATION IN THE ANTIPODES: THE SETTLEMENT OF AUSTRALIA AND NEW ZEALAND

J. B. Condliffe and W. T. Airey. *A Short History of New Zealand* (Christchurch, N.Z., 1954)
R. M. Crawford. *Australia* (New York, 1960)
W. K. Hancock. *Australia* (New York, 1931)
Keith Sinclair. *A Short History of New Zealand* (New York, 1961)*

Chapter 4. THE INDIAN MUTINY: THE GREAT WATERSHED IN THE HISTORY OF BRITISH INDIA

R. C. Majumdar. *The Sepoy Munity and the Revolt of 1957* (Calcutta, 1957)
W. H. Russell. *My Indian Mutiny Diary* (London, 1957)
S. N. Sen. *Eighteen Fifty-Seven* (London, 1958)

Chapter 5. IMPERIALISM AND THE IMPERIAL PROCONSUL

C. A. G. Bodelsen. *Studies in Mid-Victorian Imperialism* (New York, 1960)
Lord Elton. *Gordon of Khartoum: General Charles George Gordon* (New York, 1955)
J. E. Flint. *Sir George Goldie and the Making of Nigeria* (New York, 1960)
J. A. Hobson. *Imperialism: A Study* (London, 1902)
K. E. Knorr. *British Colonial Theories, 1570–1850*, 2nd ed. (Toronto, 1963)
W. L. Langer. *The Diplomacy of Imperialism*, 2nd ed. (New York, 1951)
Parker Moon. *Imperialism and World Politics* (New York, 1926)
Roland Oliver. *Sir Harry Johnston and the Scramble for Africa* (New York, 1957)
Margery Perham. *Lugard* (New York, 1956, 1960), 2 vols.
Bernard Semmel. *Imperialism and Social Reform* (Cambridge, Mass., 1960)
A. P. Thornton. *The Imperial Idea and Its Enemies* (New York, 1959)
Philip Woodruff [Mason]. *The Men Who Ruled India* (New York, 1954), 2 vols.*

* Available in paperback.

Chapter 6. CECIL RHODES: PROTOTYPE OF AN IMPERIALIST

W. K. Hancock. *Smuts*, vol. 1: *The Sanguine Years, 1870–1919* (New York, 1962)

J. G. Lockhart and C. M. Woodhouse. *Cecil Rhodes: The Colossus of Southern Africa* (New York, 1963)

Sarah Millin. *Cecil Rhodes* (New York, 1933)

Basil Williams. *Cecil Rhodes* (London, 1938)

Chapter 7. THE BRITISH ACQUISITION OF THE LOWER INDUS VALLEY: A CASE STUDY IN IMPERIAL EXPANSION

R. A. Huttenback. *British Relations with Sind, 1799–1843: An Anatomy of Imperialism* (Berkeley, 1962)

H. T. Lambrick. *Sir Charles Napier and Sind* (New York, 1952)

Chapter 8. INDIANS IN SOUTH AFRICA: THE IMPERIAL PHILOSOPHY ON TRIAL

W. K. Hancock. *Smuts*, vol 1: *The Sanguine Years, 1870–1919* (New York, 1962)

W. H. Hancock. *Survey of British Commonwealth Affairs*, vol. 1: *Problems of Nationality*, 1918–1936 (New York, 1937)

Chapter 9. THE FASHODA INCIDENT AND THE SCRAMBLE FOR AFRICA

J. E. Flint. *Sir George Goldie and the Making of Nigeria* (New York, 1960)

W. L. Langer. *The Diplomacy of Imperialism*, 2nd ed. (New York, 1951)

Roland Oliver. *Sir Harry Johnston and the Scramble for Africa* (New York, 1957)

Ronald Robinson et al. *Africa and the Victorians: The Official Mind of Imperialism* (New York, 1961)

Chapter 10. FROM EMPIRE TO COMMONWEALTH

Alexander Brady. *Democracy in the Dominions*, 3rd rev. ed. (Toronto, 1958)

A. G. Dewey. *The Dominions and Diplomacy: The Canadian Contribution* (New York, 1929), 2 vols.

W. K. Hancock. *Survey of British Commonwealth Affairs* (New York, 1937, 1940), 2 vols.
Nicholas Mansergh. *Survey of British Commonwealth Affairs* (New York, 1952, 1958), 2 vols.
K. C. Wheare. *The Constitutional Structure of the Commonwealth* (New York, 1960)

Chapter 11. THE AMRITSAR MASSACRE AND THE RISE OF THE NEW INDIAN NATIONALISM

Michael Brecher. *Nehru: A Political Biography* (New York, 1959)
Jawaharlal Nehru. *Toward Freedom* (New York, 1941)*

Chapter 12. END OF AN EMPIRE: THE PARTITION OF INDIA

Abul Kalam Azad. *India Wins Freedom* (New York, 1960)
Hector Bolitho. *Jinnah: Creator of Pakistan* (New York, 1955)
Michael Brecher. *Nehru: A Political Biography* (New York, 1959)
Alan Campbell-Johnson. *Mission with Mountbatten* (New York, 1953)
V. P. Menon. *The Transfer of Power in India* (Princeton, 1957)
Penderel Moon. *Divide and Quit* (Berkeley, 1961)

Chapter 13. THE LEGACY OF IMPERIALISM

Richard Gray. *The Two Nations* (New York, 1960)
Philip Mason. *The Birth of a Dilemma: The Conquest and Settlement of Rhodesia* (New York, 1958)
Philip Mason. *Year of Decision: Rhodesia and Nyasaland in 1960* (New York, 1960)

* Available in paperback.

Index